*Selected
News Guardian
Columns*

Peter Mortimer

First published 2008 by IRON Press and
North Tyneside Libraries and Museums
5 Marden Terrace, Cullercoats
Northumberland, NE30 4PD
tel/fax: +44 (0)191 253 1901
ironpress@blueyonder.co.uk
www.ironpress.co.uk

ISBN 978-0-9552450-4-6
Printed by Field Print,
Boldon Colliery

© Peter Mortimer 2008

Typeset in Garamond
Cover artwork by Sally Mundy
Cover design by Brian Grogan
Madman at typewriter logo by Gus Stewart
Book layout by Kate Jones
Proof reading Eileen Jones

IRON Press books are distributed by Central Books
and represented by Inpress Limited,
Northumberland House,
11 The Pavement, Pope's Lane,
Ealing, London W5 4NG
Tel: +44 (0)20 8832 7464
Fax: +44 (0)20 8832 7465
www.inpressbooks.co.uk

Mortimer at Large

Acknowledgements

With thanks to Ian Arkle, Sue Slattery and Pam Smith of the *News Guardian* for their patience. Also for patience in setting, Kate Jones and in proof-reading, Eileen Jones. *News Guardian* readers for keeping me on my toes.

Mortimer jumping in Cullercoats
Photos by Gemma Marriner, News Guardian

Author's Lowdown

PETER MORTIMER was born in Nottingham too long ago to be of much interest, and despite spells of commercial work and three years studying economics at Sheffield University, partly abandoned gainful employment by becoming a journalist. He then totally gave up working for the man to concentrate on his own writing. Twenty of his plays and around ten books have appeared mainly to a respectful silence. In moments of inadvisability he set up both IRON Press (1973) and Cloud Nine Theatre Company (1997) both of which refuse to lie down and die, whatever their creator's intention. The *Mortimer at Large* column began life in the Spring of 2003, and despite the occasional hint of seizure, at the time of book publication, survives. The author lives in the North-East coastal village of Cullercoats, not famous for windless states.

Other Books by Peter Mortimer

Poetry

A Rainbow in its Throat
I Married the Angel of the North
Utter Nonsense

Documentary

The Last of the Hunters
Broke Through Britain
100 Days on Holy Island
Cool for Qat
Off the Wall

Children's

The Witch and the Maiden
Croak, the King and a Change in the Weather

Foreword

I started writing the *Mortimer at Large* column in the North Tyneside based *News Guardian* in Spring 2003, and while the rest of the world has been getting on with matters of some practical use, and despite much advice to the contrary, I have continued to do so virtually every week since. My thanks to the newspaper's editor Ross Weeks for his regular indulgence of the idiosyncracies, and for the many readers who have refrained from throwing half-bricks. This book represents a cross-section of the columns. Readers who would like to see more are urged to engage in a mass protest march through the centre of Whitley Bay with placards bearing my name in 144 pt bold type. I did ask Robert de Niro to write a foreword, but he never replied. News of this impending collection produced a small flurry of letters, and it seemed apposite to start the book with a few of these.

Dear Mortimer,
Is it true that a selection of your columns is to be put into book form? May I say we need more newspaper columns like we need a hole in the head. I cannot open a newspaper except to see staring out at me the face of some bigoted reactionary, second rate celebrity from Big Brother, numbskull of a petrolhead, illiterate sports personality (these last two words being a contradiction in terms), skinny brainless society bird with a double-barrelled name, or loud-mouthed DJ with bleached teeth. And what do they have in common? They're all writing a damned column! Ba! Do something interesting and worthwhile for heaven's sake! Yrs etc...

Dear Mortimer,
So they're intending to bring out a collection of 'your' columns. What a farce! Everyone knows that all these newspaper columns are not written by the peo-

ple whose name they bear. The whole thing is a sham and a farrago. Some poor hack beavers away in a darkened room, then all the publicity goes to people like you whose face stares out as us every Thursday. I say produce the real author of these columns, and stop this pretence immediately. Yours, etc…

Dear Mortimer,
A book of your columns? Why not mine? I have been writing a diary of some 3,000 words every day for the last 25 years covering every topic you can imagine. I am a misunderstood genius who is ahead of his time, but that time will come, and when it does and the world really acknowledges my talents, you and your own spurious efforts will be seen for what they truly are – little short of pathetic. Excuse faint writing, I am running out of green ink. Yours etc…

Dear Mortimer,
Can you please include a column in your book about the state of the bus stop outside my house?
It's rather wobbly. Thank you very much. Yours etc…

Dear Mortimer,
I note that your book of columns is co-funded by North Tyneside Libraries and Museums, this despite the fact that North Tyneside Council are often lampooned in your work. Might I suggest this shows a generosity of spirit and maturity which you might take on board as an object lesson.Yours.....

I could go on (*you often do – Editor*), but I have a phobia about books with long forewords. Do enjoy the journeys these columns take you on, and please buy another copy for a friend, or, if you find the whole book abhorrent, buy it for an enemy.

Peter Mortimer
Cullercoats, February 2008

The Columns

Of grannies, tomatoes and traffic cones

15th May 2003

YOU'LL HAVE read the local headline: 'Granny Scoops £300,000 Book Deal!' But why 'Granny', I wondered? When did you last see a headline: 'Second Cousin wins Lottery Jackpot!' or even: 'Uncle Crosses Sahara Single-Handed!'

The media are obsessed with the stereotype of females whose offspring also have offspring. Newspaper hacks, who are tuned to all caricatures, have been told to go into paroxysms of excess should any of said species NOT simply be sweet old ladies in shawls who spend all day crocheting by the fire.

My partner is a granny. And has more vitality than all those hacks put together.

On the broader front, how delightful to be at large in the News Guardian, where, week by week, this column pledges to examine matters of huge import, or, equally as vital, those of absorbing trivia.

In which category is my Uncle Turnip? A small greengrocer of distinction, he has recently been persuaded to install on his premises – or corner shop – a hi-tech automatic phone system.

Ring the shop and you now get a recorded voice with the following: "If you wish to enquire about tomatoes, press one; for cucumbers, press two; for radishes, press three..." and so on until finally, "...or please hold for the operator".

The 'operator' is Uncle Turnip himself, who sits listening to each message perched on his cos lettuce. He speaks: "Your call is now parked and will be dealt with in due course".

At which moment, he goes off to trim three sacks of savoy cabbage, before reconnecting with the caller. According to the system's salesman, this gives the impression of a busy multi-national organisation. Uncle Turnip seems unsure whether it has led to an increase in customers.

All this has no connection whatever with my newly discovered reason why, week after week, miles of the Coast Road are coned off with absolutely nothing happening!

I learn that the Ministry of Transport is now adopting the medieval crop rotation method for its roads. You'll remember from school how one field in three annually was allowed to lie fallow for regeneration. Thus it is with motorway and dual carriageway lanes. With crops, the system was abandoned once they discovered soil nutrients, and I am reliably informed by the MoT that once a tarmac nutrient is discovered, the cones will similarly be a thing of the past.

In weeks to come, I shall be taking an outrageously partial look at our very own headless chicken, North Tyneside Council. You might wonder why all their telephone lines are always engaged, and why all employees have been sent off on high-powered courses in not answering correspondence.

And what is the post-modernist significance of their newest piece of installation art, 'A Set of Rotting Teeth' (aka Whitley Bay seafront).

And why are all our seafront pubs closing? How I rue the coming demise of The Bay, Cullercoats, where that paint-ball entrepreneur, Winslow Homer, would once sit and take in the splendid view, while indulging his favourite breakfast of sparrows on toast.

Our poor North Tyneside citizens, seen slouching their way through the streets in hunched serfdom, seem resigned to their fine domain crumbling before their eyes. But take heart! All is not lost!

I predict absolutely no loss of efficiency in the twice daily tides! And where the sea sets an example, we, good readers, can follow. Onward!

Saddam spotted – but will the synchronised swimmers explode?

23rd May 2003

THE WORLD has been stunned by the news that weapons of mass destruction have been found inside a Cullercoats seafront litter bin. Locals are almost incredulous. As one resident put it: "Ah cannat believe it, me, man. Whey – ah divvent knaa how tha cud hev fund a litter bin in the forst pleece. Ah knaa we cannat."

Members of the public have not actually seen the WMDs, which were whisked off in a black bin liner. But reports came in of similar finds in other areas of the world – at the back of a cupboard in a Hong Kong bungalow, in a Belgian garden shed, behind a settee in Mogadishu. Again, the public were not allowed a viewing.

The news follows months of frustration for the USA when the only things coming close to WMDs discovered in Iraq were a bent peashooter and a catapult that only fired backwards. Defenders of the USA policy have been quick to point out that searching Iraq is no easy matter. It is a country twice the size of – well a country half its size.

There is more. There have been reported sightings of Osama Bin Laden at the karaoke night in the Furry Lemon (he was singing 'Tie a Yellow Ribbon'), and, talking of Iraq, there were several people who claimed to have seen a portly figure with moustache, blotchy face and black beret wearing army fatigues, doing a three under par round on the Whitley Bay pitch 'n' putt course.

Again, none of this is confirmed. But I'm not sure what to make of the official Government loudspeaker van which has been touring our streets blaring out the words, "There is no need for too much panic. A terrorist attack at the coast is not absolutely inevitable!"

And what about the army Saracen tank that was suddenly parked outside Woollies?

But my main concern is exactly how all this activity will affect Cullercoats' bid to land the 2012 Olympics. The bid has been put together by various local fat cats, and hundreds of copies of the promotional video, narrated by Pamela Anderson, have been despatched world-wide. The fat cats have already been whizzed to Cullercoats Olympic Selection Committee, where they were feted with a slap-up supper at Bill's Fish Bar (batter no extra, teapot refills included).

I managed to catch a word with one committee member at Newcastle Airport: "The Olympics movement enshrines the pursuit of fitness and physical excellence", he told me. His 24 stone frame, bloated on an endless succession of freebie meals from the different competing cities, was then shoe-horned into his airline seat.

Should Cullercoats be chosen, the Olympic stadium will be built at Beaconsfield, much to the relief of the council, plus all those vested interests pushing for a new Metro station there (which will be called Olympia, naturally).

All well and good. And the plan to make St. George's Church hall the Olympic Village is sound (spare mattresses required, please). But what about these latest developments?

Could the Cullercoats Olympics be sabotaged? Do we risk exploding synchronised swimmers or marathon runners taken out by Exocet missiles?

And yesterday in Seaton Sluice, I saw a man carrying a decorated bag which definitely came from the Middle East.

Is this the al Qaeda advance line? Have you checked your own garden shed recently (asylum seekers, etc.)?

Red alert, dear readers, red alert.

Time disappears on the Metro so become extreme!

5th June 2003

BOB HOPE is 100, and it's 50 years since Edmund Hillary conquered Everest, then founded the double glazing company. I shall make the connection later.

I'm confronted by someone 41 years older than me. Hope was born the same year Bertrand Russell wrote the Principles of Mathematics, which has got fewer laughs.

Being funny AND very old is wonderful, and can make us forget

Tennyson's cheerful couplet, "time driveth onwards fast, and in a little while our lips are dumb." Ta very much Alfred.

Alfred had obviously never been on the Metro. At the same time as Tynemouth Station has a clock festival, all other Metro timepieces have disappeared.

Or hadn't you noticed? Your eagle-eyed correspondent asks where have all the stations' digital clocks gone? Not one to be seen.

I pressed the enquiry button at Cullercoats Metro. There have been times in the past when by mistake I pressed the adjacent emergency button. Within seconds the station was swarming with black-clad SAS men firing tear gas and arresting anyone who'd spent a few hours on a sunbed as a suspected asylum seeker.

They also employed that new fangled electrical stunning weapon which reduces its victim to the same kind of mental and physical paralysis induced by four consecutive nights of Big Brother.

"Where have all the stations' digital clocks gone?" I asked, and the answer came, "I don't know."

This reply produced two reactions in me. Firstly, I was relieved not to be given some bureaucratic doublespeak, the likes of, "As an ongoing experiment, we are measuring the reactions of our customers to the removal of visual temporal facilities."

"I don't know." Concise.

Secondly, I considered the crackly nature of the intercom connection. We are in an age when we can ring a call centre, which is located in India, and be connected with a crystal clear connection to a Bombay cockney who will put us at ease with the following; "Gor blimey – nar then, me ole cock sparrer, bin duckin 'n' divin, bin a ball of chalk dahn the old frog 'n' toad, nahmean?"

Yet the voice travelling from Gosforth Interchange to Cullercoats seemed from a giant pan of frying bacon.

Removing time from the Metro system is an extension of removing human beings. Not a single one on a platform, and those spotting that rare species, an inspector, on the trains themselves can fill in their I-Spy books and claim a prize.

Don't panic though. Classical music comes to our aid, and if you feel apprehensive to be alone on a platform with a gang of soured yoofs, declaim clearly, "Aha! You wouldn't dare attack me while Beethoven's Ninth is on the Tannoy!" Works every time.

I mentioned Everest. Since that momentous first ascent in 1953, you can hardly move on the damned mountain. A number 42 double-decker leaves base camp every 20 minutes, and should you wish to travel the final 2,000 feet the lovely Sharon will act as your guide. A light lunch is accompanied by a short promo video at the summit before returning the same night to traditional Nepalese dancing in the Pointy Top Hotel.

Attempts on Everest are part of the trend for 'extreme' holidays: treks through jungles, traversing huge deserts, braving white water rapids.

Whitley Bay, which has lost out to the Tossa del Mar mob sipping their poolside sangrias and hastening skin cancer, should not miss this marketing opportunity.

You've got what it takes? Extreme holiday? The Ultimate Challenge? Book now! One whole Saturday night of unrivalled daredevilry! Travel the entire length of South Parade!

Extreme or what?

You want culture?
I'll give you culture

12th June 2003

SO TYNESIDE didn't get the Capital of Culture prize. When it came down to it, the Scouse cultural giants, Jimmy Tarbuck and Lily Savage, just inched it from the Geordie cultural giants – Ant and Dec.

At least we beat Oxford, a city already so cultured the football fans chant in Latin. But Newcastle and Gateshead's main mistake was not to include Whitley Bay in the bid.

Culture at the coast is more than the Miss Wet T-shirt competition at the now defunct Idols. The area is a haven for artists, misfits, poets and dreamers and other admirable people incapable of holding down a nine to five job.

You can hardly pause by the tinned tomatoes in the Co-op without bumping into a painter, musician or installation artist.

This was once reflected in a Coast Arts Festival, which was run in the 1970s by Mike and Norma Tilley who were in charge of Whitley Bay's long-gone Spectro Arts Workshop.

At the Coast Festival I was once invited to read my nonsense poems in Panama Dip, and you can't get more cultured than that.

It's time we made a come-back, time for the Bohemian coast to reclaim culture from people in dinner suits falling asleep at the opera. Try these events for starters.

St Mary's Lighthouse is one of our great icons, but all we do is look at it, or occasionally climb it.

Each year we should scaffold it and invite the region's best graffiti artists to practise their controversial art on it.

Not the moronic DAZ IS A GIT quick spray, but the real, brilliantly coloured stuff.

For one month in the year people from throughout the world would flock to see this unique rainbow tower, after which the artists would spray it back white.

Festive events could be held on the island in this month, and they might even re-open the café.

It would become an annual event of some note, and give the graffitists a real focus.

Most people ignore modern poetry. Select 1,000 people at random, each one in turn to write a four line verse reacting, in their own way, to what's written immediately previously.

Stand these 1,000 people at several yard intervals in a line stretching from Tynemouth Priory to Seaton Sluice. The poem is then shouted one to the next, and in around four hours will pass the coastal length of the borough. It will make the Guinness Book of Records for the longest poem in transit.

People will take up roadside seats to hear the poem pass. There will be hot dog stalls etc; devotees might cycle alongside to hear the whole thing. Folk would queue to take part in this annual event.

Publish the poem as a souvenir book. A minimum of 1,000 copies guaranteed sold. Probably ten times that number. Poetry publishers would die for such figures.

Arts Festivals should attract people to new places. We all live close to the sea, also close to a theatre, but how often do we go in either?

Sub aqua drama solves this at a stroke. A 15 minute play will be performed at regular intervals underwater in King Edward's Bay, Tynemouth.

Audiences, fitted out in diving gear, will be dropped into their seats from small boats, and each person will have a specially fitted audio tape through which the actors' dialogue will be synchronised with their movements.

Actors too will need breathing equipment, but can wear specially adapted costumes. Waterproof lighting will enhance the effect. Applause, by necessity, may be muted. A unique experience.

Who will want to travel to dreary old Liverpool when they can come to the magic of North Tyneside?

More suggestions invited from readers to help make us the cultural capital not only of England, but the world. I'll publish any inspired ones, as we get the ball rolling.

A man's gotta do … so get that marmalade open!

26th June 2003

THE NEW jar of marmalade would not open. I struggled and heaved like a Sumo wrestler. No effect. I imagined in the marmalade factory a disaffected worker employed at the lid tightening machine. Maybe a broken marriage, or promotion rejected. He/she turns the dial a couple of extra notches. "That'll teach 'em!"

Or was it just me growing old and weak? I rang the doctor's surgery to be told that Marmalade Lid Syndrome could now only be treated privately, before which I would need a £100 thirty second consultation at the Nuffield Clinic.

So conventional medicine was now just about profits. Maybe I needed spiritual help. I thought of the Spanish City mediums and fortune tellers. Except, along with much of Whitley Bay, they'd all recently been bulldozed into the ground.

But this was June – the time of the Hoppings. I hurried along and chose Madame Zelda's caravan with its countless testaments from the stars including Roland Rat and the Teletubbies. Like Big Brother, Madame Zelda boasted a talent of communicating with the dead.

Before consultation she insisted I crossed her palm with a Natwest Switch card. Then she said: "Have you considered switching your electricity account to me?"

Did she have a crystal ball?

"One moment." She disappeared out of the door and returned with a somewhat damp affair. Outside on the grass I could see a goldfish flipping and flapping its last.

"Does the marmalade jar predict Mortimer's senility?" she intoned. There was a series of loud tappings. It was only Madame Cartomancy from the next caravan after a cup of sugar.

From Madame Zelda's mouth came a strange substance which I realised was the chewed-up remains of the McVities digestive she'd been eating.

"Give me a message!" she intoned, and before our eyes a figure began to materialise. It was none other than John Wayne!

"Howdy pardn'r." He doffed his ten gallon hat.

"Damn," hissed Madame Zelda. "I've told those psychic marketing people."

"Me and ma buddy, that's rootin', tootin', fast shootin' lil ole Dubja from Texas, we wanna tell all you critturs about the Whitley Bay Wild West Summer Spectacular!" He lobbed one in the direction of the spittoon.

"Yup. In the Wild West, a man's gotta do... we shoot first ask questions afterward. Only good injun's a dead injun – or is that an Iraqi?"

I jumped to my feet. "But Mr Wayne!" I cried, "Isn't this festival just more propaganda for your country's gun culture that's threatening the stability of the whole planet!"

"Them's big words pardn'r." said John, his eyes narrowing. "You better step outside the saloon and repeat 'em. Or maybe you gotta yellow streak wider than a buffalo's belly?"

He started doing tricks with his six-shooter, but already his image was dissolving, and Madame Zelda was yelling, "No more commercial breaks, I've told you!" "Madame Zelda," I said, "what about the Marmalade Lid Syndrome?" But already she was handing me a glossy brochure, and saying, "I can save you 20 per cent on telephone bills. All you have to do is sign here and..."

But I was gone. Weak, ageing and marmalade free.

It's high season! Time to get away to it all!

14th August 2003

THE STRANGEST statistic of the week was that 18 per cent of Italians pretend to go on holiday. They take the time off work, buy jazzy shorts and sunglasses, cancel the newspapers and milk. Then don't go anywhere.

The story suggested they were ashamed to admit their non-vacation. Maybe. But if you live in Italy, why bother going away? Plus which, these 18 per cent may be ahead of public opinion in the growing awareness that most holidays suck.

Better to stay at home. Plus which we live at the coast, so we're on holiday all the time. And while the rest of the country fries like a burger, we can boast of that thin ribbon of sea fret keeping us all chilled out. Ambre Solaire – Who needs it?

So narrow is this fret at times you can stand with one foot in it, one outside. And without it, our coastline might become the plaything of the idle rich, so don't knock it.

Here's Mortimer's picture of the average 2003 holiday.

Day 1 – Arrive at Heathrow. Baggage handlers' strike has grounded all planes for three days.

Day 4 – After three nights sleeping in the terminal, finally it's take off. Plane circles Europe for three days due to air traffic controllers' strike.

Day 7 – Arrive in Portugal to discover entire country ablaze with forest fires.

Day 8 – Redirected to a new destination in Greece where they've just started building the foundations of the hotel described in the brochure.

Day 9 – Five hour suffocating coach journey to another hotel, which stands alone at the bottom of a two mile, one-in-five hill, has two inches of shingle beach and a bar stocked entirely with out of date warm beer.

Day 10 – Two hour sweaty trudge up the hill to the village where your wallet is snatched. Sunstroke.

Day 11 – A local bus service brings another five hour suffocating journey to the next resort, which is full of pot bellied, loudly swearing drunks from Leeds watching 24 hour giant screen satellite football playing in every bar.

Day 12 – For relief you book on the courier's recommended luxury Mediterranean cruise. This day long event promises unlimited wine, food, and free cabaret on a sun soaked liner. The boat is a 30ft rust bucket, the wine tastes like spent diesel and the food is dried-up egg sandwiches in stale bread. A Greek junkie twangs tunelessly on a one stringed bouzouki till the frustrated passengers throw him overboard. Diarrhoea.

Day 13 – Flight home is 3am the next day. You are told to vacate your room by midday. Wander all day in extreme heat clutching five large suitcases.

Day 14 – Five hour delay at two-shack airport. Arrive back in England in sweltering heat which has melted every line of railway track. Mortgage your house to fly home, unable to face the rigours of National Express buses.

Home – Go off in relentless search of friendly Cullercoats sea fret.

I must go down to the sea again – come to that, so must you

21st August 2003

ALRIGHT. Get into that North Sea. All of you. Look, it's just down the road. Twice a day it comes up, invites you in, shrugs its shoulders and leaves. And what do you do? Absolutely nothing. You may as well live in Birmingham.

You will have noted a certain messianic zeal this week, an aquatic fundamentalism. It is born of an unexpected dip on the Long Sands, a hot early evening, caution suddenly cast to the wind (as were outer garments).

It had been years since I'd done more than paddle. As the water hit my skin, buffeted limbs and groin, I let out small gasps. Total submersion was shocking, ecstatic, freezing, life changing. The temperature on my skin changed in a microsecond from around 28 to 14 degrees. My blood rushed inwards seeking warmth. I pranced and danced, shrieked, shivered, yelped. I ran out the water. Ran back in. Went under. For two minutes I was a shrieking cold-impregnated buffoon, Tynemouth water torture. And then suddenly, a calm announcement from my body. 'OK, got through that, I'm cool now (literally), enjoy yourself.' And I was bobbing in a gentle green embrace, I was lifted and lowered. Waves rolled in, broke over me, dissolved, slithered back like snakes.

This was a moment of epiphany, the startling realisation after all these years that to live at the coast and not go in the sea was absurd, a denial of what formed us. Not connecting.

At that moment I gained an enlightenment known only to a few. These few include the Tynemouth photographer Sirkka Lisa Konttinen, the legendary one-legged man of Cullercoats, and Panama Swimming Club of Whitley Bay, all of whom submerge themselves in the sea every day of the year.

It was unlikely I could emulate such consistency. But the die was cast. No going back.

I bobbed and knew I had temporarily broken my link with the mainland, that place where humans were stressed out over mortgages, careers, thinning hair, thickening waists. I bobbed and waited for the next wave to lift me, knew that these waves, unlike those at the leisure pool, were unlimited and dependent on no electronic timer.

Day and night they came, regardless of wars, divorces, catastrophes. They had no need of business plans, marketing; they were gloriously indifferent to humans.

Like all of life's best pleasures, this one was free, simple and shortlived. For just as the sea gradually accepts you, so eventually it tells you time is up, begins to chill your limbs and turn its friendly embrace into a potentially fatal hug.

I ran out, shook myself, dripped my way home, showered. My body zinged and zapped with energy. Things were more vivid, more alive.

Post dip, your perspective on the world changes. People pay a lot of money trying to change their perspective on the world – drugs, psychiatrists etc. You can get it for free.

You're on therapy? Give the sea a shot. Sniffing substances? Try taking the plunge. Antidepressants? Let the waves roll over you.

But would I prove a one plunge wonder? I hope not. In the next seven days I was in the sea four times, feeling a part of it I never did staring from the cliff top. You could be a part of it too. There's plenty of room.

Go on. Respond to Mortimer's messianic zeal. Get off that settee. Risk missing one episode of Eastenders. Try the sea. It's why you live here.

Ain't nothing in the world like a big eyed girl

4th September 2003

THOSE OF you who missed my version of *Chantilly Lace* in the Queen's Head, Cullercoats on Bank Holiday Sunday must now spend the rest of your lives in regret.

At some future date you will bounce your grandchildren on your knee and inevitably they will ask you "Were you there?" to which you can only shake your head in resignation.

Word spread rapidly once I'd filled in the karaoke sheet and was waiting for my turn. Traffic was soon snarled up around Billy Mill and the entire coastal stretch of road from Blyth to Cullercoats was nose to tail with potential audience. Ingenious folk parachuted in and Madonna got there via a hovercraft landing in Brown's Bay. She missed the first verse, but as every verse is the same, no big deal.

The song was a hit for The Big Bopper, whose only other claim to fame was unwisely touring with Buddy Holly and Ritchie Valens in 1959. The Big Bopper's real name was P J Richardson, and he also recorded a song called *The Purple People Eater Meets the Witchdoctor,* which sold two copies. He wrote the song Running Bear, a hit for Johnny Preston, and – hang on, why am I telling you all this? (*We have no idea. Ed*)

A few people may remember my previous Cullercoats renditions of the song, on the old stage of the Crescent Club concert room in the 1970s. Soon afterwards the club banned me. The incidents are unrelated.

Chantilly Lace has a small range of notes, so is perfect fodder for people like me who want to show off, but have limited musical ability. The Three Tenors rarely perform it, and its demands on the vocal chords are little more than *Wandering Star,* sung by that rusty lawn mower Lee Marvin.

I'd always been a bit snobbish about karaoke, but found it great fun. It has no truck with such nonsense as good taste, and people can make fools of themselves without being exposed to the nastiness of Simon Cowell. In Japanese the word means empty orchestra, and its practitioners fall into two camps. Those who get up, and seem to regret it immediately, weakly bewailing their chosen number as they shrink inwards, and those who know only a quirk of fate has seen them denied showbiz fame; these strut about, punch the air, blow kisses, take an overlong bow. I am in the second category.

Why was it more enjoyable than most poetry evenings I go to? There again, would any poet get away with the words, 'Makes me feel real loose, like a long-legged goose?'

Prominent among the Queens Head singers was the landlord Julian. In fact he pulled rank and sang twice.

Singing is good for you, and we don't do it enough. Singing ten minutes a day reduces risks of heart attacks, increases memory, improves sexual performance, triples the chances of winning the lottery, and is a guaranteed cure for baldness. Most of us in England are too repressed to sing, apart from the drunks' weekend tuneless bellowing of 'here we go, here we go, here we go'.

I'd no sooner stepped off the stage than agents were rushing forward with contracts for world tours, record deals, Las Vegas booking etc; unfortunately I'd promised myself to cut the hedge.

Several of my friends sang too, most of them I confess with much better voices – trilling larks to my growly bear. One man who sang could have been Dean Martin. Another sounded like a cement lorry with busted exhaust.

But basically, if all karaoke singers performed well, it wouldn't last. And as any writer will tell you (or painter, musician, sculptor or whatever), there's something slightly disconcerting when you spend your life striving for perfection only to realise that often bad art is really good fun.

Like the man said, "Hey baby, that's what I like."

It's good to talk. Really?

18th September 2003

PEOPLE ARE objecting to the four mile high phone mast proposed for the Links, Whitley Bay. Such masts are a vital part of our modern communications systems. Without them how could the rail passenger in the next seat shout loudly into his mobile, "I'm on the train."

Mobiles are now the size of a matchbox. Everyone owns one. Six month old babies, the occasional goldfish. I know people whose double glazing has its own mobile.

I don't own one. I don't know what it is, this strange quirk, this realisation that when walking along the sea front, lying in the long grass, or journeying on the Metro I have little desire to say anything to anyone.

People ask if I'm a Luddite, and in response I take them to my study and point out, right next to the Imperial typewriter, such hi-tech miracles as my pencil sharpener.

I am looked on with incredulity by my son Dylan and his mates who regularly text one another while sitting on the same settee.

One of the great delights in life is to settle into a long train or bus journey with that novel you've been meaning to start for three months and know that ahead lies several uninterrupted hours.

Uninterrupted of course, apart from people shouting into their mobiles "Just leaving Peterborough" or "The train's stopped next to a field".

A welcome innovation is the quiet coach, supposedly phone free. Even here at times one will trill opposite me and the person answers (loudly of course). At such moments, I politely lean forward, quietly explain the situation and sock them in the gob.

'Quiet coach' isn't strictly accurate. Between each station are 25 announcements from the customer care leader, the catering efficiency officer, the ticket resource manager, every station en route is listed, also date of its construction. Buffet announcements include each item available, temperature of the tea and coffee in Celsius and Fahrenheit, the date the chef last washed his hat, plus news of his assistant's sciatica.

Eventually you decide to visit the buffet. You squeeze past the fat man who's calculating, on his laptop, the UK's entire defence budget for the next 20 years. At this moment a further announcement comes that the buffet is now closed for stocktaking, which means counting three Mars bars, but will take 90 minutes.

At times like these, I wander into the next carriage, cadge a mobile phone and attempt to ring home for a nice fried egg sandwich on arrival. Recently I have been thwarted by the following recorded message.

"We are unable to connect you with Cullercoats due to the continuing objections of local people to the proposed four mile high mast at the Links in Whitley Bay. If you want future fried egg sandwiches prepared in advance, I suggest you see such objections are withdrawn."

It's soon after this I hear the announcement, "We are now arriving into Newcastle."

Hang on – arriving into Newcastle? Into? This verbal vandalism has spread

through the entire rail network, a whole generation of announcing illiterati are unaware the adverb (or is it preposition?) for 'arriving' is 'in'.
Oh, well. Not the end of the world, I tell myself as I splutter indignantly in my pedantry. But has no one else noticed? I look around the carriage. Every person has glued their mobile to one ear. Their lips are moving in extraordinary synchronicity. As one, they are mouthing the words "I am just about to get off the train".

The shocking secret behind the pub quiz world!

23rd September 2003

SOMETHING IS happening to that strange phenomenon, the pub quiz. *(Any phenomenon is by definition strange, your sentence is therefore a tautology, and I suggest you watch your grammatical logic – Ed).*
The harmless, gently social pastime has been infiltrated by shadowy bodies who are making off with the loot. Who are they? What can be done?
Quiz strategists have come up with Quizgo, where your answers go on to a kind of bingo card, and no matter you might get the first ten questions right, if they ain't in a line, tough.
Quizgo is partially successful. But the shadowy bodies are buying up cards en masse. On your behalf I have been sampling the coast's quiz haunts, and offer half a dozen quick summaries below.
The Piper, Cullercoats: A mixture of Quizgo and home-grown questions, regular teams, unflamboyant. Not a free crisp in sight. The odd shadowy body. Mondays.
The Dolphin, Tynemouth: Held in the beautifully wood-panelled back room. Resident teams hard to beat. Amount of free grub limited by how much you can carry in a napkin. No Quizgo. Tuesdays.
Rockcliffe Arms, Whitley Bay: Jovial, lively atmosphere, good turn-out, alternative Quizgo and non-Quizgo nights. Giant platefuls of grub passed round. Music round has real sounds. Possible shadowy bodies. Final snowball/mega-prize open to all. Rarely won.
The Quarry, Cullercoats: The pub divided between quizzites and non-

quizzites, the latter keeping up a regular babble. Other distraction is the widescreen telly. Small portions of cheese and biscuits appear. Snowball question (again open to all) up to £400, virtually impossible to win. Shadowy bodies? Maybe. No Quizgo. Tuesdays.

Delaval Arms, New Hartley: Cosy, friendly, a mere handful of teams, a back room that requires no microphone. First prize of £4 and second prize Maltesers deters shadowy bodies. No Quizgo, little sense of a competitive cutting edge. Nibbles. Tuesdays.

Magnesia Bank, North Shields: Hugely popular, possibly due to voluminous quantities of hot half-time grub, which produces an unceremonious stampede of quizzers. Competitive, shadowy bodies a definite possibility. Real 'sounds' music round, eye-catching homegrown quiz sheets. Sundays.

Plenty more of course, but sometimes I have to stay home and vacuum the carpet. My own performances are inconsistent, a definite Achilles' Heel with the picture round. "Is that Ronald Reagan?" I asked recently. "No", came the reply, "it's Madonna".

In a supposedly dumbed down age, I'm amazed what people know. Also how, despite us loathing tests or exams, we can't get enough of quizzes.

But what of the shadowy bodies? It took some delving, but I've discovered the truth. These teams consist entirely of school teachers. They have spent years in school, university and teachers' training college honing their specialist knowledge.

Now they find an educational system that has failed them, and as one told me, pupils whose main aim is to burn down the building and spit at them. Thus they take refuge in the pub quiz.

"It's not the money", one shadowy team member told me. "It's just the chance, if only for a few hours a week, to have our knowledge affirmed. Without the pub quizzes most teachers would go bonkers."

To end in the right spirit, Mortimer's quiz question; first right answer here gets a box of liquorice all sorts, and fame in this column.

Q. In what year was commercial television first seen in Britain, and where? Open to all, teachers included.

Oh Little Bohemia by the Sea – Where to now?

2nd October 2003

I WAS TRAVELLING back by Metro from the wonderful Cullercoats Exhibition at the Laing Art Gallery, Newcastle, when who should plonk himself down in the opposite seat, but the ghost of Winslow Homer himself.

Homer was the great American painter who for 18 months in 1881-2, lived in Cullercoats and created remarkable pictures of its inhabitants, fisherfolk especially.

"Hi, Winslow", I said, (American-like informality), "Just visiting?"

"Sure am," he replied, "what with the exhibition and all, thought I'd take a li'l look at the old place."

I offered him a salt 'n' vinegar crisp, which he'd not previously experienced. Homer was among a whole colony of artists who made Cullercoats their home at the end of the 19th and start of the 20th century. People such as Robert Jobling, George Horton, Frank Holl, Isa Thompson, Henry Emmerson and the wonderfully named Victor Noble Rainbird, created a large, often fantastic body of work and Cullercoats was described as "a little Bohemia by the sea".

I kept Winslow amused on the journey. He'd never seen mobile phones, fare dodgers, graffiti, and I was able to show him how far we'd advanced.

He first wanted to see the Lookout House, that famous Victorian landmark featured in his and other artists' work (try Robert Jobling's magnificent *The Day is Done and Darkness Falls from the Wings of Night*).

Blood drained from his face as he surveyed his beloved building.

Its windows were grimy, those offering the view up the coast to the north were boarded up, half the latticed fencing lengths that framed the building were gone. Winslow peered into the shadowy interior.

"What's that?" he said, pointing to the object that almost filled the room.

"A snooker table," I said.

"A snooker table – in the Lookout House?" He steadied himself. "I need a drink. Let's go to The Hudleston." Winslow had lived his 18 months in The Bay Hotel (then known as The Hudleston), and had favoured the occasional tipple.

I set him up with a pint of Guinness. He spat out the pork scratchings.

"Some changes around here," he said, "but at least we can still sit here and look across the bay."

"Actually, Winslow", I said, "they might be knocking The Bay down."

"Knocking it down?" His jaw dropped open. He had a small layer of froth on his top lip.

"Developers want to rebuild it as luxury flats", I added.

"Knock down the centre of the whole village?" he gasped, "and who'll be able to enjoy these views then?"

"A few rich people, I suppose", I replied. "They'll be pulling down those unique fishermen's cottages next," he joked.

"Gone," I said, "back in the 70's."

Winslow stared into his stout, "You know," he said, "one thing I learned about this area. It's either trapped in its history, or it's mindlessly destroying it – always one or the other."

This might have just been the Guinness talking. We went outside and Winslow took a last and painful look around his little Bohemia.

"They call it progress, Winslow", I said, "plus which – ", but the artist was no longer there.

I sensed his presence in the soft moan of a lonely wind which touched my cheek, blew itself westwards, and was gone.

How Nexus can net a million plus while keeping us all healthy

16th October 2003

HURRAH, North Shields is to get a new Tyne Ferry terminal. The present version is a glorified corrugated shed with two sides missing. You wouldn't even grow a leek in it.

Across the water, the distinctive red and blue light sculpture at the South Shields terminal mocks us nightly. Once more the south side has stolen a march over the north.

I find myself fantasising over their modern landing. You can sit in warmth and comfort and buy a drink (albeit from a machine).

Maybe you can order a bottle of Moet Chandon, take a sauna or Jacuzzi, have your trousers pressed, seek counselling about that troublesome neighbour, have the dog de-flead, undergo a body building crash course, get a bikini wax, receive advice on filling in tax forms, pay for a head massage. Thus, in Mortimer's perfect world (and what is life without dreams?) is the ferry landing we should aim for.

The difference in the north and south sides of the river over recent years is symbolised by these landings. South Shields was once Whitley Bay's poor relation. While we have slowly turned the town into a rotting tooth, over there they have a lovely funfair, attractive seafront and a pleasant pedestrianised centre. Whitley Bay once pedestrianised its centre, but in a fit of madness not equalled since George III took to eating grass, tore it up again.

But are we on the move? Two adjacent stories in last week's News Guardian claimed we had both turned the corner and were on the crest of a wave, a double whammy metaphor conjuring some bizarre images of right angle surfers. So let's be positive.

As a man given to harmony more than discord, I offer Nexus a revolutionary new idea for the new terminal which would unite both banks.

Since it's five months since I first reported the disappearance of all Metro clocks, and Nexus have failed to replace a single one, I have a few small doubts about their dynamism, but I'll let that pass.

Here's my scheme, which after extensive market research (i.e. staring into a pint of Magus), I am labelling Tyne Skim.

Nexus will introduce, to complement the ferry service, a new water-ski service across the river, terminal to terminal.

The service would cost £2 each way and include the use of a quickly donned wet suit. The journey would take two minutes (the ferry takes seven) and passengers would travel four abreast holding the towing bar.

A boat would travel from each side, two boats, 30 journeys an hour per boat equals 60 journeys at £8 equals £480, ten hours a day, £4,800 a day, £33,600 a week, or £1.65m a year. With boats, operators, training, fuel etc., it might take £1 m to run, leaving Nexus well in the black.

Quicker, healthier and more exhilarating, water skiing across the Tyne would leave stressed executives pink and zingy for their meetings and would keep passengers in close contact with that vital element to we coastites – water.

Tyne Skim would soon become famous world-wide. Nexus could run short courses on technique and adventurous passengers might even try water-ski acrobatics. Some commuter groups might travel in a pyramid like those police display riders.

As passengers became even more adept, they might push for an annual Tyne Skim Festival to show off their talents. Doing this kind of thing twice a day would soon hone the skills, so why not a challenge cup for the annual Skill Supremo?

Nexus claim to lose a million quid a year to fare dodgers. To combat this they have recruited a large army of ticket checkers whose main talent thus far seems to be invisibility. No matter. Here's a fun-filled idea which will halve that deficit at a stroke.

How can they refuse?

Priory Heights is progress dear boy, progress!

23rd October 2003

A LETTER arrives bearing the photo of a well-known soap star. It is from the previously unheard of Friends of Property Developers Benevolent Fund and reads as follows:

Dear Mr Mortimer, Like most of us, you are a busy person, but can I ask you to take a few moments to read this heartfelt appeal, which I'm sure will touch a chord.

I write on behalf of the Friends of Property Developers Benevolent Fund which supports those unfortunate property developers who have fallen on hard times. This can happen in various ways, but most often via local councils' refusal to support members' valuable development schemes. In some cases this has led to our members selling the second holiday home, downgrading to a new BMW and mortgaging the yacht.

We were most concerned of late at resistance to the exciting redevelopment of The Bay Hotel, Cullercoats, but we are now delighted that the powers-that-be have seen the light. The Bay will soon be razed to the ground and replaced by luxury flats, news that affirms our efforts are not in vain.

One argument against pulling down The Bay was its historical importance to the village. We are delighted this aspect was given the scant regard it deserves and this moves us to seek your support in our latest bold venture.

For many years Tynemouth Castle and Priory have been in a state of disrepair (much worse than The Bay). There is no roof, the stonework needs attention. There is a complete lack of double glazing and central heating, the flooring is inadequate. In short, it is an eyesore. To bring it up to acceptable modern standards would, we are informed, cost a fortune, and we propose a more suitable alternative, which is to knock down the Castle and Priory and build a whole new exciting luxury home 'village' complex on the headland.

The location offers unrivalled views up and down the coast from the spectacular 50ft high cliffs, is within easy reach of all local facilities, and with our plans to convert the present castle gatehouse into a high security entrance, will afford residents the kind of privacy and security the modern successful man (and woman) deserves.

Our initial enquiries suggest an impressively large list of potential purchasers, many of them from the south. With up to 30 dwellings, this would bring much needed income to the area and aid prosperity.

It will also bring to this headland a true sense of modernity. Many people believe that it has tended to lag behind the times, and that a crumbling ruin is hardly the right symbol if we are to attract the brightest and best in our enterprise culture.

Our benevolent fund now asks you for your support. A similar campaign for The Bay, Cullercoats project, which was initially thrown out by the local planning committee, eventually saw the committee members re-educated and, as you well know, The Bay redevelopment now has the green light.

Property developers depend on schemes such as this. Too many rejections and they are forced to send their children to state schools and cut back on the BUPA and shares portfolio.

The creative members have already come up with a name for the development which is 'Priory Heights', acknowledging both the historic and religious aspects, plus the location's unrivalled position and you will find enclosed an artist's impression of the finished scheme, complete with landscaping and various slim looking figures drawn in.

Please do what you can. A letter of support to the local authority would help us, or any informal contact with known councillors. If you are able to do anything of this nature, do let us know. We shall of course be happy to put you on our exclusive list of potential purchasers, who will be given first

option on these exceptional properties.
Thank you for your time and attention etc. etc.

Don't shoot until you see the whites of their eggs!

13th November 2003

THE MOST memorable quotation from last week's *News Guardian* came from Northumbria Police, for whom a spokesperson said, "Any kids found walking the streets with eggs can expect harsh punishment".

I conjured up the street scene, as surly yoof is stopped by the bizzies.

"Alright son, you're in possession of an egg. We need to establish large, medium or small, free range or from imprisoned hens and – what's that? You say you were just off home to scramble it? A likely story! Sergeant – the bracelets!"

Eggs have become, if not quite weapons of mass destruction then at least offensive objects. Throughout North Tyneside, it appears, Hallowe'en was marked by incidents of surly yoof lobbing eggs at people's doors and windows.

Surly yoof is increasingly looking at ways to relieve its boredom, but unlike half-bricks, grass sods or snowballs, eggs cost. Any surly yoof unleashing a regular salvo at an unsuspecting house could face a hefty bill.

In some countries of the world, facing daily starvation, throwing food at windows might seem a bit bizarre. This is unlikely to upset surly yoof. In surly yoof's defence, I'd say there are worse weapons around than eggs.

The headline 'KILLED BY AN EGG' is mercifully rare. One man died when he erroneously boiled and ate a 12-year-old egg; another when for a bet, he tried to swallow an egg whole, shell and all, and choked.

Actually I just made both of those up.

A boiled egg was once described as the perfect food; you add nothing, take nothing away and it is untouched in the cooking. I once had a friend (and this is true) whose method of eating a fried egg was to balance it unbroken on his knife, then swallow it in one. The sensation, he assured me, though brief, is almost orgasmic. I have yet to try it.

In his little known TV cooking series, "Cordon Bleu (or was it 'Rouge'?) Cooking on a Budget for Revolutionaries", Lenin said: "You cannot make an omelette without breaking eggs", an interesting phrase as none of Vladimir Illych's omelette recipes appear to have survived and have never been mentioned by Jamie Oliver.

But I'm digressing. I would like to find something positive in this relationship between surly yoof and eggs. Disciplinarians are often calling for the return of national service to solve the problem of surly yoof. Some call for rhino whipping, rolling in salt or straight decapitation, but we'll stick with the moderates.

While surly yoof is more surly and yoofish in the UK than elsewhere, it IS a problem for all western society, which has given us high technology, but no aim in life.

So why not recruit all surly yoof into the armed services, but instead of deadly bullets, load all weapons with eggs? I've never understood why, when two states fall out, as against two individuals, killing each other's citizens seems acceptable. Egg weaponry would solve this.

Eggs could be fired from tanks, lobbed like grenades, launched from ground to air missiles, or dropped from a great height.

Damage would be more messy than terminal, and even if one hundred million eggs were used in any one year, the cost would be minimal compared to the cost of present weaponry. We might build more schools and hospitals.

International treaties would need to be drawn up ensuring armies use only eggs, but why not?

The victors would be those who could best stand to be continually covered in albumen (the white of the egg to me and you).

Nobody would actually die, but cleaning the uniforms would be a major logistical exercise.

Surly yoof of the world unite. Go to work on an egg.

Bush in Bullerboats – the real truth revealed

20th November 2003

I CAN NOW exclusively and sensationally reveal that President Bush has not been in London! Nor has he been up meeting the Prime Minister in his constituency.

My secret sources disclose the White House's nervousness about the unpopularity of the visit led to Plan B. Even with 25,000 security guards, one hundred hovering helicopters, 145 sniffer dogs, a full salvo of anti-ballistic missiles, three tons of liquid napalm, not to mention a check on every shaving brush in the country for hidden semtex, the CIA were not satisfied about the president's safety.

Thus he was substituted on all occasions by a life-size robotic doll. A computer glitch meant the doll mispronounced words, and talked in clichéd tosh, but this only made the ruse more effective.

Bush himself was still determined to meet the Queen and get her signature, so a secret meeting was organised in a Cullercoats seafront shelter (sorry, you've just missed it).

Both had to be disguised – Bush as a human being and the Queen as a fresh sea trout. Ceremonial presents were exchanged in the shelter. The Queen gave Bush a solid silver serving dish with engraved crest of the House of Windsor, and Bush gave the Queen a Texas t-bone steak.

As ever, this column was ahead of the press pack and managed to secrete a tiny microphone inside the shelter. Here is the transcript:

Queen: "One is moderately pleased to meet one, Mr... Mr..."
Bush: "You just call me Dubja, Queenie, yes sirree! Hot diggety, when I show them your signature back home, they'll move to re-elect me faster than a coyote that's sat on a cactus."

(Gang of surly youths arrive, drink 20 cans of Foster's and tear out the shelter seating. Before leaving they spray their graffiti tag on the back of the unsuspecting president's sheepskin coat.)

Queen: "One is slightly apprehensive about Iraq."
Bush: "Don't you go worrying your li'l head about Iraq – or anywhere else in India. We bombed them so much they know we're on their side! Say, you got any chuck round here?"

(Move off for state banquet in the Copper Kettle, egg, chips and peas plus pot of tea for two.)
Queen: "One is smaller than one imagined."
Bush: "Ain't got my Texan hi-heels on today Queenie. Why, they make me nearly as tall as Madeleine Albright. What is this one horse town anyway?"
Queen: "One believes the nomenclature is Bullerboats, in a remote and uncivilised part of my empire."
Bush: "It's kinda cute. No shopping mall, no Toys 'r' Us, but kinda cute. Has it got any oil?"
Queen: "One suspects not."
Bush: "See if this Bullerboats had oil, we could liberate it. I can have a whole squadron of B52 bombers airborne in minutes! Did you bring your crown, Queenie?"
Queen: "My crown? Certainly not!"
Bush: "Aw shucks – no photo for Laura."
(Despite the security, news of the visit has leaked out. Demonstrators begin to gather outside the cafe. Five Sherman tanks rumble down John Street and squash them.)
"Say, Queenie, how about you just sign your name here in my crayon colouring book. 'Queenie from Killerkites' will do just fine!" *(She does so.)*
Ok, that's Mr Pres. outta here! *(Black helicopter lands outside the cafe, Bush jumps on board and it ascends. The Queen is left to finish her chips and pay the bill.)*

Please throw those knickers in an orderly fashion. Thank you

18th December 2003

ROLLING STONE Keith Richards is 60 today (Thursday). The occasion has attracted a deal of publicity, mainly through his disparaging remarks about fellow Stone Mick Jagger, who, poacher turned gamekeeper, accepted a knighthood from the palace.

I'm with Keith Richards. Sir Mick should have taken his cue from poet Benjamin Zephaniah, and sent the award back to their Satanic Majesties.

Keith Richards also said that despite his age, 20-year-old women still threw their knickers at him. I was 60 yesterday, and though a day older than

Richards, thought I'd chance my arm in the centre of Whitley. I sat with a bag of chips on the seat outside Tom Owens, walked round Woollies, supped a pint in Dundee's, but not a single pair of briefs was lobbed in my direction – probably explained by the cold weather.

No-one expected Richards to make 40, never mind 60, his annual consumption of drugs at one time being more than the average NHS hospital. I'm curiously envious of the fact he's still a character women wouldn't dream of taking home to meet mother, and, as far as I know, he's one of the few celebs (the word itself insults him) to resist making adverts.

In short Richards is a reassuring presence as your correspondent reaches an age always previously viewed down a long tunnel, the length of which only other people travel. Sixty. It's only four years younger than doddery old curmudgeons patronized in Beatles songs.

And there is an anomaly here. We are the generation that invented the power of youth (along with rock 'n roll), we were no longer content with the 'speak when you're spoken to', 'adults know best' philosophy. Nor did we want to grow up humming 'How Much is that Doggy in the Window?' or some vacuous Perry Como number. Youth culture was born.

And we're none too keen to let it go either. Last week at a rock concert at City Hall (see what I mean?), I noticed how things had changed, and how many of the audience had bald heads and pot bellies. The men were even worse. This baby boomers' refusal to grow old is either admirable or pathetic, and I don't know which.

But our youth revolution also unleashed a demon, so that now 'yoof' is worshipped blindly, setting totally unreasonable expectations on people still too immature to fulfil them. Watch a night's telly and count how many people in the adverts are over 25. You'll still have five fingers left. Consumerism, culture, pubs are all geared ridiculously to the young, who meantime are still living at home at the age of 30, unable to afford scandalous house prices.

Age is simultaneously the least relevant and most shattering fact in anyone's life. It's irrelevant because it's beyond our control, and therefore not worth worrying over. It's shattering because despite all the world's thinkers, philosophers, and poets, the older we get, the less comfortable we are with its gradual, though incessant progress.

Still, we are all immortal till the moment of death, and as someone once said, the soul doesn't age. Trouble is, the knee joints do.

Growing old gracefully means slowly disappearing into the anonymity of beige. Alternatively, be like poet Jenny Joseph; wear purple and be slightly disgraceful.

While the latter is to be applauded, we've all seen the ridiculous spectacle of a man of a certain age flailing about on the dance floor in a pathetic aping of John Travolta. Half the time, it's been me.

Sixty is the age when people say to you heartily "You're looking well!" as if at this age their expectation is of some shambling semi-cadaver. Worse is, "I would never have guessed you were THAT old!" At this point I'm tempted to slap them in the gob.

Things have changed though. Fifty was once seen as more or less the end of it. Now welcome to sixty – the Age of the Knicker Thrower.

The unholy trinity – three things to be shown the door at Christmas!

25th December 2003

ACCORDING TO a local news report, a Byker supermarket one week before Christmas had sold only 650 brussel sprouts. The wonder (apart from who's counting) is not how few, but how many. The sprout is my first nomination for Yuletide elimination, a vegetable that inflicts untold misery on us all.

First, preparation: each sprout is individually prepared, the base sliced through, the outer leaves pulled off. No-one is ever quite sure when a sprout is ready.

There is always a hint of discoloured leaf, so you pull off more till the whole thing's no bigger than a marble and you chuck it out.

We are then expected to cut a cross in the base. Again, we do this with no other vegetable.

Boiling the sprouts is a joke. They float, jostling shoulder to shoulder on the water surface. Spuds don't float or carrots, cabbage. Why sprouts? Despite floating, cooking turns them the consistency of soaked blotting paper, the awful texture only forgotten when you encounter the even more awful taste (the cooking smell has stunk out the whole kitchen by now).

The taste is fetid, decayed, unsavoury, and means inevitably some sprouts are left in the dish. For some reason we put these in the fridge, and stare at them for several days, increasingly troubled by their presence, for eating a cold sprout is even less savoury than eating a hot one.

During these few days, we suffer flatulence – the dreaded Brussels Revenge.

Finally we throw them out. Despite all this the sprout survives as an essential Christmas vegetable.

I now move on to bread sauce. Bread sauce is one of life's great mysteries to me. Not only have I no idea how to make it I'm also unaware who eats it.

At every Christmas meal I can remember, a bowl of bread sauce has been put on the table. Likewise at every meal the same, untouched bread sauce has been taken away at the end, and either put in the fridge (next to the sprouts?) or chucked in the bin.

I may have got it all wrong. Bread sauce may well be a table decoration, like a bunch of flowers. It may be placed there to drive away evil spirits.

My suspicion though is simply that no-one has clicked, and that before too long the bread sauce chef is going to turn round and say "Hang on, did anyone eat any of the bread sauce this year?" A shaking of heads. "How about last year?" Again. "The year before that?" Same. "The one before that?" Ditto.

At which point the chef will ask the vital question.

"So why do I keep making it?"

To which no-one has a satisfactory answer.

Finally, those small plastic presents in Christmas crackers. I've already had a dog and a motor cycle.

You snap the cracker, unroll and don the paper hat; read the awful joke, then pick up the tiny item.

What then? What exactly is one expected to do with a plastic pressed motor cycle less than an inch long? What purpose does it serve?

I ran my motor cycle across the table cloth a few times (the wheels don't move of course) and went 'vroom, vroom!' The dog I held up in front of people and went 'woof woof!'

As seasonal entertainment it ranked pretty low, and the glazed looks suggested it might just possibly not keep us all absorbed for hours. Within a few moments most of these tiny treasures are usually in the bin. At least if there's any room left after all that bread sauce, all those brussel sprouts.

But sprouts, sauce, and plastic nonentities apart, do have a good Christmas – assuming such a thing is remotely possible.

Salvation lies in the lollipop – its renaissance is now overdue

15th January 2004

CONSIDER IF YOU will the humble lollipop. I am not writing here of iced lollies. These are sophisticated beasts with names like Space Rocket, Twister, or Launch Pad, a complex mix of ice-cream ingredients and each with enough content to feed an Ethiopian village. Or at least render them less hungry for 20 minutes.

The lollipop I refer to in shape and colour is like a traffic signal and led to the most user friendly job description in the world – that of lollipop lady.

The genuine lollipop is unburdened by a famous brand name or marketing trivia. It is often found in those heavy glass jars once the preserve of every sweet shop, but now normally replaced by the plastic variety so lightweight they blow away in a gentle wind.

The true lollipop costs little. My local cafe, the Copper Kettle in Cullercoats, often gives them free to kids.

But what, you ask, is the reason for considering this item?

Because the lollipop, as produced at the coast, is under threat. In a quote which resonates with foreboding, a spokesperson at the House of York (still known to all sensible people as Welch's), in Norham Road, North Shields, said: "It takes about four people to run the lollipop machine and they are concerned for their jobs."

I read this and was filled with yearning. I wanted to be an eight-year-old boy and in the early morning have my father kiss me on the brow and say, "Well, son, I'm off to run the lollipop machine."

When I was eight my father worked in a furniture shop.

The very word lollipop is cuddly. It is something from an Edward Lear nonsense poem. The word waddles in front of us even as we speak it, suggesting an innocent world where estate agents, user options and unopenable milk cartons are non-existent.

Many sweets are now targeted at adults as well as children, ensuring we remain the fatties of Europe. Some (consider the Cadbury's Flake) are blatantly sexual.

Yet an adult walking down the street licking an old fashioned lollipop would still command a second look. It is time to give the lollipop its due and – who knows? – maybe save four jobs in North Shields.

I suggest at every high powered business meeting, conference or summit, those attending (who will be mainly white, middle-aged, middle-class and male) be actively encouraged to lick lollipops throughout, bringing a much needed playful air to the proceedings.

It is well known most meetings serve no purpose and the more meetings a human being attends, the more miserable he/she becomes. It is hard to think of a cabinet declaring war while licking a lollipop.

Note I use the word lick and not suck. For here now is the advertising campaign to give the lollipop a new life. As far as I know (readers' letters welcome), it is the only foodstuff that can be eaten without ever being put in the mouth. You may think this unimportant, but the advertising world survives through trivial gimmicks.

And because a lollipop is in full view while being devoured, it could be more interactive, maybe a series of visual images appearing as you lick through it – a short episode of *The Simpsons* with each lolly maybe?

The lollipop renaissance is overdue. Soon the lollipop machine will be sold off and the four operators will have only their dreams.

Come on Welch's (or House of York). Surely you're not licked yet.

Revealed – the surefire way to fill all those empty soccer seats

22nd January 2004

ON THE SAME day the new boss of Whitley Bay FC declared his intention to win back the fans, the global soccer supremo offered a curious slant on increasing the game's popularity.

The Bay's Ian Chandler put his faith firmly in playing entertaining football. Fine principles, sir, but listen a moment to Sepp Blatter, FIFA president, one of the world's least loved men, whose name smacks of contagious vomit.

Mr Blatter believes women footballers should wear sexier, skimpier outfits. Hotpants were mentioned. In his defence he mentioned other sports which have adopted the 'less is more' philosophy. Women's beach ball is played in bikinis, though suggesting most spectators watch it for the sporting content is akin to claiming millions of men tune into Bay Watch for the post modernist dialogue and tight plot structure.

In case Ian Chandler had not read Blatter's suggestion, I not only offer it free of charge, but would claim it is nowhere nearly radical enough. The professional male game is in crisis.

Thus far, spectators at premier league games have still not twigged how much they are being ripped off to feed the immoral salaries of soured and spoilt young men.

But those insomniacs who, like me, watch Nationwide League highlights late on Monday night will have spotted the empty seats and the ability, if you have a relative at any game, to be able easily to spot him or her.

It is obvious to me that the best way to lure back the fans and win new ones is to play every game naked. Free thinkers have so far only flirted with such large things in sport. Sky offered us topless darts, though concentrating for some reason on female players, whereas male dart players usually have much more rounded breasts.

The original Olympic Games were competed for in the nude, though as ancient Greeks were made of white marble and often had missing arms, this may have merely been an eccentricity.

A nude premier league would pull in whole swathes of new female fans, but my plan does not end there.

Thus far, male and female versions of the game, despite films such as *Gregory's Girl,* have been kept apart. This has been justified on the grounds that men can commit fouls more strongly, but it's time to bring down the barriers.

Each team could have five male, five female players, with an option on the goalkeeper. And even if there are differences, who will give a hoot?

In fact who will give a hoot about anything apart from seeing naked people? This will bring football into line with the current fad of pseudo-serious television documentaries on *The History of the Gusset,* or *Nipple Sociology Through the Ages.*

Ours is a market economy, and anything that fills grounds, and TV schedules is fine. The trend could soon spread to other sports, though nude crown bowls might not immediately take off; Formula One car racing wouldn't mean much unless the drivers stood up at the end. Sumo wrestling, with the need to find a grip on your opponent, might prove problematic. I'm not sure about chess.

Cable and satellite stations are locked in fierce combat to grab the viewers' mindless attention, and I'm only surprised this has not been thought of before. Now this column's powerful influence has unleashed the idea, it will spread like wildfire, and as well as sport, it can't be a long wait before I'*m a Nude Celebrity Pillock – Get Me Out Of Here*, or even *Changing Genitals*.

But first football, and the need to fill Hillheads. Make the right selection, Ian Chandler. Watch the fans flock.

Shedding blood – for Queen, country or a bourbon chocolate cream

4th February 2004

CASS COMMUNITY Centre, Whitley Bay, seems a much more suitable place to shed blood than the corner of some foreign field. Plus which you get a biscuit.

It appears they do not take blood from amnesiacs. Four times during the process I was asked date of birth and address and presumably had I forgotten even once, I'd have been hoyed oot.

For two days after my splendidly unselfish act I stared at the small Elastoplast on my inner arm, wondering what was the officially designated EU time for removal. I was afraid that whenever I peeled it off, a hand would be placed on my shoulder and a voice of some officialese pronounce, "Not so fast if you don't mind sir."

A sticking plaster blood duration officer is a little known occupation, but an important one.

The Blood Transfusion Service seems to have escaped the main horrors of modern life. By this I mean the 'There is no society' philosophy, which suggests the best way to help others is to trample them underfoot in your rush for self-improvement.

Not only does blood giving generate no income, there is also no financial gain whatsoever for the donor. How on earth does it all survive? The 98 per cent of the population who don't give blood miss out. Not just the tea and biscuits, but the exciting lives lived by all donors. Why, just look at the exotic list of diseases they're asked about, and equally exotic locations they have been, or whether in the last six months they've had sex with a Malawi alligator.

My main reason for donating has little to do with altruism, more the only chance I get to fall asleep in a public room with 12 other people. Once I lay on that couch, I never want to get off. Let them take the whole eight pints if they want.

Out in the real world, there's a play to finish, letters to write, people to see. So what? I turn the small object in my hand, as requested (no idea why).

I stare at the cork ceiling, hear the occasional voice, or footfall. I am totally at peace and I think of ways to attract the missing 98 per cent.

An enterprising TV producer could produce a programme called Blood Lines. This would link pints of blood through from the donor to eventual recipients and bring the two together.

More than that, it might take five such groupings and place all of them in a sealed house or an Australian forest where they'd risk being eaten by poisonous scorpions or a model with over sized breasts.

Meantime, the nurse approaches, checks my bottle, and says "Almost done." I am filled with disappointment. Is she sure? There's really no rush.

Another idea comes to mind. The service is highly worthy, but slightly staid. Instead of those certificates, how about a large badge, red garish print on a black background and the legend 'I'm a right bleeder'.

Or a Rhesus Negative Club, where the minority group can meet up every three months for common solace. I'd like a few statistics as well. Fastest pint. Slowest pint. Surely the boss person could appear on Parky with some jolly tales of transfusion disasters?

Or do I really want to sex it all up? "Get your drink now," says the nurse kindly and I know my twice-a-year brief sojourn of utter tranquillity is almost over. I know, in a hostile world, I never really want the Blood Transfusion Service to change.

I munch on the bourbon, wondering if cycling home comes under the 'strenuous activity' forbidden for at least an hour.

A whole pint of blood. That's nearly an armful, as Tony Hancock said.

And of course, our Tony was rhesus negative.

Scowl, please! You've been captured on a special Metro (fuzzy) camera!

19th February 2004

ACCORDING TO last week's *News Guardian,* extra loot will he made available to maintain the Metro network of CCTV cameras. I thought I'd get out on the system and gauge reactions. Choosing 10 a.m. was a mistake, as most passengers were half buried under discarded copies of newspaper, but I dug out an American academic doing a thesis on 'People v Technology.'

He had heard rumours of an inspector spotted near Shiremoor station in November 2003, but this was unsubstantiated.

"I'm intrigued with your security camera system," he said. "Are there statistics for the number of tickets checked by the cameras, or number of times the cameras step in to prevent trouble?"

"The cameras are a deterrent," I said. "They identify wrong-doers."

"So those fuzzy out-of-focus pictures can actually identify people?" he asked.

"No" I confessed.

We were passing through North Shields, 200 youngsters jumped on the train and ran up and down the aisles bellowing and knocking old men's hats off. "Don't you realise you're on camera?" I yelled. "And there's a remote chance one of you may be identified at some future date."

In response they all lit up a fag, while an 80-year-old woman had a heart attack (luckily captured on camera).

I was keen to impress our American academic friend.

"When the inspectors do have a blitz," I said, "the fare dodgers are fined and their names are published on large posters and shame them."

"Yes," he said, "I hear those posters are collector's items with the fare dodgers."

He produced a table of statistics which he guided me through.

"A fine will cost you £10 and you can expect to be checked once every two months, or 60 days. Paying the £3 daily fare over that time would cost you £180. Interesting yes?"

The figures made an uncomfortable, if immoral kind of sense.

The train had now pulled into Howdon and was being bombarded by a group of youths with half-bricks.

"You fools," I yelled at them. "Don't you realise that if you stick around for 30 minutes, or put your face really close to the camera for ten seconds, you could be in big trouble?"

"My research also tells me," continued the learned one, "that vandalism always starts when you replace people with machines – or in this case cameras."

We were at Walkergate, and fighting had broken out by youngsters too stupid to realise the presence of cameras. In the hubbub the academic shouted: "£1m annually lost to fare dodgers. You could buy a lot of inspectors for £1m. And make people feel safer."

"Look," I shouted back as someone's head was banged against the carriage window.

"It has been shown that riding the Metro is less dangerous than walking the rim of Vesuvius. And Vesuvius has no cameras. Case proven."

The fighting was spreading and we were in danger of being sucked in.

"A handy tip" I yelled. "Cushion your body against the blows with a dozen discarded copies of the Metro newspaper."

"And for Heaven's sake, do smile." I urged, as his face went into panic mode. "You're on camera."

I've felt more apprehensive in Whitley Bay than I do here

4th March 2004

Sana'a, Yemen

MY CLICHED IMAGE of visiting a British Embassy in distant climes is of sitting with the Etonian blazered ambassador on the Embassy lawn with tea and cucumber sandwiches while he (sure to be a he) enquires, "So how is old Blighty then?"

The reality in Sana'a is somewhat different. In front of the Embassy building is a ten foot wall topped with an iron fence, itself topped with barbed wire.

In front of the wall is a series of huge concrete blocks linked by chains to prevent a car bomber. Entrance to the Embassy is through this zig-zag of blocks and a series of armed checks, into an ante-room where you are checked from behind a glass screen, then allowed access via a series of steel doors that operate on an air lock system; one automatically closes before the next one opens.

Inside there is a garden of sorts, but stacked three deep with massive bales of a material called hesco, which is designed to absorb the impact of an explosion.

"Al Qaeda tried to blow us up before and they may well try again," said the official who looked me up and down as if to suggest his own clichéd image of a British playwright was fixed with J.B. Priestley.

All this makes Yemen sound like a violent country, as does the sight of many male Arabs with the long traditional dagger – the jambia – stuck down the front of an ornate belt.

Others walk around the street with a Kalashnikov rifle slung over the shoulder, and most statistics say there are more rifles in Yemen than there are people. The population of this little-known country on the southern tip of Arabia is 20m.

The truth is I have felt more apprehensive walking down South Parade, Whitley Bay on a Saturday night than I have being on the night streets of Sana'a.

Few westerners here, and I look strange to the locals, but their curiosity is of an extremely gentle kind. Part of this may be explained by the national habit of chewing qat, the legal stimulant leaf indulged in as far as I can see on a daily basis by a majority of the population, at least the males.

My own qat session, seated on large cushions round the edge of a long room with up to 24 other men (no mixed sex qat sessions, mixed cafes, or even mixed banks in this Muslim country), lasted three and a half hours.

Qat tastes (and looks) like hedge clippings; it's both bitter and foul, and for the first 30 minutes I feared I might disgrace myself by vomiting in front of my hosts, who had welcomed me warmly.

Thereafter, as I slowly pushed in enough leaf to acquire the distinctive swollen cheek, we talked religion, politics, sport, culture, the Iraq war, the UK, Yemen – a long uncompetitive meandering discussion which I couldn't imagine having with 24 men of various ages over three and a half hours in the UK.

I drank gallons of water with the qat, and that night was awake until the early hours, then up again at 6.30 a.m. It is said both to root you and to clear the mind, and if I can get over the goddam awful taste, I may try it again.

Sana'a, said by some to be the world's oldest city, is full of uniquely decorative high buildings that seem to be made out of pink icing sugar. Some 8,000 feet above sea level, it's a teeming chaotic city of small souks, and it's surrounded by yet higher mountains.

My hotel room, on the fifth floor, and with a broken window (and a prayer mat) overlooks one of the busiest highways; up and down whiz an endless procession of the city's battered cars, some seemingly held together with string or sellotape.

They honk their horns endlessly in a way Brits only do after we've won the World Cup.

This all night horn symphony, plus the thin air mean I'm continually knackered, but in laid-back Sana'a no-one bothers if you fall asleep for a few hours.

Tomorrow I'm taking the no-doubt battered bus up over the mountains on the scary and spectacular road to Aden, the former British Protectorate and port through which the Yemeni seamen passed. It was the same seamen's riot of 1930 in Shields that will form the subject of my play, and that brought me here in the first place.

The journey is 200 miles, around seven hours and I'm told there'll be a lot of qat chewed.

More next week.

One of three columns from the Yemen trip.

It's good news for the trees – and good news for us, too

8th April 2004

A SMALL RENAISSANCE may be underway. I am trying not to get over-excited (never having mastered the envied art of being laid back), but three separate stories in last week's *News Guardian* give cause for cheer.

The newly formed Friends of Brierdene are looking to return the site to its former splendour.

Marden Quarry, thanks to English Nature grants, and Community Service action is back to mint condition: new fencing, footpaths, landscaping. No Safeway bags caught in trees, plus ducks, geese and swans chortling with delight – if birds can chortle.

Oh, and Tynemouth Park is undergoing a £170,000 facelift via its new owners, Ron and Carol Scott.

Possibly parks are making a comeback. Parks were once a national treasure. The Victorians saw the provision of green open spaces as essential to the national well-being.

All towns and cities had large, well-kept green lungs where you could roam free and let your imprisoned spirits soar. To youngsters, the park-keeper was as well-known a figure as the local bobby.

And if the man in the ice-cream kiosk turned a few bob, as did the pitch 'n' putt course, not to mention the boating lake, no-one seriously expected parks to be money-makers.

Round about 1980 it all changed. Society was abolished, and we were told all our problems could be solved by the market economy. Parks don't fit easily into the market economy. Where's the profit in trees and shrubs, and fresh air and squirrels?

You might possibly get developers eyeing a park enviously but only if (as recently with Brierdene) they saw a chance to build on it.

In this new age of commercial brutalism, parks were easy pickings. Old ladies who fed the ducks, kids who kicked a ball about, and the odd fisherman constituted no sort of pressure group. Parks became neglected, overgrown, bandstands rusted, as did swings and slides.

Only one kind of park was in favour; the National Garden Festivals flared briefly in the 90s. But they were moneymaking ventures, and when the money was made, they were allowed to rot.

As parks declined, leisure centres mushroomed. The new mandarins were more at home with leisure centres, and multiplexes. They sat nicely on the balance sheet.

They were nothing like parks. Parks are truly egalitarian: paupers can enjoy them as much as millionaires, there is no means test, no entry fee. You cannot jump the queue, privilege or influence count for nothing. As far as it is possible, parks are incorruptible.

I want parks. Lots and lots of them. I want a high priority on people who look after parks, pick up litter, skim the lake surface, plant flowers, remove plastic bags from trees. I want accountants to have nothing to do with running them. Nor multinationals.

I want sitting under a tree, or roly-polying to be seen as vital activities. I want people who seethe in rush-hour queues en route to jobs they hate to spend time in parks, or even climbing the same trees they also sit under.

"Only God can make a tree," said the poet Alfred Joyce Kilmer. But human beings can make parks.

For almost a quarter of a century it has been a neglected and forgotten art. And we have all become more lonely, more paranoid, more stressed. GNP soars, the human spirit shrinks.

Bring back the parks! And maybe, just maybe, it's happening.

Revealed: The long hidden secret. King Edward's Bay and me

15th April 2004

OK, OK, I KNOW grammatical pedants will fume that the above headline should read 'King Edward's Bay and I', but finishing a sentence on 'and I' makes it sound like the Queen talking.

Naturally, news that the above bay has been selected among the country's top ten beaches has been greeted with loud hurrahs. I have little idea on the voting process, who voted, or when, but no matter.

King Edward's is now up there (or down there geographically) with the best of 'em and I only wish I could run across it, chest swollen with pride, joyously waving a Cadburys 99.

But I cannot. I am forbidden ever to set foot on King Edward's Bay. I have never once walked upon that beautiful beach, nor, in the years that are still allotted to me (105 will do) will it ever happen.

I shall explain this curious state of affairs. Some 25 years ago, when I'd lived at the coast only a couple of years, I stood looking down on King Edward's with the realisation that it was the only beach between Tynemouth and Blyth I'd not set foot on.

In dramatic fashion, I stood back from the railings and declaimed "Nor shall I ever set foot on it. This shall be, for Mortimer, the untrodden territory, the place never visited. Always seen, never experienced."

Now this was an unusual thing to shout from those railings. People usually shouted down the likes of "D'ye want batter wi' yer chips, like?" or "Ah'll see you aal in the Porcy."

The ensuing quarter century has not been easy. On occasions I have stood at the top, a sense of severe exclusion, waving at friends happily barbecuing below.

Chrisy, aunt of my son Dylan, gave me a jam jar labelled 'Sand from King Edward's Bay', so that at least I could get close to the stuff. I stroke the glass regularly.

And seeing news of the award on *Look North* was strange, camera shots from the beach itself, tilted angles of the Priory and the cliffs I had simply never seen in my life.

The biggest test came in the late 70s when I wrote a series called *Beachcomber* for the *Newcastle Journal*. This entailed walking every inch of beach from Berwick to Tynemouth accompanied by a frisky Jack Russell, Che.

I suffered for my art on this eight day journey. Unable to traverse the wild shoreline of Budle Bay, Che and I headed out directly across the low tide wastes, unaware the treacherous quicksand had in that lonely spot trapped many people who simply drowned with the incoming tide.

I still wake in cold sweats over those moments, with Che clutched to my chest, and at every stride the cloying mud coming closer to the Wellington tops as we struggled to keep going. Somehow we made it.

I'd also resolved to do the journey without using bridges.

As we needed to cross the rivers Tweed, Coquet, Wansbeck, Aln and Blyth, this was a bit reckless, but again by wading, scrounging rowing boats etc, we did it, the most scary moment edging like a tight-rope walker across a round pipe that straddled the deep cut at Seaton Sluice, the wriggling Che again in my arms.

"You do all this, and then tell me you can't walk across King Edward's Bay," roared the editor as I phoned in near journey's end.

"Sorry boss, it's just a personal thing," I said. The phone went dead and the next week my expenses were halved.

King Edward's unique place in my life has made it a site of mystery and allure, which, despite their obvious attractions, Tynemouth Long Sands, Cullercoats Bay or Whitley sands can never equal. I was there again over Bank

Holiday, leaning on the railings, staring down at the paddlers, the sand castle builders, the strollers. And close though it is as regards accessibility I may as well have been staring at the moon.

Half century up – and at last I'm off to the moon!

6th May 2004

THERE'S A GROWING sense of euphoria at the coast this weekend. It is explained by the feverish anticipation for this – the 50th *Mortimer at Large* column.

Thank you... thank you... all donations gratefully received. Fifty columns is around 30,000 words, which is part way towards a decent novel length, and possibly the birth of a new genre – git lit.

It was while looking back over these past 50 columns that I received a recent copy of the *Slovenian Sun*, with its front page headline 'Stop These Scroungers Now!'

Let me quote. 'Now that Slovenia has become part of the expanded EU, there are fears of a massive influx of foreign workers swamping our social services, molesting our women, and generally having bad breath.'

'Rumours are rife of up to 20m Brits planning to cross our borders. It is well known hardly any of them will speak a foreign language, and they are musically illiterate apart from bellowing "Here we go! Here we go! Here we go!" They have been driven from their own bleak shores by rising crime, astronomical house prices, low pensions, rain, obesity, a violent yoof culture, and increasing drunkenness.'

'*The Slovenian Sun* says BOG OFF BRITS! There is no place in our modem Slovenian society for such types, even if they are fleeing a repressive Christian fundamentalist regime intent on wiping out the Muslim world. We do sympathise, but still we feel bound to say, TOUGH LUCK BRITS! STICK IT UP YOUR YORKSHIRE PUDDINGS!'

Watch this space for future developments.

Meantime, I look back on highlights of those 50 columns. These included afternoon tea with Osama Bin Laden in Whitley Bay's Cosy Café. He ate two portions of lemon drizzle cake, and left me with the bill.

I also enjoyed the arm wrestling competition with the North Tyneside mayor.

And while Linda Arkley may have pretty good deltoids, in a best of three contest, there could only be one winner.

I was also disappointed only to finish second in the London Marathon, a good two minutes outside the world record. Running in one shoe, plus the severing of an artery by a rottweiler near Tower Bridge didn't help, but hey – no excuses here.

Writing for the *News Guardian* brings its own celebrity status of course, and I was pleased to take part in the TV programme *Weekly Columnists Go Through Their Dustbin*, where I was only just pipped for the title of most boring content by some geezer writing for *The Seghill Thunderer*.

Being chosen for the first Whitley Bay moon shot was an honour I will always cherish; blast-off some time in June from Panama Dip, and though in some ways it's an economy moon shot (I'm asked to bring my own beetroot sandwiches), I'm thrilled at the thought of writing this column's dateline as The Sea of Tranquillity.

Many thanks to all those thousands who week in, week out declined to write to me, and thanks also to the spirited gentleman who engaged me in animated conversation down South Parade last Bank Holiday. My jaw's almost healed.

Columnists are terribly insecure folk, waking in cold sweats as deadlines approach with naught but the blank page to show. We sit in our lonely rooms and purport to make some comment on the world. Like everyone else we want to be loved, appreciated and paid more *(now cut that out – Ed.)*.

But let's face it, things could be much worse. I could be writing editorials for *The Slovenian Sun*.

Happy 50th to me.

Someone watching over us – that'll be £2.90 a week

20th May 2004

LIKE THE REST of you on North Tyneside, I'm busy filling my piggy bank to make sure I can afford the new security protection coming our way. You'll already have read how this has started in the leafier suburbs of Whitley Bay.

Participants pay £2.90 a week for which they can sleep safer in their beds knowing a watching eye is on hand (is that a mixed metaphor?).

The scheme is reported to have sent a shiver down the spines of hardened criminals, fleeing in their droves in the general direction of East Sleekburn.

Naturally there have been teething problems, as with any radical venture. I am told of the householder who ran up the street yelling, "Stop thief!" in pursuit of the obvious ne'er-do-well clutching the family jewels.

Our poor victim was intercepted by a man in a dayglo jacket holding an enrolment form.

"Sign here, pay your first month's instalment, and such unfortunate incidents could become a thing of the past," he said.

"But the thief's getting away!" yelled the robbed one.

"The moral being, of course," said the form-waver, as the ill-shaven ruffian disappeared over the horizon, "sign up earlier! Always plan ahead!"

The scheme is only the start, the tip of the iceberg, the merest hint of things to come.

Unleash the power of market forces into our public services!

Let the strong winds of competition blow through the corridors of our social fabric (hang on, that's a bit of a strange metaphor too).

Picture this. Somewhere in Shiremoor a fire rages. From the house's top window people are yelling to be rescued. One brave person manages to struggle to the phone and ring the new-style 'market aware' fire brigade.

"Ah, 23 Acacia Gardens – we don't actually seem to have you on our books as signed up for our blaze rescue scheme."

"We'll all be burnt to a crisp if you don't hurry!" yell the trapped.

"You have my sympathies of course. But I'm sure you'll agree it would be financially imprudent for us to make our scheme retrospective. That way, everyone would wait till their house was on fire before signing up – just like you're doing."

"My eyebrows are beginning to smoulder!"

"As far as I know, there may still be some remnants of the old-style fire service in the borough, though they may have had to flog their engine. As a special favour, I'll give you their number."

"The budgie has just exploded!"

"On the understanding that if you do get rescued, you sign up with us straightaway. Surely £5 a week isn't too much to be confident of staying singe-free?"

At which point the phone went dead.

Ambulances could operate on the same principle (and often do in the USA).

And while we're at it, while we're looking to introduce a vibrant market economy, and not some stodgy nanny state in which people just sit back and expect everything on a plate, how about the mountain rescue service, or the coastguard?

Do you really expect to be rescued from a blizzard half way up Ben Nevis or plucked from the icy waves of the North Sea if you haven't subscribed?

We've almost managed to eradicate 'state interference' from the dental service, and we're well on the way to a 'you want it – you pay for it' system in the NHS, and quite frankly I can't see the anachronism of state schools lasting that much longer.

So come on all you citizens of North Tyneside. You know it makes sense.

Humbly I stand before you – your duty is clear

27th May 2004

LOCAL ELECTIONS loom and I have only one thing to say. Vote for me. Yes, that's right. Voting for anyone else would be foolhardy, misguided, errant, calamitous, wrong, ill informed, reckless, absurd, dodgy, divisive, counter-productive and a bad idea. Vote for me.

What do I stand for? A very good question. A question I am extremely glad you asked. A question that gets to the heart of things. A question we all need to address. A question that pulls no punches. A question relevant to our children, and our children's children, and our children's children's children and their pets.

Look around you. Exactly.

Search deep in your hearts. Explore your consciences. Need I say more?

Can there be even a flicker of doubt that I am wrong? Of course not.

The time has come. On this we are all agreed. Pulling together. Nose to the grindstone. Shoulders to the wheel. A stiff upper lip. A clenched fist.

We live in modern times. This much is certain. Great challenges lie ahead.

All we need fear is fear itself. And falling trees. Painful decisions have to be made. A tightening of belts. Sometimes we have to say 'yes'. Or 'no'. Or 'maybe'. Or nothing at all.

I shall not rest. I shall not flinch. Read my lips. Stroke my chin. Drink my coffee.

Ask yourselves this. At the end of the day, in the final analysis, given a level playing field, when push comes to shove, what goes around, comes around – right or wrong?

If you can't stand the heat get offa my cloud. Exactly.

Vote for me. I have never met you. You have never met me. Here I am. This is my photograph. Knock, knock. Who's there? It's your councillor. Councillor who? Exactly.

Tynemouth Long Sands. Spanish City. St Mary's Lighthouse. Brown's Bay. The Leisure Pool. Cullercoats Crescent Club. Need I say more?

How honoured I am. It gives me great pleasure. Point of order. Land of Hope and Glory. Chirpy chirpy cheep cheep. Shuddupa ya face.

Vote for me. That's right. This is my pledge. And this is my shaving brush.

Let there be no doubt. Can I say quite categorically? Exactly.

You know it makes sense. Does what it says on the tin. You can't get quicker than – clunk click.

Tynemouth Boating Lake. The Priory. King Edward's Bay. The Bonga. Wandering Willy. Land of Green Ginger. Need I say more?

A new beginning. Marks & Spencer. A land fit for heroes. Marks & Spencer. Exactly.

You're too kind. I stand here before you. Let me say quite categorically. High tide. Low tide. In my lady's chamber.

Long term. Short term. Medium term. Statistics prove. Right there. A neat cross. Thank you.

I have no hesitation. I am the answer. I am the eggman. Your humble servant.

Who am I? Another good question. So pleased you asked it. Point One. Point Two. Exactly. On the other hand.

Vote for me. This is my leaflet. This is my rosette. This is my poster. This is my budgie. Let no-one deny.

Absolutely. Unequivocally. Irrefutably. June 10. Day of destiny. Vote for me.

Another burger. More lager? Time for an extra Mars Bar?

3rd June 2004

I BUMPED INTO my occasional acquaintance Slob Foster on South Parade, Whitley, Bank Holiday Monday. He was making his way top to bottom via every bar and burger van.

Slob's dedicated drinking and junk food consumption have left him with the ability to balance a pint jar, unsupported, on his pot belly.

"Well, Slob," I said, "all this talk of obesity – what do you think?"

"Obesity?" he retorted, opening a tube of Pringles which he poured down his throat in one go. "I can't stand their music."

"No, Slob," I countered." Obesity is not a band, it's an epidemic, with now one quarter of the population dangerously overweight."

By this time a pack of salted peanuts had disappeared and he was banging on the bar for another lager.

"You see, Slob," I continued, "people are eating and drinking too much and getting too little exercise."

"Hang on," he said, and reached for his mobile. He dialled. "Hello, Foxhunters Taxis?"

"Where are you going Slob?" I enquired. "The gents," he replied.

When he returned I took up the conversation again, though he was puffing and blowing from the exertion of getting out of the car's seat.

Slob was pretty excited. He'd been invited to appear in the new reality TV show *Fat People Get Fatter* where a series of highly overweight people in a sealed room are fed unlimited burgers, chocolate, doughnuts, milkshakes and chips, and the last fattie to explode walks (or waddles) away with one million pounds.

"I'm forced to win!" said Slob. "I've never exploded in my life!".

"You should listen to these warnings Slob," I said. "Those experts know their onions."

"Their what?" he asked.

"Onions. A vegetable you can buy in a greengrocers, old fruit."

"Old what?" asked Slob.

"Fruit, Slob. They're like vegetables but sweeter. Bananas, oranges, apples, that kind of thing. Never eaten any?"

"Not sure," said Slob. "What flavour are they. Smokey bacon? Barbecue chicken? Salt 'n' Vinegar?"

Suddenly he grew excited and pointed to the TV where Garry Lineker was extolling the virtues of fat-saturated potato crisps.

"See!" yelled Slob. "If it's alright by Garry, it's alright by me!"

I wanted to discuss with Slob the scientific theory that with the average UK citizen putting on an average stone extra weight a year (which came to 300,000 tons), our island was expected to sink beneath the waves by 2011.

But Slob poo-pooed the idea. Fat bulged from his trouser top like cream squeezed from a cake, and I could swear even his eyebrows were gaining weight.

"Maybe you should try to lose a few pounds, Slob," I ventured.

"No problem," he said and immediately squeezed one of the many zits his diet had deposited on his face. The zit burst, he wiped away the pus and said, "See? A few grams gone already!".

He'd made his way (via another taxi and the next burger van) to the next bar when a flicker of concern ran over his face.

"I've just remembered," he said, "the batteries on the TV remote have packed in. Three times last night, I had to get off the settee and change channels. You don't think all that exertion will put an extra strain on my heart?"

"I doubt it, Slob," I said. At this he looked relieved, ordered a large pack of Quavers, another pint of lager, and got on with his short life.

Russian assistants' smiles as expressionless as Rushmore

10th June 2004

NOW HERE'S something to smile about; all our local beaches have been given the blue flag, and the chances of swallowing a rotting dog while bathing are severely reduced.

I have once again taken up my weekly dip, and can be seen bobbing like a wine cork at the North End of Tynemouth Long Sands.

Will I be smiling? Maybe. I'm intrigued by a news item saying Russian border guards have been ordered to smile more when checking passports.

I have been to Russia several times and love the people. But they are not big on smiling.

You could blame the Siberian winters, Rasputin, the ice pick in Trotsky's head, or the gulags.

These Russians do have British sympathisers. There is a breed of shop assistant whose lips never seem to stretch horizontally. No matter how cheery your "hello!", no matter how you compliment them on their efficiency, the quality of their goods, their faces remain as expressionless as those on Mount Rushmore.

They have obviously been rendered mirthless at birth – perhaps an errant use of forceps causing the facial muscles thereafter forever to malfunction.

Other obligatory non-smilers are rock bands on album covers or publicity photographs. Any hint of happiness severely dilutes the required sense of tortured genius the mastery of four chords brings. Their street cred is gone and they're linked with such family entertainers as Val Doonican or Des O'Connor. So these latterday Malvolios adopt non-smiling as a style statement.

Not to smile from one angle is a signal you are deep, serious and beyond the comprehension of lesser mortals. Alas, it could also mean you're a miserable git.

Against these are the excessive smilers. As with most modern vulgarities, the blame lies with the USA and PR. In America, a smile is superglued to any counter assistant's face. You could bite off his or her leg, and while the severed artery pumped its last, the assistant would still have the Stepford Wives smile, and the sing-song greeting, "You have a nice day now!"

Marketing people now see the smile as politically advantageous. The more odious the politician, the bigger and more artificial the smile. Michael Howard, who for 30 years had the demeanour of a soured dishcloth, now smiles constantly, albeit the activity seems as natural as a giraffe limbo dancing.

In her latter years, Margaret Thatcher was 'made over' to stretch those lips. Her frozen smile coupled with the *Dawn of the Undead* staring eyes exuded the same kind of warmth as a blast of dry ice. Ian Duncan-Smith (remember him?) was persuaded to go further; a series of gurgling chuckles when asked an awkward question. It made him seem bonkers.

Basically, a smile has to be real. Which is why a baby's smile turns the most hardened criminals into quivering jelly.

Just how 'real' the Russian border guards' smiles will be, I'm not sure. For some reason we are all told to smile when posing for a photograph, unless it's a passport photograph, when we're ordered not to. Imagine how miserable are the passport photos of rock band members.

We North Tynesiders have more reason to smile than most. The politicians may have done their best to ruin our coastline, but somehow it survives.

And I'd like you to remember that baring our teeth was originally a sign of aggression, not friendliness. It only took on its present significance with the collapse of the NHS dental service which left most of the population sporting ill-fitting dentures incapable of biting through a soft marshmallow.

Not many people know that.

Jazz on a summer's day but not where you might expect

1st July 2004

ACCORDING TO reports in the last week's *News Guardian,* this year's Whitley Bay Jazz Festival, 'will be the best yet'. That's the ticket! Post Euro 2004, post Chester-le-Street debacle, post Rugby Union trouncings, the country is in deep gloom and in need of uplift. It is the job of any festival organiser to claim this year's will be 'the best yet'.

There is no room for an organiser speaking as follows: "This year's events will be atrocious; we've booked a line-up of sad has-beens, ticket prices are extortionate, flat beer is on sale at £3 a pint, and the £10 programme is stuffed with useless advertisements."

The description, I would add, does fit many festivals I've attended, though I'm sure not what's coming up in Whitley Bay, with 40 concerts from 25 bands hailing from five countries in what is claimed to be among the country's four top trad jazz festivals (don't ask me where the other three are).

I'm not very hot on jazz. Music has to release me, whereas jazz often asks to be intellectually appreciated. My housemate has a voluminous collection of jazz albums with such obscure (to me) artists as Muggsy Spanier, Fats Navarro and Ben Selvin. He considers anything post-1950 a mite common, but the sounds of his early jazz big bands wafting through the house tend to get me out of my rock 'n' roll rut.

I accept a certain anti-jazz prejudice born from teenager years, when, as a likely lad from Sherwood council estate in Nottingham, I once went to a rowing club dance and saw a load of chinless Hooray Henrys stomping around in big jumpers to what they called 'trad'. I took an instant dislike to them, and went off to play my Chuck Berry. The stigmata have remained.

I realise I risk becoming a grey haired dinosaur permanently tuned to the station Planet Rock, with its diehard 'We're still rocking!' appeal to rock geriatrics misty eyed about Led Zeppelin II.

This though isn't why I'm worried about Whitley Bay Jazz Festival. The more music the better I say. Music is much more important than economics.

My problem is location, location and location. Edinburgh Festival takes place in Edinburgh; the London Film Festival is in London. But Whitley Bay Jazz Festival is not in Whitley Bay, and those folk flocking to a seaside town hoping to hear the sounds of jazz wafting out across the promenade will be disappointed.

There is one event in Whitley Bay, the 10.30am parade from the Playhouse to the town centre where it will be joined by a procession of jazz-loving classic Jenson cars.

From then on, the Festival ups sticks and hides itself away in the Menzies Hotel, Silverlink, close to a US style shopping mall, and a geographical setting guaranteed not to stir the blood. In previous years it was at the Park Hotel, Tynemouth and is slowly removing itself further from Whitley. Soon it may be in Patagonia.

There is an event in Cullercoats, and one at Saville Exchange, North

Shields. But Whitley Bay this weekend, the weekend of the Whitley Bay Jazz Festival, will have no street corner trumpeters, no saxophonists wailing in bars, no seafront drum solos.

What it will have is hundreds of stag night revellers, great swarms of youngsters with the sole dedication of maximum drunkenness in minimum time. For it is to this section of society that Whitley Bay has sold its soul, and now it must reap the reward or lack of it.

And the reward – though I'm certain there would never be any official recognition of this – is the unfeasibility of holding any kind of arts festival in the centre of Whitley Bay on a summer's weekend.

Imagine a group of stompers setting up somewhere on South Parade, Saturday, 9pm.

And the further irony is that, having sold its soul in this way, Whitley now sees more and more pubs, those very centres of the booze that fuels it, closing up and falling into decay.

So despite my jazz prejudices, I extend a welcome to all those musicians. Let them blow and sing their hearts out. It's just a pity that as a part of the Whitley Bay Jazz Festival, they can't do it in Whitley Bay itself.

The ghost in the white satin dress – but how well do I know my onions?

8th July 2004

AND NOW, something completely different. I refer to an e-mail forwarded from the publisher of my book *Broke Through Britain* ('An exceptional read' – Sod Cutters Weekly).

It comes from a man who says his mother has just read the tome and realises this is the same Peter Mortimer she knew as a child in Nottingham more than 50 years ago.

The woman's name is/was Susan Onion. I stare at these two words and silently mouth them. Susan Onion.

I must have been six or seven. Who did I want to invite to my party asked my mum? I lived on Sherwood council estate and a few streets away lived a little girl who'd smiled at me in the school playground. Her name was Susan

Onion, and (I argued) she obviously thought I was terrific. Could we invite her?

The day arrived and so did Susan Onion. She was a very shy girl who knew no-one else there. She wore a beautiful white satin dress obviously bought for the occasion.

Seven-year-old boys being pigs, I got caught up with biffing and bashing and shouting and wrestling and paid Susan Onion no attention whatsoever. She stood on her own in a corner crying quietly for two hours after which her mum came and took her home. Meantime I was still biffing and bashing and shouting and wrestling.

That was more or less the end of the relationship. I did grow to know Susan's brother David Onion, who in later years would take me on the back of his BSA Bantam to Notts County away matches on the slag heap grounds of the football league lower reaches, where the team remain to this day.

Thus I would sometimes call at the Onion establishment, and in brief passing might utter "Oh, hi there Susan," though as she grew from child to girl and young woman, the birthday party was never again mentioned.

And from Sherwood council estate, life's winding road led me to various destinations until I arrived in Cullercoats, a village which despite my many trips on the Bantam, was previously totally unknown to me.

And on that winding road I had given scarcely a thought to Susan Onion, nor ever imagined she could feature again in my life. Until the e-mail.

An exchange of e-mails with the son revealed Susan Onion was planning to walk the Roman Wall during the summer and would like to call and see me. And here was her phone number.

The number threw me into a tizzy. We were talking of a gap of more than half a century. We were talking about a little boy still in short trousers. We were talking around the time of the coronation, the conquest of Everest, Churchill as Prime Minister. This had been pre Suez, television still in its infancy, the first explosion of an atomic bomb. Susan Onion, who I had not even known, belonged down the far end of a long, long tunnel. She belonged on another planet.

I rang her and was secretly relieved to get an answerphone. With an enforced casualness I said: "Oh hi there Susan. It's Peter Mortimer here. Your son gave me your number. Do give me a ring if you get a chance."

Part of me had wanted simply to replace the receiver. Another part had wanted to blurt out, "Look Susan, I'm really sorry about the party. I mean, you looked lovely in your white satin dress and I know my behaviour was appalling, but I have improved a bit and..." How ridiculous it would have sounded.

And if she did knock on my door, what would I say? "Why hello Susan. My, you haven't changed a bit!"

Last year I bumped into a man I hadn't seen since my student days in 1968. There was a short but significant silence as both of us took in the mischievous joke which time plays on all fresh-faced youth. But 1968 was just yesterday compared to the vast temporal distances associated with Susan Onion.

Yesterday her return message was on my answerphone. Perhaps we two are destined never to talk or meet. Perhaps this fits neatly with my own philosophy, 'never look back'.

I'd never been interested in school reunions. Never wanted to go chasing after the past.

Now the deep and distant past had materialised, like a spirit in a seance. What exactly to do about Susan Onion?

Terrorist alert! National debt threatened! No FA comment!

5th August 2004

THE NEWS THAT Newcastle United manager Bobby Robson will be asked to stand down at the end of the season has rocked Tyneside. This column reveals the true reasons: Robson once knew a man who knew a man who once went to a football match while having a fling with his own secretary, hence undermining England's chances of qualifying for the prestigious Robocop Cup.

As a nation we are already reeling from the news that together we all owe more than one trillion pounds. Even worse is the news that this one trillion quid has become an Al Qaeda target!

The info comes from the same intelligence forces that warned us of a salvo of WMDs raining down in 45 minutes.

A spokesman for MI5, Colonel Nut said: "These damned terrorists will stop at nothing, and in one year have already killed almost as many people as cars kill in a week."

Nut was last seen handing out sandbags in Station Road, Whitley Bay. His advice for anyone spotting an Al Qaeda suspect is to close the window immediately and turn the radio up loud.

I feel guilty about my part in the trillion quid. Last week I borrowed a quid off my son Dylan for the Tyne Tunnel toll, and forgot to pay it back.

A trillion quid is a lot of money. More than some Premier League players earn in a season. If you laid one trillion playing cards end to end you'd probably get a good hand.

A trillion quid has been estimated as a £17,000 debt for every man, woman and child, though for a six-month-old that's a lot of Farleys rusks to borrow.

As a Government spokesman put it from behind a sandbag: "We've never been so well off, that's why we owe so much."

Much of the blame is that of daytime television. This is full of advertisements offering easy loans. Daytime TV was invented for people who have no idea what to do. They see these advertisements and think, "Hey! That's a good idea. I could borrow £20,000 and it would give me something to do!"

It's not as if they need a new washing machine, carpets, stereo, three piece suite, deep freeze, wallpaper or central heating, but buying them and thinking they're cute for a while does give them something to do. For a while. Soon though they realise it's not making them happy, they're back to watching daytime TV, and there's an advertisement for easy money, and they're thinking, "Hey..."

And soon they're a trillion pound in debt.

If only someone knew the secret of what made us happy – well, it would make them very happy. Seaton Delaval ice-cream and the giant soups at Castaways Cafe make a brave stab at it, but all is fleeting. But here's a thought. Should the terrorists get their way and wipe us all out, then we get the last laugh, because it means we don't have to pay the trillion quid back!

Governments both side of the pond are sounding alarm bells. Only one thing is certain. There will never ever ever be a terrorist attack at the times and in the places the Government identified as top risk. So we can remove that tank from Cullercoats beach.

This week comes the announcement of a new crime of pre-terrorist activity. This could, I suppose, be identified as coughing suspiciously, stirring a cup of cocoa the wrong way, or wearing odd socks. You have been warned.

And of course all the time the terrorists are getting closer, as are Bobby

Robson's retirement slippers. As he faces an uncertain future devoid of Garth Crookes asking him 25 minute questions, I have a small piece of advice as to what he should, or in this case, should not do.

Bobby – stay away from daytime television.

Hip hip hooray! Here comes the sea fret!

12th August 2004

YOU MAY not believe it, but quite often this summer, folk in the north east have woken up to blue skies and sunshine. "Oh, it's good to be alive!" they chirrup as they leap from their beds, get dressed and rush off by car or Metro to the wonderful coastline of North Tyneside, for verily it is such.

They are part of that great unstoppable British desire to sit all day by a huge expanse of water they will not venture into. During their day, sand will find a way into every orifice, and come sundown their red angry skin may peel off like old wallpaper.

They have crammed themselves into packed Metro cars, or sat staring long spells at the number plate in front before arriving at their destination.

On the beach several minor skirmishes may be fought over towel territory, until they finally manage to locate their own piece of gritty heaven close to a family who boast the following attributes:

1) The loudest transistor north of Puerto Rico.

2) Four young children who fight, scream and punch continually.

3) A large smelly dog that digs down 20ft into the sand, leaving a three inch covering on everyone within a medium sized radius.

4) A loud and uncomplimentary marital row about who forgot the Ambre Solaire.

No matter. Our heroes stretch out on their towels and drift away. They have covered themselves with a variety of chip fat given a fancy name and bottle, as sun tan oil. Its main attribute is to ensure the entire body is soon covered in sand which clings on for dear life.

The four hulking yoofs playing beach football close by means our valiant trippers are trodden on six times and twice the ball drops from a great height direct onto the groin.

Hang on though. Help may be at hand. What is about to arrive is normally greeted with howls of frustration and disapproval. My own theory is we should welcome it with open arms.

Here it comes, rolling in off the North Sea like some giant tumbleweed. Its arrival is announced by the sonorous tones of the Miss Fenwick fog horn. Soon it has sliced off the top of St George's Church steeple in Cullercoats, and, in a trick worthy of Houdini, caused both Tyne piers to disappear.

The sun, which had come to the coast for a full day out, shrugs its shoulders, wraps up its towel and goes home. The great grey curtain that is the unique north east coast sea fret has arrived.

Let me list a few advantages. You can now change into your bather without fear of embarrassment – no-one can see you. You can get rid of that glorified chip fat. The sea fret is a much more effective sun blocker. You can let your imagination run wild. The fret, plus foghorn, create a genuinely spooky atmosphere in which all manner of ghostly ghoulish things can be summoned up.

But most of all, it is this very same sea fret that prevents our coastline being turned into some monstrous tourist hotspot of ugly concrete hotels.

For some reason most holidaymakers require the tedium of non-stop sunshine. Probably because it guarantees skin cancer much swifter. But the north east coast? You simply can't rely on the weather!

Which is why there are miles and miles of unspoilt coastline. Which is why we should offer up thanks to the Great God of Sea Fret. Possibly we should have an annual sea fret festival and celebrate its misty magnificence.

Except of course, no-one seems to have the slightest idea just when it will arrive.

Wonderful, isn't it?

Rejoice! For now we are truly a two greetings card town!

9th September 2004

PEOPLE CAN be seen dancing through the streets of Whitley Bay in brightly coloured hats. They are serenading one another in Panama Dip, performing spontaneous Irish jigs on the crossing to St Mary's Island. A few have been heard to whistle favourite ditties.

Whence comes this glee, this sense of ecstasy? Is it to celebrate the end of the summer holidays, and our coastline returned to its inhabitants? Is it merely the infectious sense of fun generated by the latest Newcastle United FC manager?

Neither. It is the opening of the new Park View shopping centre. Walk through this gleaming new emporium and you can hear audible gasps at the massive strides we have all taken into the 21st century. (*If you could hear the gasp it was by definition audible, your sentence is therefore a tautology and I'm watching out for any more grammatical sloppiness – Ed.*)

I was fortunate enough to encounter a council spokesman on my visit, and he was keen to say the following. "Let no one accuse us of letting the coast fall apart, selling valuable green sites, and dumping Linskill in the face of total opposition. If they walk into this new shopping centre, they will find not one...", and here the poor chap, obviously overcome with emotion, had to steady himself, "I repeat not one, but two greeting card shops."

And verily, he spoke true. The evidence was there for all to see. A greeting card shop. And then another one. The spokesman was now in full flow.

"A measure of any civilisation is a healthy choice in greeting card shops" he said. "When word gets out, we confidently expect a massive influx of visitors from throughout the world."

Even as he was speaking I spotted a group of Swedes, eight foot tall and with long blond hair, and that's not to mention the men! Each wore a t-shirt with the legend, *I went to both greeting card shops in Park View!*

As if that were not enough, we are promised shortly a brand new Boots and Superdrug in the centre.

"Some people may claim Whitley already has these stores," added the spokesman, "but these two are in a different place!"

"Plus which, we promised a new Marks and Spencer, which is exactly what you have got."

There were reports on the opening day of endless middle-class housewives flocking to Marks to replenish their knicker stocks, but returning only with a bottle of balsamic vinegar.

"It's true some people expected a proper M&S store, not just food. But if they're disappointed, they can always walk out and take their pick of two greeting card shops."

Rumours the recently closed and much missed Park Bookshop might find a replacement in the centre were ill-founded.

"Against which," added the spokesman "there are twice as many greetings cards as anyone could have wished for."

The centre was crowded this week with the filming of a new reality TV game show called *Guess Where You Are*. Contestants are plonked blindfolded, into a modern shopping centre, blindfolds removed and asked to guess which town they're in.

"Doncaster? Inverness? Halifax? Rotherham? Bury St Edmunds?" There were some ingenious guesses, but not one contestant won the £10,000 prize by guessing Whitley Bay! Which, as the spokesman affirmed, proved the universality of Park View Centre.

This, it must be added is a warm haven for those less fortunate in society who can get in out of the cold and rain a good 90 seconds before being moved on by security.

The benefits, as you can see, are manifold.

Hip hip hooray – a unique opportunity for medical care

23rd September 2004

CAN IT REALLY be two years this week that I was trundled into the operating theatre at North Tyneside General Hospital for a hip replacement?

Two years since the malevolent Arthur (departing hip) grudgingly gave way to Mr Charnley (new hip on the block)?

To be sure it is, and here's a smart looking letter and leaflet from a private organisation recently recruited to move the health service towards a brave new world.

Dear Mr Mortimer,

We sincerely hope that your hip operation, performed thus far without a single penny outlay from yourself, has continued to be successful. And you will be aware that this government has been examining ways of streamlining and rendering more efficient the entire system, thus bringing better value for money to the taxpayers.

A management consultancy team has now completed its feasibility study, and we are pleased to inform you that you will be among the first fortunate benefactors.

Firstly let me assure you there are no plans to demand a one-off large payment for your new hip (which costs in total £8,000). But in our present healthy market economy, transactions have to make economic sense.

Thus we are introducing a rental system similar to the ones that have operated successfully with cars or mobile phones. Let me assure you this will not be backdated, and you can look on the last two years as a wonderful bonus with our compliments.

But hips are an expensive item of capital expenditure, and as from November will be subject to a monthly rental fee of £50. Pay an entire year's fee in advance and we offer an amazing discount of five per cent (or £30).

What do I get for my money, you may ask. For one, peace of mind. The hip is now fully insured. Should it become detached, torn from your thigh by rabid dogs, or be unexpectedly dissolved by body acids, we shall be happy to replace it free of charge. You will pay only the surgeon's labour costs (£1,000 per hour).

And though all future hips will have to be paid for up front, existing customers will be offered an unbeatable 50 per cent discount on either a second hip or a replacement – that means an £8,000 hip for £4,000!

Our aim is to drive DOWN the real costs of the hip in your leg. We fully understand that our customers can be confused by too much financial jargon. What does it cost, they want to know, and we can assure them that our rental terms are fully competitive, being 10.25 per cent APR, 12.3 per cent AGP, 9.8 per cent HMV, 7.65 per cent MFI, and a staggering 11.6 per cent B & Q.

Our sole aim is your customer satisfaction and we are here to answer any of your queries. For instance, people often ask us, yes, but what if for any reason, I am unable to keep up the rental payments? Does this mean I no longer keep the hip?

Not necessarily. Should you fall into financial difficulties our advisers are happy to call on you and discuss possible solutions. With this in mind, in extreme circumstances we are even prepared to freeze the monthly payments for up to three months – yes, that's three months – before we embark on a necessary repossession process.

Naturally we do this reluctantly as it involves a lot of blood, pain and sharp knives, and we can assure you that it is only necessary in a minority of cases.

Ask yourself this question. Just how valuable is a new hip? How much can it transform my life? Much more so than say a new dishwasher or vacuum cleaner, consumer items we are all more than happy to buy on easy terms.

I enclose our rental agreement which is in seven point type. Please sign and return immediately along with the bankers' order form. Should you have any queries, please do not hesitate to ring our help line number. This is available 24 hours a day, seven days a week to give you an unrivalled automatic robotic response.

We remain your humble servants etc......

Time for a spring clean, Polly. Dust clouds are gathering over Cullercoats

30th September 2004

IT HAD BEEN several months since the house had been properly cleaned. Time for a purge. Polly the dog helped me. "You know Polly," I said, as I carried several large cushions outdoors and beat them within an inch of their lives, "this Linskill business must be the biggest piece of political chicanery in a long time".

"Woof," said Polly.

The resultant dust clouds were so huge and dense that three flights from Heathrow to Newcastle were delayed, and several ships off the north east coast ran aground on the Black Middens.

"I mean," I added, thwacking a few carpets for good measure (my front gate was beginning to resemble an Eastern bazaar), "do you know a single person in the borough, a few politicians apart, who doesn't find the proposed closure nothing short of a scandal?"

"Woof, woof," agreed the canine.

The vacuum cleaner had packed up. Taking it apart with a mechanical deftness for which I am famous, I discovered an impacted brick of dust which when pulled apart contained two hair grips (only one of them mine), two Smarties, the top of a ball point pen, a false eyelash, the remains of a chocolate digestive, half a dog chew, and a Metro ticket (day saver).

I switched the vacuum back on. It ran across a carpet, then picked up some metal object, the resulting noise like two skeletons fighting in a steel dustbin.

"One of two possibilities," I continued, "either those local politicians are so stupid they can't see what's glaringly obvious to everyone else, or" – and at this I pointed the vacuum hose at Polly dramatically, "there's a hidden agenda."

"Woof, woof," retorted Polly, then as an afterthought, "woof."

Years ago a Mr Dyson made a fortune from vacuum cleaners by getting rid of the bag. Now everyone gets rid of their Dyson.

The bag on my old machine, a paper one, says in large letters DO NOT REUSE. For the tenth time I empty it and put it back in situ.

Oh, the therapy of cleaning the house. It takes me two days, but feels as good as finishing a play. Half an hour after completion my son Dylan turned up with a couple of mates.

"One moment," I said and checked them for the odd speck of dust.

"The trouble is Polly," I continue, as I wipe dust off the top of picture frames as thick as the ermine in the House of Lords, "everyone's too damned polite about the protest. Me, I'd occupy the building, and I'd sit in front of the bulldozers holding a baby."

"Woof" responds the pooch, which probably means, "Why don't you then?" "I might just" I say.

An interesting exercise is the removal of the settee cushions. It reveals a long forgotten area, and down there I discover Lord Lucan, the racehorse Shergar, and that missing one from the Manic Street Preachers.

In moving this same settee around, I realise that the world's worst invention (surely a TV series in there somewhere?) is the furniture castor. This small irritating item manifests one of two behaviour patterns.

Either (a) it falls off, and you require four copies of *Penguin Modern Poets* to prevent the settee listing at 20 degrees, or (b) it resists all attempts at removal when this is the only way to manoeuvre the item through a narrow doorway (fact of domestic life – all items of furniture are three inches wider than all door frames).

Wiping clean the front of the television brings the startling discovery that the BBC studio for *Look North* has not been fogbound these last months.

"Sometimes Polly," I conclude, "the injustice is so appalling, and the refusal of the authorities to listen so stubborn, that a programme of non-violent civil disturbance seems the only answer. You can write letters to the paper till you're blue in the face."

Actually Polly was blue in the face, having swallowed the false eyelash. She coughed it up and went to lay down on the bit of carpet recently vacuumed.

"Anyway, that's what I think," I added, but already she'd dozed off, dreaming no doubt of her first ever sit-in.

Why tunnel vision can work – depending on the choice of tunnel

7th October 2004

MOTIVATED BY Muriel Green's letter in last week's *News Guardian*, I biked to the Tyne Pedestrian Tunnel. Though I often use this under-rated wonder, I'd yet to see the double sculpture installation at the northern end. Lovely stuff.

Giant chubby fish, glistening and glorious with their turquoise and purple scales leap right out of and dive back into the grass and make you feel like breaking into dance (go on, do it).

Slightly more formal is the stainless steel construction, like a flattened boat shape on end which lists the 14 different ways of crossing the Tyne from Shields to Newburn. My only complaint is no reference to my own commuter water-ski proposal (*Mortimer at Large,* October 16, 2003).

The tunnel houses the world's longest wooden escalators. Each one takes three minutes 36 seconds to travel. I know because I timed them (you see what a sad life I lead).

On the south side is a photographic exhibition marking the tunnel's opening on July 15th, 1951. It is full of important looking people, stiff-backed in that distinctive 50s style, and misspelt in the caption as 'dignitories'.

When the pedestrian tunnel opened, the Tyne Ferry still carried cars. Their subsequent removal ranks as possibly the pedestrian's only major advance over the motorist in the last half century.

I have walked through the pedestrian tunnel, run through it, cycled through it. Walking gives the chance to sing the entire Roy Orbison repertoire. Like being in the bath, the tunnel invites mediocre singing talent such as myself to explode into song with Pavarotti-like delusions.

When I ran through the tunnel as a solitary padding figure, I was reminded of Keir Dullea in the film *2001* on that great lonely spaceship, endlessly jogging his way round the white perimeter.

There is also a lift. This feels like the most isolated place on earth, the sense of being inside an empty corned beef tin, and everyone breathes a sigh of relief when the old clanky thing reaches journey's end and the door opens.

You can take bikes on the lift, but more than two and you spend an eternity trying to fit machines and riders in, ending up with the front wheels up against the ceiling.

Contrast the pedestrian tunnel with the main one. There's great satisfaction for the cyclist approaching the former at rush hour. You weave merrily through the grid locked cars and lorries queuing for tunnel number one, you slip past the 'no entry' gap onto Tyne View Terrace, leave behind the seething frustrated mass of nose-to-tail motorists with their thickening arteries, and prepare for the great solitary descent on the pedestrian's escalator.

This squeaks a bit like a mouse. The walls sport no advertisements; too few people to warrant them. The slow nature of the descent imparts a dreamy state, a sense of Zen Buddhist calm.

Descend in the lift and when the door clanks open you're confronted with a sign saying No Cycling. This is the signal to get on your bike and whizz round the corner to where bikers and walkers are segregated into separate tunnels. You're 85 ft below high water, and on a bike there's scarcely time to sing *Pretty Woman* as you zoom past the white and green tiling. But it's free, whereas somewhere close by, motorists are paying £1 to crawl through the fume-infested hell of tunnel one.

My fear is some feasibility study Johnnie suggesting the tunnel's closure. It was built mainly for the thousands of shipyard workers, now but a trickle.

No one suggests closing the other tunnel, which is about as pleasant an experience as sour milk. In fact they suggest doubling the misery by building a second one. And when that gets full, why not a third, or a fourth?

Meantime the chubby fish leap in delight, the mouse squeaks on, and every journey through the pedestrian tunnel leaves the impression it is mine alone. This does not happen with the Tyne Tunnel proper.

Why the odds are stacked against Slob

14th October 2004

WHAT HAS the huge upsurge in gambling to do with my associate Slob Foster? Stay tuned. According to news reports, the internet is responsible for gambling increasing by something like a trillion per cent. People suddenly realise, "Hey, look, if we go on line, we can throw our money away much faster and in the comfort of our own homes!"

This hi-tech advance is slowly nudging out the tobacco-stained corner betting shop where some wizened geezer in a shabby mac, with the remnants of an old roll-up between his lips happens to know a dead cert in the 2.30 at Wincanton.

The next day the horse is reported to be still five furlongs from home. Furlongs! Now there's a word only bandied about in the Sport of Kings, (the kings of course being the bookmakers, and the paupers those who bet).

As my dear old mother told me at an early age, "Arthur" (names weren't her strong point) "you'll never see a poor bookmaker."

Plus which I slowly came to realise that if you want to gamble in life, why not do it on something exciting and unpredictable, rather than in willingly offering up your money to slick organisations who have scientifically worked out how to fleece you?

Mind you, I did hear about this dead cert in the 3.30 at Doncaster…

Back to Slob Foster, I discovered him in front of a Metro ticket machine on Whitley Bay station. He was in a state of some excitement. I would say he was jumping up and down except his junk food and lager diet meant it was more a case of his rolls of fat rippling to and fro in a vertical fashion.

Slob was putting a series of coins into the machine slot which is positioned high enough to make anyone of challenged stature need a trampoline. No sooner had the coins gone in than they were regurgitated into the glass-fronted aperture positioned low enough to ensure strained back for anyone not regularly practising yoga.

He would press one button, A, B or C, then another DAY RETURN or CHEAP DAY SAVER. Always the same result. Out came the coins.

"This is brilliant, Mortimer!" he enthused.

"I don't understand, Slob," I said, "what exactly are you doing?"

"I've been playing this for about an hour now!" he chortled, his various chins wobbling in delight, "and I'm still breaking even!"

A line of impatient would-be travellers was slowly growing behind him.

"Slob," I said, "are you not here to travel the Metro?"

"Travel the Metro?" A confused look came across his face. "I'm playing the bandit, Mortimer – and I can tell you something, if I'd been in the slots in Whitley Bay or Cullercoats arcades, my money would never have lasted this long!"

I took the poor inflated fellow to one side. "Listen, Slob," I said, "what you have here is a Metro ticket machine. In theory you put in your money and out comes a ticket. But recently a great number of them have been malfunctioning and simply chucking the money back out. This has afforded the Metro traveller the almost perfect excuse for not buying a ticket, hence adding to the already huge amount of lost revenue brought about mainly by Nexus's head-in-the-sand policy over many years of relying on CCTV cameras rather than people to regulate the system. Cameras, Slob, can not check tickets."

Had he listened to my speech? I fear not. A look of sheer horror had spread over his face.

"Are you telling me this is not a machine for gambling?"

"Well no, it's not."

"There's just no point to any of this then, is there?" he wailed.

"Some might say the same about gambling, Slob," I added.

He let out a loud wail, and within minutes was already waddling back to his PC, and a system of losing his money he KNEW he could trust.

I sighed a deep sigh, and stuck in my £3.30p for a DAY SAVER. Know what though? It threw it straight back at me. You win some, you lose some.

Oscar Wilde, empty seats and the poetry of the sausage...

28th October 2004

LAST WEEK, the musical *Oscar Wilde* opened at The Shaw Theatre London, and closed the very same night. The show left town, as it were, even as the calamitous reviews of the morning papers were appearing.

Oscar Wilde was written by Radio One DJ Mike Read, and a brief extract shown on television suggested here was a mercy killing. A total of five tickets had been sold, exactly equalling the number sold for my own poetry reading at The Customs House, South Shields, the same night.

Radio DJs will be unused to such indignities. Not so poets, who see such public shunning merely as a refusal of the big bad world to recognise their great genius. Ah well.

One of my five audience was an eccentric woman dressed gypsy style who would shout 'yes' or 'no' after various lines. This was a bit of unplanned audience participation, but somehow added to the night's bizarre nature.

I am fairly stoical about small audiences, having once launched a children's poetry book where no-one turned up. That's right. Millions of souls on the planet and not a single one arrived to celebrate my new book. The illustrator had hung his originals round the room, the barmaid had opened up, we'd put out 50 seats. Ten minutes after the planned start a man poked his head round the door, and we leapt on him like wolves. He was just looking for directions. Later that night I lay down in a darkened room and seriously considered the attractions of becoming a chartered accountant.

Most people don't know a single line of modern poetry, and you never see anyone reading the stuff on buses or trains. Every year National Poetry Day sees a small number of people make an enormous effort while the rest muddle along without a thought.

But it does bring a day's labour for the odd versifier, and this year (just gone) a group of north east poets was each commissioned to write a poem inspired by food, which we then performed in a poetic feast at Newcastle's Literary and Philosophical Society.

Quite a big audience actually. We were asked to dress in the spirit of the occasion. I wrote a poem called *Sausages* which I read while wearing a butcher's apron and a (pretend) pig's head.

I've decided to donate a framed copy of *Sausages* to the Cullercoats butcher Peter Darling. Two reasons. His own sausages, including black pudding, and lamb and mint, are the world's best. Plus which if he hangs the poem on his shop wall, my readership will multiply many fold.

No poet can expect a mass audience except by selling out to mammon. Thus Benjamin Zephaniah wrote a rap for a Barclays Bank TV commercial, and the Barnsley poet Ian McMillan can be heard on the current Oats So Simple ad. No-one's ever asked me, but I wouldn't do it.

Not that I don't want to appear useful as a poet. Another of my poems adorned the walls of the then Nouveaux Restaurant in Cullercoats. The owner Willy Carruthers cooked the best burger this side of East Sleekburn, a quality Ronald McDonald could only dream of. I was moved to eulogise it in the *Ode to the Willyburger*.

Plus which if you go to Holy Island where I spent a winter to write a book, you'll find various Mortimer poems carved onto rocks and even one on the ex-vicar's bathroom wall. And there have been poems for birthdays, weddings (a wedding poem is called an epithalamium) etc. A poet will never be as useful as a plumber, but the *Penguin Book of Useful Verse* does contain such gems as 'A pint of water weighs a pound and a quarter' – the kind of information that can change your life.

And while people may not read poetry, loads of them write it. I edited a poetry magazine for 27 years, and sometimes in a desperate attempt to escape the daily torrent of submissions, I'd flee to the edge of Saddle Rocks and pretend to be a herring gull.

No matter. Writing poetry is a more benign activity than beating up your neighbour or declaring war. And whether anyone else wants to read your work is out of your hands. And remember, rock climbers don't demand an audience, or pot holers, deep sea divers. Why poets?

To end as we began, with Oscar Wilde. He wrote his final work, *Ballad of Reading Gaol* as a broken, disgraced and exiled man. No expectation of an adoring audience there. It's become a classic. My advice to all you tyro poets. Just keep writing. Expect nothing in return. Not a sausage.

We sit, we stand we kneel – O come all ye faithless!

4th November 2004

OFF TO St Paul's Church, Whitley Bay, for a wedding, passing *en route* the growing line of shuttered shops towards the top end of Whitley Road.

These have graciously closed down to make way for the new Park View Shopping Centre (twelve units and climbing!) which at times attracts customers in double figures.

But if Whitley Bay still needs a lift-up, luckily help is at hand with the government's latest regeneration plans. Build a casino! Yes, that's the answer to urban decay, drug and alcohol abuse, unemployment and buses that never arrive, then turn up in threes. And should we get a casino complex at the coast, a plaque can be attached to the 1,200 one armed bandits, 'Thank you for throwing your money away on this machine, thereby helping to regenerate your town'.

But I had other fish to fry. The joining of two people who thereafter no man (or woman?) should put asunder.

Asunder! What a splendidly archaic biblical word! Has anyone ever uttered the word aloud outside a wedding ceremony?

I confess often to enjoying myself more at funerals than weddings. Weddings are planned for so long, and to such meticulous detail that every ounce of spontaneity can be squeezed out. Funerals on the other hand announce themselves at short notice, everyone turns up disorganised and bewildered, and somewhere mid-wake someone decides to crack a smile despite it all, after which people start to relax.

Plus which weddings themselves can be endless. The service, followed by the reception, after which we're all knackered, but hey, here comes the disco! Enter a spotty DJ with flashing lights, in-yer-face manner, and the delusion that the definition of the British having fun is them dancing to *The Birdy Song* or *Agadoo*. Meanwhile poor Aunt Elspeth from Sidcup, who's been having problems with her bowels, hasn't a clue what's going on, and everyone stares at the empty dance floor.

Good to report then that Saturday's was one of the better receptions, and we all got to sit down to eat! This is a miracle in the age of the buffet where the country's main growth industry is the firm making that strange contraption allowing you to fasten your wine glass to your small plate, thus making the eating of a tiny sausage possible. Eating while standing is as daft as dancing when sitting.

And of course every church wedding has its strange rituals. We sing hymns but have no idea of the tune, the church filled with an indeterminate warbling. Only born-again cousin Mildred impresses, as her god-fearing tones ring out above the rest.

God-fearing we are not. Most of us enter churches only as babies to have our heads wetted, to tie the knot, or to be wheeled in, in a wooden box. Oh come all ye faithless.

And when exactly do we sit/stand/kneel? Some mysterious system is at work which no-one understands. On Saturday at one stage, the suspicion grew we'd been left standing when we should have been sitting. People glanced round, shuffled their feet. Finally one brave soul took the plunge and sat. Others followed, first singly, then in groups. Later the reverse suspicion was true.

Again one stood nervously, maybe expecting a thunderbolt from above. Then another. Slowly we all rose like saplings in a forest.

Wedding photographs are interesting. It has been calculated that there are 28,564 possible combinations of the two sides' relatives, and take care the photographer who does not snap them all! Meantime the rest of us stand by and shuffle, or adjust rarely-worn ties.

Tin cans tied to the wedding car seems a forgotten fashion, and I'm not sure if people still take honeymoons. No matter, we threw our bio-degradable confetti, and got in the cars to follow the beaming bride and groom to the reception.

And passing down Whitley Road, I could swear yet another shop had put up its shutters.

'Shop till you drop' promotion deserves a little taste of success

11th November 2004

SATURDAY APPROACHES, and a certain street in Whitley Bay will be dolloping out the booze. No fewer than 24 outlets along a small stretch, and if this weren't bad enough, all the drinks are totally free! Plus which, they're even encouraging you to bring your car! Blimey! But don't jump to conclusions. This isn't a case of wobbling in Whistlers, boozing in Banana 10's, heaving in Havana, or feeling decidedly odd in Origin.

These, plus other drinking haunts in South Parade WILL be open for business as usual this Saturday of course.

Stag and hen parties will descend from Scunthorpe, Todmorden, Brampton and all compass points with the serious intent of getting bladdered.

Drinkers will rush (and later stagger) from bar to bar fuelled on the special offers, three gallons of Southern Comfort for a tenner, a large bucketful of vodka and Red Bull on production of a metro ticket. Later, vomiting may be in evidence, plus occasional fornication against a hotel wall.

The long arm of the law will cast an eagle eye from their large vans, and occasionally emerge to collar the worst culprits and chuck them in the cells.

But what I'm talking about is Park View, geographically only a short distance from South Parade, but culturally many galaxies. Should you wish to do so, this Saturday you can call in a whole host of different shops in Park View and they'll give you a free glass of wine.

In theory the determined swiller could down 24 glasses, or about five bottles. Is this why the promotion includes the phrase, 'Shop till you Drop?'

There's an attractive oddity about the thought of a small Chardonnay in the butchers, slurping St Emilion in the jewellers, or sampling the Merlot in the wallpaper shop.

The concept of shops offering a hospitable glass of wine comes from Italy, a country which still sees alcohol consumption as cultured and refined rather than a frenetic and somewhat desperate rush to oblivion.

I'm trying to remember the last time I saw an Italian totally blotto. I can't.

My sense is that Park View is not anticipating that Saturday will turn into mayhem, where great gangs of drunken shoppers moon their way up the middle of the street, chanting "Ere we go, 'ere we go, 'ere we go", or other operatic arias; they seem little concerned fighting groups will fall through shop windows, or vomit up a variety of kebabs.

Park View deserves good fortune. The further north it goes, the more interesting, individualistic and less corporate it becomes; hardly a chain store to be seen; cafes, book shops, art shops, clothes shops, soap shops.

Compare this to the blandness of the new shopping mall (which ironically shares the same name) or the wasteland steel-shuttered grimness that is much of Whitley Road.

When people talk about the 'devastation' of Whitley Bay (with some justification), they forget Park View.

But none of this explains why on Saturday, with booze being offered freely in Park View, everyone knows the drunkenness will happen in South Parade. Is there a thesis to be written on this conundrum?

Age is one factor. Another is expectation. Once you're on South Parade at the weekend, getting pie-eyed seems the only ambition. This is exacerbated by an industry which over the years has cynically encouraged and fostered binge drinking in young people unable to handle the consequences.

If you go blotto in Park View, and started falling all over the place, you'd look daft. Which is what all drunks do, look daft, unless they are surrounded by other drunks. Which is why they gather on South Parade. The trouble is, sometimes they're dangerous as well as daft.

I once got drunk quite a lot, until it all began to seem a waste of time and money.

I'd rather pop into Heaven Scent on Saturday, try a few tricks in Now That's Magic, or play with the toys in Selling Smiles. With the odd tipple of vino, naturally.

Farewell, long seat – it is the return of the butter pats...

25th November 2004

TYNEMOUTH LONG Sands on a Saturday morning, a clear blue sky, a clean flat beach, and waves come crashing down like horses over Beechers Brook. Oh, it's good to be alive!

Across the sands comes one Brian Knox of Cullercoats, who hails me with the enquiry as to what has happened to the long seat on the western platform of Cullercoats Metro station.

The seat, maybe 30ft long, and an original part of the station, is no more. It has been replaced by those small yellow groups of miserly plastic creations which look like oversized pats of butter.

These modern seats actually despise the idea of being sat on, which is why they swiftly retract, the second bum pressure is released. We sit on them feeling as comfortable and secure as someone squatting on top of a pole.

The butter pats are in groups of three. This ensures no four people can sit and chat. It also ensures no poor down-and-outs can lie down for a kip. Unless they're vertically challenged. Plus which they'd need to be as skinny as Kate Moss not to roll off.

The butter pats grudgingly accept the necessity of some people needing to park their carcass while waiting for the train. But this acceptance comes with a meanness of spirit that seems to define our age.

I engage Brian Knox in the butter pats conversation. The sun sparkles on the wave tops. I unwisely turned my back on the sea, which the next second was ankle high over my black suede boots. Score – North Sea 1 Mortimer 0.

Somewhat damp of foot I returned to telephone Nexus about the long seat. It has apparently been removed for health and safety reasons. It is not, they assure me, a listed seat.

I now travel the system spreading the good news. "Your health and safety is no longer threatened by the Cullercoats Long Seat!"

Those passengers who are not being berated by disconsolate yoof, suffering cuts from bricks through windows, or being tumbled on by drunks staggering down the aisles, join me in shouting a loud "hurrah!"

To my untrained eye (and bum), the Cullercoats Long Seat was not unsafe. It is however worth reminding ourselves that it did not fit Metro's corporate image. The butter pats do.

Another victim of the corporate image was the original CULLERCOATS STATION sign. This metal marvel was dismantled in favour of the somewhat bland orange and black replacement back in 1980 when the system opened. I discovered it was to be melted down.

My friend John Oliver and I decided to steal it, which we did in the early hours. We carried it along to my house but the sign was so long it went all the way up the stairs and was still sticking out the front door.

We hacksawed it in half. John kept Station, and I kept Cullercoats, which I painted in bright colours, though its full potential is as yet unrealised hidden away in the back yard. The long term plan is to stick it on the roof to replace my poem that sadly rusted away more than a year ago.

I accept the removal of the Cullercoats Long Seat is unlikely to provoke protest marches. People will not handcuff themselves to railings, or throw purple powder at the Prime Minister. It is unlikely a press campaign (the phenomenal influence of this column apart) will be organised on the seat's behalf.

Yet like Brian Knox, (who has drier feet), I am sad to see its demise, sad that Cullercoats Station has lost something that made it different.

I wobble on top of my butter pat.

I am attempting to console myself, while I wait for the train, that corporate uniformity, and hence efficiency has probably been advanced by this change and that somewhere in the bowels of Nexus's headquarters, accountants are being congratulated. In this attempt, I am not totally successful.

On daft names, sexy colours and the significance of rubber bands

9th December 2004

RUMOURS THAT the British Olympic Bid is to include foxhunting as an official Olympic sport are, I can state quite firmly, utterly untrue, and I have no business circulating them.

Plus which there is the matter of the rubber bands to consider. They have begun to appear on the doorstep. One, maybe two per morning, at times three.

They originate I know, with the postie. The postie used to be a security rock in everyone's life. You waved at the postie, who arrived punctually at 8:15am, a return smile, and you knew everything was OK. Today's postie is likely to be a spotty 17 year old wandering the North Tyneside streets with a lost look on his or her geographically challenged face. The postie might now appear at 8am or when you're cooking tea.

The postie may possibly bring the second-class mail, but will inform you the first class now takes a little longer. It is after all Christmas, and it's not as if the Post Office has had many years experience of dealing with Christmas mail.

Each day I pick up the rubber bands; I keep them in a small compartment of a desk drawer where they now resemble worms in a fisherman's tin. Sometimes I make use of them. I may place one round my wrist for no apparent reason.

For even less reason I stuck one around my head the other day. I used one as dental floss. It snapped painfully. I even pinged one against the back of my hand which made me yelp. I have absolutely no idea why I did this. I always put a rubber band round the book I am reading in case it thinks of flapping its pages and flying away.

It is just possible to make some sort of musical note with a rubber band. It's not very exciting which is probably why unlike vacuum cleaners or dustbin lids, no rubber band has ever been used in a symphony.

Have you ever seen a rubber band factory? Of course not. Have you ever met a person who makes them? The idea is absurd. Do you have the slightest clue how they can be made without a join? NO.

They are one of life's small mysteries. They have never been fashionable, yet are not quite as old-fashioned as elastic. Magicians can make one pass through another.

And now they are appearing on my doorstep. Unlike generations of rubber bands which have been a dull brown colour, the present doorstep variety are a dusky pink. It's quite a sexy colour, and I am left to ponder the true nature of all this.

In short, are these rubber bands simply carelessly discarded by the postie as he/she is otherwise distracted in applying the Valderma to the acne, or are they a deliberate marketing ploy?

Could they be dropped there as the front-runner in a campaign to 'sex up' the Post Office? Once we start noticing how attractive and erotic their rubber bands are, it's only a short step to us viewing the entire organisation in such a light.

You might think this as absurd as most of what appears in this column and you're entitled to your opinion. But consider the following. A few years back, with similar motivation, the Post Office employed a whole host of totally useless marketing people to give them an image make-over.

After spending a great deal of money these hapless Harrys came up with the idea of changing the company name to *Consignia*. It cost millions and millions to alter all the vans, letterheads, machines and endless other things, and it all got done just in time for the realisation that the idea was totally stupid, something a six-year-old or a goldfish of average intelligence could have told them in the first place. Consignia? It sounds like a Roman emperor's wife! Everything had to be changed back. More millions.

My supply of rubber bands grows. What to do? Tie 150 together to make a flexible dog lead? Melt them down to make a rubber ball for the kids up the street? Chew them?

Readers' suggestions are welcome. Meantime, if I just ping one here against the back of the hand.... ouch!

Bin and gone – and a new year, a brand new sport

6th January 2005

Note: *written a few days after the tsunami*

OUR OWN words come back to haunt us; in the 1980s I made a short film with Tyne Tees Television about living at the coast. Included in this was my poem about Robin Rigby, the painfully thin old man who endlessly walked the North Tyneside cliff-tops.

Part of the poem reads:
And if one day
that sea should tire
of its steady breathing, should fill
its great lungs to drown

walkman, chip shop, tranny
and sweet wrapper, then
it will carry him, like a twig
on its swollen back, far, far out...

On to other matters; a new year and in the back lanes of Cullercoats the game of Find the Wheelie gathers pace. It is still a game more than a sport, no trophy, no championship, no sponsors, no sign of interest from Sky, but these are early days.

Who could have predicted its rise? In the old days you put out your dustbin, it was emptied, you brought it in. Pretty boring. Now I await each Thursday morning with a growing sense of anticipation.

It begins earlier than this. On Wednesday night I walk up and down the back lane. The wheelie bins are lined in serried ranks. I give a nod here, a word of encouragement there, like Henry V the night before Agincourt.

Though all identical in design, the bins have developed their own characteristics. My own had the house number neatly printed. Others have great swashbuckling white numbers painted on. A few have the name of the terrace. No one had been pedantic enough to put the post code. Some of the bins are in a poor state, as if rolled in builders' rubble. Others have a Rolls Royce gleam, having taken advantage of the region's latest growth industry, the £2 wheelie bin clean.

Occasionally I lift the lid of a neighbour's bin, nosey about their rubbish or just to check an elderly relative hasn't fallen in.

There are three tell-tale signs that Thursday's game is about to begin.

Around 9am we hear the low thrum of the wagon's engine. There is the flashing light above the wall top. And that distinctive beep-beep of the alarm. The temptation now is to open the gate and take a look, but this would ruin the game. I hold my ground till all evidence of the binmen (are there any bin women?) is gone.

Out in the lane the serried ranks are no more; bins face this way and that, a few huddle together, others stand in splendid isolation. And now comes the real excitement. Finding your own bin. Possibly (and somewhat anti-climatically) it may still be near your back gate. Or it could be one house up, or two, or on the other side of the lane. Occasionally I encounter another bin hunter and light pleasantries are exchanged.

People who do real jobs have gone to work, so bin finding is scattered. This is a pity. Part of me wants to organize it properly. Blow the whistle and we all emerge from our back gates; the first with the bin back *in situ* gets maximum points.

Why not a league table, interbacklane competitions? A super cup? It would do wonders for community spirit. With wheelie bins now being national, even international, the opportunities are limitless.

I have yet to discover if the binmen work to some algebraic formula in bin redistribution, or if it is random.

I am keen to know the maximum distance a wheelie bin has travelled from its original home. Is there any record of a bin ending up in a different lane entirely?

And in all this wheelie excitement, spare a thought for the poor old 'retro' bin. My own still sits in the back yard. Occasionally I lift and replace its lid to ensure it feels a minimum of neglect. It has never known the thrill of the game, the uncertainty of where it will be plonked each Thursday morning. It is like some old pit pony put out to grass.

Maybe I'll donate it to Beamish Museum. People can grow misty-eyed at its quaint size, its immobility.

For it is this very mobility of the wheelie bin that has made the new game possible. As the philosopher might have said: "Put a bin on wheels, and it will discover new horizons."

Happy hunting.

How we can make the coast great again!

13th January 2005

I TAKE NOTE of a letter in last week's *News Guardian* from a J H Carr who mentions Panama Dip, and concludes, "did you know Lulu won her first talent contest there?"

I did not. This is the kind of information we need. All local authorities are desperate for links with the famous to lift their prestige.

My own home town of Nottingham bangs on endlessly about Robin Hood who, even if he did exist, was probably a common thief. In South Tyneside, the Catherine Cookson Country tour will see you staring at various flattened car parks on which (reputedly) once stood a house mentioned in *The Fifteen Streets*.

County Durham boasts of being The Land of The Prince Bishops, although most visitors haven't a clue who the Prince Bishops were, or when.

Kylie Minogue did pay an impromptu visit to the Queens Head Cullercoats some years ago, but what other claims to fame have we?

I have unearthed various previously unknown yet astounding facts which will transform the status of North Tyneside, so that very soon Whitley Bay will have a new theatre, Linskill Centre will be saved and extended, the shuttered up seafront pubs will re-open, and all talk of closing the Delaval Arms will cease. Hurrah.

St Mary's Lighthouse: It is little known that before conquering Everest in 1953, Edmund Hillary did a 'dummy' ascent up the lighthouse. This took ten days, was achieved without oxygen and with 12 Sherpas in base camp on the rocks, where their tent peg markings can still be seen. The strange stone monolith on the rocks was erected to mark this event, but an amnesiac town clerk forgot to attach the brass plaque.

Beaconsfield: Largely unreported is the world record roly-poly speed achieved on the Beaconsfield slopes by the distinguished, slightly loopy astronomer of uncontrollable eyebrows, Patrick Moore.

Moore was staying at the Park Hotel Tynemouth, where he delivered his lecture, 'The Solar System – Donut or Big Mac?' In the small hours he suddenly challenged other guests to time his descent which knocked 22 seconds off the existing record. The entire gathering was somewhat inebriated and the details never officially documented.

The Fish Quay: An event took place at North Shields Fish Quay in 1986 which somehow has never received the acknowledgement it deserves. Fishermen and dealers at the early morning market were astounded when a trawler docked and revealed part of its catch to be none other than Harry Secombe, well known singer and Goon.

Secombe had been pulled up in the nets somewhere off Scarborough after falling asleep on, then falling right off, an inflatable Lilo, after which the tides had carried him many miles north. In front of the incredulous gathering, the oversized Welshman proceeded to sing *We'll keep a welcome in the Hillside* and do a 45 second performance of Neddy Seagoon. Old sea dogs chew over the incident even now, though thus far it has been ignored by the borough.

Billy Mill: The borough has never celebrated one of its most unusual sons, and the world's first 'roundaboutist'. Determined to bring down traffic accidents, Billy Mill stood at the end of the Coast Road for 23 years banging a loud drum and wearing a bright coat, directing the traffic in a circular manner. Collisions dropped slightly, the authorities were forced to admit traffic islands were the way forward, built one on the very spot and named it after its creator. But where is the statue?

Where indeed is the acknowledgement for any of these unique events? Over to you, North Tyneside.

Two gold rings and why charity begins in the shop

20th January 2005

AN ITEM in last week's *News Guardian* had Barnardo's appealing for volunteer workers in their North Tyneside shops. That's for me, I thought. A few hours later I was made aware what dangerous work it was. Dangerous? Read on.

I'd cycled into Whitley Bay for one of my regular forays into the coast's charity shops. I'm the sad creature you see crouched on the floor flicking through the battered vinyl albums.

I whizz past endless Top of the Pops compilations, scan *Val Doonican's Greatest Cardigans*, *The Grenadier Guards Play Mott the Hoople*, *Favourite Nursery Rhymes in Esperanto*, or *Meatloaf Does Perry Como*. Who knows – maybe I'll find a little-known Brian Eno or Kraftwerk?

I could easily live in a charity shop. Every shirt I own comes from one. The shirts normally cost £3, then £4 to have the collar removed at that dying breed of outlets, the dressmakers (where I am the only male customer), for truly, I am of the religion that forswears collars.

I'm less keen on most conventional shops. More than one trip per decade to the MetroCentre, and I disintegrate into a strange red powder, and I have a special voucher that frees me from visiting the January Sales.

The women who run charity shops should be running the country. I love all of them.

When things feel bad, I have only to walk into their premises, and see these women of a certain age to feel comforted. No matter that most of the goods on sale do not interest me, the shapeless grey suits, the small glass bowls that produce a snow storm when shaken.

Nor dare I buy the second-hand books, for my house already rivals the British Library, due in no small part to a fellow house mate whose biblio excesses now see him stacking books next to the breakfast cereal.

These charity shop miracle women work unpaid, yet seem much more at ease than their salaried, often stressed counterparts in the city centre chains.

Come to that, amateur footballers often seem to be enjoying themselves more than their scowling-faced, £60,000 a week professional counterparts.

Which is not to recommend that everyone should work for nothing. Just that doing something for others is good for you.

For these women lack the normal ambition we are encouraged to nurture. They are disgracefully uncorporate, have probably received no training in retail psychology and have no interest in clawing their way up the company ladder. Yet they seem strangely content.

This is a small observation but one that could change your life. The nation's most potent sense of wellbeing lately came not through the announcement of a record GNP, but when we donated £200m to the tsunami appeal with absolutely no thought of personal advantage.

But what about this danger element mentioned previously? That same Saturday I walked into the St Oswald's Hospice shop on Park View only minutes after a young ne'er-do-well had walked out with two gold rings, valued at £45. The women of a certain age behind the counter for once (and understandably) were shaken, and there was quite a commotion.

Stealing from charity shops ranks pretty low, and I hope the young fellow slept well. I doubt it, and though our initial gut reaction might be of the flog 'em, hang 'em, disembowel 'em tendency, just remember, if only such people had the sense to know it, working in a charity shop can bring much more satisfaction than stealing from one.

Now then, about that job application...

When one (automatic) door closes so does another...

3rd February 2005

CONSIDER IF you will the case of the Natwest bank door. This is the main door to the Park View, Whitley Bay branch in which have been stored for more than 20 years, the Mortimer millions.

Despite my two decades of loyal devotion, I have no idea if the manager has two heads, is adept at making spotted dick, or can predict the winner of the 2.30 at Haydock. In short, I have never met him/her.

Time was your bank manager used to emerge from the wardrobe – even if it were only in the TV adverts. Bank managers in 2005 are totally subterranean.

This main bank door has been automatic for some time. It opens outwards which means if you approach and attempt to enter without breaking stride, you are doomed to failure.

There is a large PRESS button at the side, but by now the door has bypassed this and opens of its own accord, shoving you back towards the street as it does so.

It makes a soft noise that reminds me of the Flash Gordon air lock opening in those Saturday morning serials.

Once you have passed through, the door closes behind you. If a second person wishes to enter fairly close behind, the door suffers a momentary indecision as whether to open or close. If there is then a third person similarly placed, the door undergoes a mental crisis, and is put on a three month prescription for Prozac.

Last week the door was non-functional. A note had been attached with two words PLEASE PULL. This proved quite simple and the door opened without fuss. Less fuss than usual if the truth were known.

I found myself wondering which were the more likely to break down, an automatic door, or a human arm?

I could reach only one conclusion. The automatic. Nor does the opening of a door via a human arm and hand need special training. You could almost say anyone can do it.

Nor have I heard of a single person complaining when required to open a manual door.

"But this is intolerable! You mean I'm supposed to open this door by hand!"

And while I confess the following is only a hunch, I am prepared to wager there is not a single article or letter to a newspaper complaining civilisation's progress is retarded through the lack of automatic doors.

But they are spreading. Doors to the new Park View shopping centre are automatic.

Automatic doors break down. For a manual door to break down, every hinge would need to fall off simultaneously, or every atom in the door's make-up instantly decide to resist movement. Physicists put the chances of this as slim.

Eavesdrop on the Metro, in the street, or the pub. You're unlikely to hear the complaint, "That blooming front door of mine's broken down again!".

I have never had a friend who has experienced a broken-down door. It's as unlikely as a broken down plate. But this techno-myopia is growing.

Impossible now to find cars without automatic windows.

Some years ago my partner Kitty and I gasped our way to Rotherham on a sweltering day when travelling in a friend's car whose automatic windows had bust. We eventually fell out the vehicle like boiled lobsters.

I feel a Sci-Fi story coming on. A totally automated world where not a single task is left to human dexterity, be it eating soup, tying shoe laces or scratching a zit. Then BANG! The super control everything computer breaks down, no-one has a clue how to do even the simplest movement, everyone staggers about in futile fashion and eventually we all die out.

It will make me a fortune. Which I'll deposit with Natwest.

Automatic door willing.

Got the sinking feeling? Then join BUBASAP immediately!

17th February 2005

THE WORST job in the world awaits me, and who will help? I turn to my son Dylan. His face pales. He apologises but feels he really must lie down for a while.

What about my partner Kitty? Normally supportive, she suddenly remembers an urgent deadline and is gone.

I could always contact President Bush, tell him his assistance would help defeat Al Qaeda and ferret out Osama Bin Laden (remember him?). Or maybe I could telephone North Tyneside Council. Except all 128 phone numbers are permanently engaged. I could always emigrate.

I have done awful jobs before. How about cleaning six dropped eggs off a proggy mat? Or wobbling on top of highly insecure stepladders trying to rewire a new light socket with screws the size of lighter flint?

This is worse. It is the removing, the cleaning and the putting back of the U-bend under the kitchen sink.

For six months I have tried to deny the obvious truth, that the bend is growing irretrievably blocked. I have stood on top of the sink pouring boiling water from a great height.

I have made strange noises with plungers. I have poked long knitting needles to the pipe's heart to no avail. Once a U-bend begins its blocking process, it will not be denied.

What that U-bend secretes is unspeakable. And to get access I have to contort myself like a circus acrobat under the kitchen sink.

I loosen off the two large plastic nuts and as black liquid emerges, I remember I need a pan to catch it. With a pan in situ, I eventually remove the U-bend. Stinking foul putrescence vomits out, most of it missing the pan.

Inside is trapped the detritus of two years' washing-up, a thick black slime that secretes hair grips, baked beans, bacon rind, half a pie crust, a two pence piece and a child's index finger (OK, so I made the last one up).

Cleaning this outranks as such a traumatic task I'm surprised Dostoevsky has not based a novel round it. It does not surrender easily.

There is boiling water, bleach, scourers. The glutinous mass is then wrapped in newspaper, thrown in the wheelie bin and a few minutes later I stare with a sense of giddy delight at the squeaky clean U-bend.

Except the job is not done. Resecuring the bend, the lining up of the two nuts and threads is a task that requires a three year HND course.

Now I have read and absorbed *Zen and the Art of Motorcycle Maintenance* and fully appreciate the need to be both artistic and practical. None of which helps as I stand and curse the bend which is dripping like a runny nose, and requires three attempts before it is properly screwed (if you'll excuse the phrase).

All of this I will face within the next few days when I finally face up to the worst job in the world. And how come the house is deserted? Where are the potential helpers?

The task is made worse by the suspicion that a U-bend serves no purpose except help make worse what it is supposed to prevent.

I have developed a new plumbing technique, a pipe running vertically down from the sink, then joined to another pipe running off at 45 degrees, and taking with it all the waste, which has nowhere to congregate.

The U-bend conspiracy has gone on long enough. We have been hoodwinked by the manufacturers of these strange, utterly useless devices for too many years. I urge you now to join BUBASAP (Ban U Bends As Soon As Possible) which I have just this moment created.

There will of course be resistance from the plumbing establishment, but as Lenin said when he appeared on Ready Steady Cook, you can't make an omelette without breaking eggs.

In years to come children will tug their mummy's arm in museums, point to a glass case and ask: "What's that strange thing mummy?"

"It was a device to ensure your sink pipe got blocked every two years," mammy will reply, and the child will be left to ponder what strange creatures grown-ups are.

The economy of crosses, and the vital issue of Whitley Hungarians

24th February 2005

SIGN HERE, please, said the counter clerk in the Halifax, Whitley Bay, as she marked a cross at the relevant place. I was intrigued by this cross. Every time anyone in a bank, building society or other institution asks you to sign, they first make a cross.

Is this cross an essential visual guide to the signature's required location? If so, why not simply pre-print every form with said cross. If not, why is the cross done at all?

If marking a cross takes one second, assuming every counter clerk in every institution performs the act 100 times a day (say 400 times a day per venue in toto), assuming 10,000 venues nationwide, that amounts to 4m seconds a day,

20m a working week (not allowing for Saturday), 1000m a year, or 16m minutes a year, or 260,000 hours or 31,000 working days.

In removing the act of cross-making, the country will save 31,000 days and Britain will once again rule supreme in the economic tables!

Moving on: two things struck me watching Newcastle United's first leg UEFA Cup tie with Heerenveen. Firstly the North Dutch team is the only football club in the world with five vowels in its name, each one the same. This leads me to a feeble joke: Clubbers' Question: Where do you go for the best 'e's? Answer: Heerenveen of course!

Secondly, at one stage the Channel Five commentator, spluttering with incredulity, said, "the third official is Hungarian, but" – and here he almost needed smelling salts before continuing – "he actually lives in Whitley Bay!"

A few missed chances, yellow cards, and Titus Bramble blunders later, he repeated it: "Would you believe it – he's Hungarian and he lives in Whitley Bay!"

Incidentally, the third officials used to be called linesmen. But then Sellafield was once known as Winscale, so we can only assume linesmen became dangerously radioactive too.

Is the thought of a Hungarian in Whitley Bay so incredible, I asked myself? Then I realised that increasingly it was. For how would a Hungarian slip through the immigration net in 2005? Or any other foreigner come to that?

Firstly they would need to undergo two dozen medical tests to ensure they were carrying nothing that might affect the entire indigenous population within hours and within days be a national epidemic.

Secondly, they would be required to sit a written examination to prove they were fully trained as brain surgeons, seismologists, astro-physicists, archaeologists and water diviners, and had won at least four consecutive series of their own country's version of Mastermind.

Thirdly, they would be sent into a windowless room where a disembodied voice would bark at them such questions as, "What year was Marlborough dismissed from command by the Tory government?" and unless they were able to reply, "1711" within five seconds they would be considered unfit for British citizenship.

Even passing this test would require them further to sing all verses of God Save The Queen word-perfect while standing on their head in a bucket of water.

Should they come through all these tests, they would be allowed into the country, but under immediate house arrest until able to prove conclusively that they had no terrorist connections and had never held a flag day for Osama Bin Laden.

Even then they could be kept under close observation. It's rumoured that Hungarians have been known to corrupt north easterners with the likes of goulash when Geordies are perfectly happy with pie and chips.

Hang on though, Hungarians and football? Wasn't there that little incident in November 1953 when the Hungarians shook us all to our shin pads by becoming the first team ever to beat England at Wembley?

And didn't we go to Budapest in May of the next year determined to show what a fluke it was, and prove that we were still world supremos?

And didn't we get tonked 7-1?

And now, say some, 51 years on, to rub salt in the wound, they're coming here and taking all our jobs as third officials. And living in Whitley Bay! You'd hardly believe it.

Great Tom is gone – we own part of him

10th March 2005

TOM HADAWAY, you're gone, and when will we see your like again? What other North-East writer could stop all the news, so that 6.30pm on Thursday March 3, the crime, the sport, the politics, the tittle-tattle and the celebrities were all put in their place on BBC TV *Look North*.

Only one item could lead that day, from York to Berwick, from Blyth to the Solway Firth – Tom Hadaway is dead.

And where now are my regular evening bike rides with a bottle of wine to visit you and your wife Barbara, chew the fat, pop a few corks. Sort out the world, then wobble home around midnight? I knew time was short, but then time always is.

I'd known you 30 years. Ten years ago we were booked to give a joint lunchtime talk at Marine Tech. South Shields, remember Tom? You spoke first, and come 2pm, and the meeting's end, you were still talking and the audience hanging on every word. You remained a socialist in a nation hardly able to pronounce the word any more.

And when Roger Burgess and I decided to stage a festival to mark your 80th birthday, you couldn't understand why. Everyone else could.

Film makers, writers, directors, theatre companies – a massive coming together of the region's talents, more than 60 plays, talks, films over a two week period, a Hadaway bonanza. Tom, you united different parts of the arts that had hardly talked to one another in years.

And here at Cloud Nine, Valerie Laws wrote *Hadaway – The Making of a Writer*, your life put on stage with such powerful emotion, a celebration of human potential directed by Anne Orwin, a founder member of Live Theatre who knew the Hadaway story so well and so instinctively that the production seemed to record every one of its subject's heartbeats.

How proud I was that my own son Dylan played the young Tom. Dave Smith played the older version, and when you three met up at your house for a photo-call, you all ended up shooting pool for an hour.

About this time I wrote you a short poem which reads 'Tom Hadaway/With words'. You did too, that remarkable combination. You described an often harsh gritty macho world, yet in a language of rich intensity. You told me you merely recorded other people's lives, just put down their words. This was not true. You wrote from the heart, but knew the heart alone is not enough. You crafted and shaped and challenged.

I published many of your plays, firstly in 1975, *Three North-East Plays*, you, Leonard Barras, and C.P. Taylor. Live Theatre launched the book with a production at The Gulbenkian Studio, Newcastle, and this sold out.

Your play was *The Filleting Machine*. Twenty five years later we restaged it at Live Theatre as part of IRON Press's anniversary. Melvyn Bragg hosted the night, and watched the play slack-jawed. He said, "more power and emotion in 25 minutes than a dozen full-length BBC plays."

I never knew how much of this you took on board. You never played the game, never bothered mixing with the influential. You were undervalued, but these things find their level.

And you spoke for people not normally given a voice in theatre. You never patronised them. How could you? You were one of them.

Tom, the Fish Quay playwright. Aye, but later on you branched out, working three months with Durham prisoners (then another six months unpaid), which led to the play *Yesterday's Children*, and also the Arab-Israeli play, *Long Shadows*, co-written with your button-bright daughter Pauline.

Some projects sat scattered and abandoned: the Australian play, the mail train play. This is a writer's lot. At the end Pauline was working with you, attempting to finish your Laurel and Hardy in Tynemouth play.

And now we feel we own a part of you. I feel it, your family, friends, Live Theatre, Amber Films, Robson Green, Tim Healy.

That's what happens with great writers. We feel we own them because the words they write touch us in a way nothing else can. In a way we do own them. In another way they are unownable, just as in a way, while their words continue to speak for them, they are immortal.

How Oscar fooled us. The bite could be worse than the bark

17th March 2005

THUS FAR this column has kept stumm about Oscar, but an amusing letter from Henna Mackie of Tynemouth spurs me to action. For those living on Alpha Centauri, I'll remind you that Oscar is the Royal Mail staffie banned from accompanying his postie owner Andrew Jamieson on his Tynemouth route following a single complaint.

Oscar did the rounds dressed in his own Royal Mail coat. The decision has produced a huge reaction and questions in the House.

Let me confess then that the single complaint came from me. Oh yes. The reasons are several. Firstly it has been scientifically proven that although wearing a RM uniform, Oscar is singularly inept at posting letters, or even reading a postal code.

He has also been known to poo in the street. OK, the owner cleans it up, but it leaves us with the question as to whether any creature sporting official RM clothing should be unable either (a) to drop a single letter through a single letter box or (b) to control their bowels in public.

I highlight these two serious canine shortcomings, but we have not yet reached the hub of the matter. I realise that in many eyes, the Royal Mail itself has come over as a bunch of brainless twerps in this, without humour, imagination or feeling.

Yet they have sacrificed themselves for a greater cause. They are afraid to reveal the true facts knowing that panic could sweep the nation.

It is therefore left to this column, fearless champion of the truth, standard bearer for integrity, campaigner for – (*get on with it* – Ed). OK, it is left to Mortimer to come clean and if the revelation results in thousands of people hurling themselves from Tynemouth cliff tops, then so be it. Brace yourselves dear readers. The awful truth is that Oscar is suspected of having strong terrorist links. It is true.

You will immediately want to know more but in the interests of national security I cannot reveal more. I may have already said too much.

I can only say that shortly Oscar will be put under kennel arrest. Already he has been denied internet access and his Pedigree Chum is being stringently vetted. Regrettably his rights of *habeas canine* are to be revoked.

You can rest assured that the authorities would not take this action without strong intelligence information – the same intelligence services who revealed Saddam Hussein had weapons of mass destruction that could be unleashed on us before half time at St James' Park, so you can have every confidence.

Oscar is the tip of the iceberg. Strong evidence exists for an entire national network of terrorist pets. There are reports of a goldfish swimming the wrong way round its bowl in Monkseaton. A tortoise in Seaton Sluice hasn't moved for a week, a definite signal that is transmitting information to Al Qaeda, while the squawk of a parrot in West Allotment has been recorded, played backwards at half the normal speed, and seems to bear more than a coincidental similarity to the phrase 'Good old Osama'. The plan is frighteningly simple but effective.

Terrorists acknowledge the British love of animals (only 30,000 Christmas pets dumped by January) and know this is the nation's soft underbelly.

Recruitment has secretly been going on for years and now, unless we take draconian measures, the pets are almost ready to strike. Like the Home Secretary I urge you all to be terrified – sorry, vigilant. Should you see an ant acting suspiciously, let the authorities know.

We may have to lock up, indefinitely, every single pet in the country, if this is the price for maintaining our freedom.

And of course Oscar was the front line, stage one in the cunning pet terrorist strategy. What better way to wreak havoc and destruction than a terrorist dog officially sanctioned to call at 300 houses every day.

But if I have reduced you to a gibbering wreck, cowering in the airing cupboard, let me reassure you. Your safety and welfare are not being neglected.

Big Brother (the original) is watching.

Men only bars and the meat draw – questions that need to be asked

24th March 2005

YOU MIGHT have caught the items on BBC *Look North* of late on the decline of working men's clubs in the north east. There were black and white films from the 50s and 60s; whole concert rooms full of sturdy looking working class lads carrying trays full of foaming beer, while on stage the 'torn' warbled her way through Delilah, and oh but how the cash tills did ring.

Cut to some modern-day concert rooms: peeling paint, holes in the roof, and just a scrunched up crisp packet or empty lager bottle on its side to suggest signs of life.

In those days, sweat pouring from the brows, miners, shipyard workers and sheet metal workers could clomp into the 'clerb' bar and down eight pints of Fed Special just to replace the eight hour shift's dehydration.

It's somehow not the same for their modern counterparts sat in front of a call centre computer, and most people today would think a welder's helmet was something worn by Darth Vader.

Not that I am a noble son of toil myself. I do occasionally get my hands dirty at work – only last week my bike chain came off while cycling up to deliver this column.

But I can categorically mark the month and year when the decline of the traditional CIU club began. It was March 1987. Let me explain.

I'd been a member of Cullercoats Crescent Club for some time, I also occasionally wrote *The Cullercoats Kid* column for *The Beacon,* that tiny organ of free speech (now defunct) put out by Cullercoats Community Association.

My light-hearted offering that particular month detailed how the three Cullercoats watering holes, The Queens Head, The Bay and The Crescent Club, all had splendid views over our magnificent harbour – or at least would have if the windows at eye-level had not been frosted, or curtained over. I suggested some entrepreneur might hire out ladders to drinkers who could climb up, and thereby still marvel at the beach, the sea and the rocks.

Reactions varied. Joe Henry of The Bay said nothing. Bill Routledge of the Queens Head sent the article down to Bass's headquarters in Leeds who promptly instructed the frosted glass be replaced by the clear variety, and tipplers have enjoyed the view ever since.

The Crescent Club wrote to me claiming I had brought 'the club into disrepute' for which I was summoned before the committee. I refused to attend and sent them a poem back. Eventually I was told by letter that I had been 'tried and found guilty' in my absence. The punishment was a six months ban and I could almost see the black cap being donned while it was pronounced.

In a great melodramatic gesture I sent to the club my CIU card which I thereby renounced. All this caused quite a rumpus and even made an article in the Daily Express with, if I recall right, the headline, 'Cullercoats Bard Barred.'

I was smitten. What kind of reward was this for a man who in the early 70s, in the old concert room had entranced all with his versions of *Chantilly Lace* and *Twenty Four Hours From Tulsa?*

And there were still questions about the club I had no answers to. Did vegetarians take part in the meat draw? What was the rule on cross-dressers in the men only bar? Why did all committee men have saggy trousers?

And thus began the decline of the working men's clubs regionwide. The Crescent Club still packs them in for weekend concerts, but generally Windowgate (as I call it) saw the rot set in.

Ten years later, my brother, himself a CIU card holder, visited me, and said: "I'll buy you a pint in the Crescent. It's all water under the bridge now." As he went to sign me in, the doorman, who I had never seen in my life, pointed an accusing finger at me and said: "He's barred." We supped in the Queens Head instead and enjoyed the view.

And on Saturday night as I walk past, the guest singer is still belting out *The Green Green Grass of Home* (or even maybe *Delilah*) and all those energetic young men who in the 70s were the alternative generation are now becoming the club's bedrock and hierarchy, as their trousers grow gradually more saggy.

And here's me still undecided if 'clerbs' are a hopeless anachronism, a lone bastion of male chauvinism, or a welcome refuge where couples of a certain age can escape the mindless binge drinking elsewhere and enjoy a dance and live music without hassle.

Oh, and one last thing. The committee never said if they liked my poem.

How I tackled 7 minute barrier and the parcel beyond recall

7th April 2005

THE POPE may be dead and St James' Park may be applying for a fight club licence, but for me the week is dominated by the seven minute barrier.

It has, I confess become a mite obsessive. Perhaps I should explain, and offer you the following telephone number (0191) 259 6953. It is not my policy to give out phone numbers without the owners' consent, but here I'll make an exception.

The number belongs to the Royal Mail and specifically the North Shields Delivery Office and Callers Office, and it is the number you ring should they try and fail to deliver a package to your house.

You could be dead, in the bath, fast asleep, on the roof, hearing aid switched off – various reasons for missing the postie. No matter, here's a card through the door saying you can (a) collect the parcel in person, or (b) have it re-delivered.

Maybe this is an urgent parcel – in my case special delivery – so you prepare to rush up to the office. Hang on though. The card states you must wait a minimum of 48 hours.

This is because in the interests of economy, the Royal Mail now employ tortoises to whose backs are strapped returning parcels. Tortoises eat very little and require no maintenance, the only slight drawback being it takes them 48 hours to cover the two and a half miles to the office.

After 48 hours you decide to pick up the parcel. The office is Cumberland Road, off Norham Road near West Chirton Industrial Estate. Hang on though. That's a bit remote. Anywhere near a Metro? In your dreams! Any bus go that way? You tell me!

Never mind. You'll wait 48 hours then catch a taxi when you've finished work. Hang on though. Parcels can only be picked up between the hours of 7am and 1pm, so they're closed.

Plan C. You ring (0191) 2596953. What could be simpler? What you'll say is, "could you please deliver my special delivery parcel tomorrow morning when I shall not be dead, in the bath, fast asleep or on the roof. I do not have a hearing aid."

Now this is where the seven minute barrier comes in. My first call rang out for six minutes and 32 seconds before I heard a not unpleasant female voice saying, "Sorry, there is no reply."

The second occasion the dialling tone stretched to six minutes 38 seconds before I was similarly rejected. Down to six minutes 16 seconds on the third attempt, and six minutes 35 seconds on attempt four. With attempts five and six there was an engaged tone.

I wouldn't like you to think I spend my days timing dialling tones. There is a loudspeaker on my phone, so I can lay it to one side, and while attempting to get through to (0191) 2596953, I can do something useful like rewire the house or paint the living room.

It could have been an off-day. I tried the next morning. Only six minutes 17 seconds. It seemed I would never be successful. I would never get the phone to crack the seven minute barrier, which had become a bit of a wild dream of mine.

Instead I took to imagining the staff at the North Shields Delivery Office and Callers Office. Two hours a week are put aside to training, part of which is the topic 'How to Deal With a Ringing Telephone from People Wanting a Parcel Delivered.'

Trainees are gathered round a phone that then rings. The supervisor says, "Hear that? That's someone who thinks they can beat our inaccessible venue, our unsuitable opening hours, and use the phone to get their parcel delivered. And will they succeed?"

There's a low murmur and half-hearted shaking of the heads. The supervisor shouts loudly, "I said, are they going to succeed?"

At which the enthused trainees, also shouting loudly, reply, "No way!"

As the phone rings and rings, not all keep their nerve. Some make a lunge at it and are restrained. The training is tough but scientific, and after four weeks every trainee can hear a phone ring up to 100 times a day with nil response. But (here's the rub), should any call exceed seven minutes, psychological damage can set in. Hence the cut-off, and the end of my dream.

After three weeks, every parcel is returned to sender, and the beautiful circular symmetry of the whole operation is complete.

Just as long as no-one ever breaks rank and answers that .phone. Which I'm pretty confident they won't do. That number again? It's (0191) 2596953.

No Mortimer Pope, but look how the money rolls in...

21st April 2005

SEVERAL THEORIES have been put forward as to why I stood for Pope. Some claimed I was a trouble-maker, intent on installing condom vending machines all round St Peter's Square.

Others said I had a thing about wearing big pointed hats. One theory had it I was indulging a strange desire to kiss airport tarmac in public.

None of these is true. I stood for Pope as it's one of the few remaining jobs likely to turn me down because I was too young. The other is a High Court Judge, and I may apply there if a vacancy comes up, though thus far I've searched the sits. vac. columns in vain.

Supermarket shelf stackers, call centre operative trainees – no High Court Judges.

The Pope's job went elsewhere, and it's their loss. We have our own elections anyway, and I am able to announce a new political force on the scene.

At present they're standing only in the North Tyneside council elections, but if their expected success materialises, they would soon hope to be a major movement nationwide.

Would you welcome please the Stick 'Em Up! Party. No, no, this is nothing to do with bank robbers. The name comes from the party's philosophy which is to stick up as much new building development as possible.

Thus far they have operated in the shadowy margins of politics, but with such breathtaking success in North Tyneside that they've decided to 'come out' and form their very own party. Just look at the influence they've exerted behind the scenes!

1) The planned demolition of Linskill for luxury housing development.

2) The demolition of Spanish City for luxury housing development.

3) The demolition of the Bay Hotel Cullercoats for luxury flats development.

4) The planned demolition of half of Monkseaton for luxury flats development.

5) The planned demolition of Whitley Bay allotments for luxury housing developments.

Impressive, eh? And there's plenty more if only space allowed. But space is among the things Stick 'Em Up! is sworn to oppose, and one of their eye-catching slogans states, 'Grass is a Profit-Free Zone.'

A Stick 'Em Up! spokesperson commented: "North Tyneside has shown itself incredibly receptive to our philosophy. So now it's time to take the next step."

And this new step includes a radical new venture in co-operation with Nexus, who, following the realisation that luxury housing is more profitable than a few mangy cabbages at the Whitley Bay allotments, want to expand in a big way.

The plan is to build stilted houses over the Metro track. Fantastic, eh? The stilts would be high enough to allow trains to pass underneath.

A joint feasibility study carried out by Nexus and Stick 'Em Up! reveals at least 100 new luxury dwellings, selling at £200,000 apiece, could be built between Cullercoats and Whitley Bay stations alone. This amounts to £20m.

Think of all the Metro track between Howdon at one end of the borough and Shiremoor at the other, and we're talking 1,000 new properties and an income of £200m.

"All that development space going begging – why, it's such a waste!" said the party spokesperson, who also expressed gratitude to the present North Tyneside Council for setting such a good example.

The 'Nexus Heights' properties will be insulated against noise, offer fine views, and be almost totally flood-proof. And of course owners will always be near a Metro station. It is seen as an advancement in designer living, and as the spokesperson concluded, "the more properties we build, the bigger the choice, the lower the price".

This can be backed up by news this week that a West Monkseaton property went on the market for only £96,000. And according to reliable reports, a first-rate dog kennel it is too.

Why we should all be walking back to happiness

28th April 2005

TWO NEWS items catch the eye. Firstly, a walking campaign has been launched in North Tyneside to encourage us all to get off the settee, put the best foot forward and stride out to better health and fitness.

This second phase of the Idle Eric project (do you need permission to use a celebrity's name backwards?) will encourage us not only to perambulate but to do it round our very own streets and environment.

This is good. For while we all jet off to gawp at the Acropolis or the Taj Mahal, few of us look closely at what's on our doorstep. When was the last time you walked round Tynemouth Priory?

The second item was comedian Vic Reeves banned from driving for 32 months for crashing his vintage Jaguar then making off without stopping. He was three times over the limit. Reeves had left his home to get cigarettes from the corner shop. The shop was a quarter of a mile away.

A quarter of a mile. Think about it. Five minutes walk. How long did it take the comedian to find the car keys, open his garage, reverse out, then drive off? You need to be pretty committed to drunken driving for such action. If Reeves didn't have a stage partner called Mortimer, I'd say he was pretty dumb.

Most car owners would prefer to attempt strangling a man-eating alien rather than walk anywhere. I was the same before I gave up my car ownership. My local pub was a quarter of a mile away, and I'd drive there for my two pints.

One day scientists will discover the chemical that prevents motorists walking. The chemical is powerful and will see them struggling into a tiny parking space when a much bigger one is only 20 yards distant.

It is not only the exercise. I have a theory that everything that's worth anything has been thought up while walking.

Thus Albert Einstein was probably taking a walk in the Black Forest or some such when he paused and said, "You know, I think everything is relative." After which $e = mc^{\approx}$ couldn't be far away. And Isaac Newton must have been walking to see that apple drop which then saw him go off to invent cider – or was it to discover the law of gravity?

Beethoven's Fifth? My money's on Ludwig out for an afternoon stroll when those opening chords came to him.

I need to walk at least 30 minutes each morning before I start writing.

The walk can be round Beaconsfield, Marden Quarry Park, along the cliff tops, or sometimes along suburban streets where I nosily peer into front windows and speculate about the lives lived therein.

And I have yet to have a collision when out walking. Signs such as 'Slow Bend Ahead', 'Low Gear Now', or 'T Junction' have little relevance. I barely notice speed cameras.

Nor, unlike many human pursuits, am I being exploited by a multi-million pound industry, unless you discount shoe leather.

Often my partner Kitty and I will walk the three miles from the Magnesia Bank to Cullercoats, a midnight ramble in the riverside and Tynemouth Long Sands.

If you know a better walk home from the local I want to know it, and the tea and toast on arrival feels doubly deserved.

I remember once going out for a walk in a leafy suburb of Austin, Texas. After 20 minutes I'd seen 32 lawn sprinklers but no humans.

Then I was attacked by a small dog that took me for an alien. It knew humans only as fat creatures in checked trousers who sat either at the car wheel or in front of the TV.

Walking has been abolished in the USA. It's one reason they bomb places like Iraq.

Go on, get off your bum and take a walk. I bet you think of something interesting while you're at it.

I keep thinking of Vic Reeves, staggering about looking for his car keys for that short but oh so costly drive.

If only he'd have walked, he'd have saved himself a 32 month ban and a fine. Plus which he may well have come up with a brilliant idea. Another dove from above as it were.

The art of good living, or why Delius and Dizzie can co-exist

19th May 2005

OFF TO The Sage, Gateshead, to see my first classical music concert in years. Who would have thought a few years ago that Gateshead, poor inferior, unfashionable Gateshead, could attract four figure audiences to international art exhibitions or the world's leading orchestras?

The town – not that dissimilar in size to North Tyneside, was famous for – well, nothing at all really. Then some people of vision arrived. First to make its presence felt was the International Athletics Stadium. Then the Angel of the North winged its spectacular way in. The huge anonymous mass that was The Baltic building rose from its anonymity. The most beautiful bridge in the world, somewhere between a harp and an egg slicer stretched to span the river and finally The Sage (known affectionately as 'The Slug on the Tyne') slithered its shiny curvaceous way into place. Hey presto – Gateshead river front is transformed by culture.

Newcastle meantime, glitzy fashionable Newcastle had the quayside vision only for more hotels and drinking shops.

And if Gateshead town centre is mainly funereal, blame the MetroCentre for sucking it dry. It's the price we pay for supporting such out-of-town monstrosities.

The interior of The Sage's 1,700 seater Hall One looks to have been sculpted out of butter. The acoustics are so sensitive you could hear the second violinist's nostril hairs vibrate.

Things have changed since my last classical concert. The male musicians' dinner suits have been replaced with open-necked black shirts and trousers. They look a bit like the man in the Milk Tray advert. There's a female conductor too, a stunning Finnish ice-maiden called Susannah Malkki whose long draped black coat could have come from *The Matrix*.

I've never been sure about conductors. All that arm waving – is it really necessary and how do the musicians take it in and read the music at the same time?

In this hi-tec computerised age, I expected the musicians to be reading from flickering screens which automatically scrolled down. But no, it's still old fashioned sheet music, still turned by hand.

And how come we have to stay silent at the end of each movement (except the last) when all our instincts are to applaud? Who came up with that idea? And why is the audience almost exclusively white, middle-aged and middle-class?

While the Northern Sinfonia perform, I find myself wondering if the clarinettist gets on with the cello player. I imagine which musician might be having an affair with which other one. I try to pinpoint who might be having a mid-life crisis, and are all musicians totally absorbed during a performance or do some wonder if they've fed the parking meter?

I freely confess that I was totally absorbed, and felt the world couldn't be such a terrible place after all if 30 plus highly talented individuals combine to create such musical beauty for we who have gathered to appreciate it. Send the Northern Sinfonia and other orchestras to all the world's battle zones and tell them to perform, to remind combatants of human potential.

Meantime The Sage offers a huge diversity of music, but audiences I suspect still stay within their own limited boundaries.

Here's how North Tyneside can capitalise. First we need a modern performance venue. The fact the borough boasts not a single one is a disgrace. To herald its opening, we should have The First North Tyneside Random Music Festival. You buy a ticket for a particular performance without knowing whether it will be Foo Fighters or the Berlin Symphony Orchestra playing Beethoven's Eighth Symphony.

Ticket holders may find themselves listening to Shostakovitch. There again it could be Dizzie Rascal. The festival would embrace classical, trad jazz, baroque, rap, electronic, ska, folk, chamber, heavy metal, ambient. A charver may find himself at a Stravinsky concert and a grandma watching So Solid Crew. Not everyone will like everything. But a few people might find themselves surprised.

The festival will happen in a blaze of publicity. Build the new venue on the Spanish City along with a new Playhouse, and make the coast a focal point for vibrant culture.

Our redevelopment plans for too long have been in the hands of the unimaginative or the purely mercenary. It's time for a bit of wisdom, Gateshead style. Plus a touch of the random.

Choose to snooze – or what the political parties have missed

27th May 2005

MY BEST JOKE of the week came on Sunday, dropping in to see the splendid efforts of Stanley Crescent residents in Whitley Bay. They're uniting to prevent Nexus's outrageous plans to sell off the railside allotments etc for property development, and their group Tracks staged a massive 'weed-in', clearing a whole swathe of open land.

The clean-up threw up about 40 different time-pieces, buried and forgotten, but some still working. They laid them out on display.

"Neighbourhood watch" I said. Oh, but I am a wag. Meantime, the insanity that is property development goes on elsewhere in the borough, the demolition men now moving in to flatten the beautifully rococo building that was the Chain Locker by the Shields Ferry, and alongside the inevitable sign 'For Luxury Flat Development'.

Rise up good folk of North Tyneside. You are being abused.

Meantime I went to the dentist. Whilst we treat our doctor (even post-Shipman) as a confidant, and token of security, a dentist we view differently, despite the fact he/she may achieve a closer proximity to us than any but our most intimates.

This is what a dentist does: fills your mouth with tubes, braces, cotton wool, suction pipes and other paraphernalia, and then casually enquires, "going anywhere interesting this summer?"

Your reply, which is meant to be 'the Lake District', is an incomprehensible "gggg-gggg-gggg." The dentist says "hmn" and carries on, leaving you to feel like an unintelligible idiot.

The dentist produces a needle longer than an Olympic javelin which when injected will turn your bottom lip into something the size of a Pirelli tyre needing a wheelbarrow to get it home. Your cheek is also inflated into a bouncy castle. Despite this, when the dentist starts drilling, the nerve in the tooth is still sensitive, but you dare not scream out for fear of being labelled a wimp. Plus which this scream would merely come out as "gggg-gggg-gggg."

Even so, I look forward to my dentist trips. This is partly because my dentist Moe is a pretty chilled-out individual. No white coat, and hanging from his dental equipment is a teddy bear.

When you arrive you get a cup of tea or coffee.

Once he tilts me back in the chair and turns his back to mix the amalgam or whatever, I fall asleep, and he has to wake me to put in the filling.

Is this rare? I also fall asleep every time I donate blood. I'm snoring almost before the first drop hits the bottle, and invariably they have to shake me awake for the tea and biscuits.

Another place I'm given to a sudden somnolence is a city centre shoe shop. The minute I sit down, and ask for a size eight boot, I feel the weariness take over, and I'm drifting off while the assistant is rummaging.

And while I can nod off quicker than some, these incidents prove how vital these daytime naps are. Being an errant scribbler, and thereby fairly unemployable, I can indulge the luxury of grabbing a quick 15 minutes.

Not so, many wage-slaves. They are condemned to stay awake from nine to five.

Which party will seize the initiative and bring in a Choose to Snooze policy?

Instead of all the nonsense about banning hoodies, beheading asylum seekers, and stamping identity cards on our forehead, why not encourage factories, shops and offices to have snooze rooms?

A quick daytime nap has been proved to be medically beneficial, but most of us drag our weary way through the day. Large stores, supermarkets and shopping centres could also have snooze rooms where you can grab a quick 20 minutes, then bounce back, more active, less stressed. This would make a bigger difference to our national quality of life than every other policy combined.

There are caveats. You'd prefer a train driver not to choose his snooze period when his vehicle is hurtling at 125mph up the East Coast. A surgeon opting for a snooze mid-operation might be inadvisable.

But who amongst us, at some time during the day has not yet yearned to let the eyelids drop. And why not? If the Gross National Product suffers slightly, so what? In fact it may increase. A snooze produces a better person.

Britain could lead the world in making systems fit people rather than people fit systems. We wouldn't need to consume all that Red Bull and Pro-Plus to keep us awake.

Snooze time should be an automatic part of every employee's contract of employment. Put the country back on its feet. Allow it to fall to sleep.

Phone pests, the errant 'E's and vandalism writ large

9th June 2005

A WORD ABOUT those telephone messages which begin with a bright eyed prerecorded American voice saying "Congratulations" or "Hi! You are a winner in our prize draw!"

The almost irresistible temptation is to utter an expletive, slam the phone down and return to whatever activity the call interrupted.

Let me advise a different tactic. Place the phone gently on the table or desk, go off to peel the spuds, mow the lawn or fill in six crossword clues. Return several minutes later to replace the phone in its cradle, by which time a much bigger charge will have been incurred by the phone pests. If enough of us do this often enough, the activity may even shrivel and die.

Meantime I have formed the pressure group SPOMME and ask for your support. This all began after seeing a large poster on Cullercoats Metro Station featuring five haiku by the north east poet Subhadassi.

I'm a bit of a haiku man myself, but I was drawn not only to the wee poems, but the small print beneath which read 'Five haiku written for North Tynside.' Yes, that's right, North Tynside. I have never been to Tynside. Spoken aloud, the name conjured images of entire streets constructed of thin shiny metal buildings entered only via a tin opener.

I found myself wondering as to the fate of that missing 'e'. Where exactly had it gone? Was it cold, frightened and lost somewhere? The answer came the following day as my son Dylan and I ate lunch in the Queens Head. "Seen that, have you?" he asked.

The posh new menus bore the legend, 'The Queens Head, Cullercoates'. Yes, that's right, 'Cullercoates'. I had tracked down the missing 'e'!

This reminded me of two similar incidents not too long back. The Candy Man in Cullercoats had seaside rock in the window.

Seaside rock is the confectionery time forgot. It belongs in the 1950s with *Kiss me Quick* hats. This does not make me feel nostalgic towards it. It is revolting sticky stuff invented by dentists to increase their trade in replacement fillings. The taste is insufferable. This rock had written through it the words CULLERCOATES ROCK. That 'e' again.

In the other incident, Whitley Bay calendars were on sale, produced by one of the town's trader organisations.

Above each month's photo writ large were the words 'Whitly Bay.' Yes, that's right, 'Whitly Bay.' Was there a pattern here? And was it spreading? Only last week I was at Chester-le-Street for the test match, a sorry affair where the diminutive somewhat emaciated looking Bangladeshis were put to the sword by the strapping Englishmen.

By the side of the pitch was a sign which read 'This stand is monitered by CCTV'. It seems the errant 'e' has grown bolder, and has now begun shouldering out other letters, in this case an 'o'.

Perhaps I lead a sad life to be spotting such things and should have my mind on higher matters such as who's next in the *Love Shack*.

But I was moved to call the inaugural meeting of SPOMME – The Society for the Protection of the Misplaced or Missing Es (members attending – Mortimer, P).

If Cullercoats, Whitley Bay and North Tyneside have all thus far been blighted, who can say the rest of the borough is safe?

We could soon have the likes of Arsdon – which could prove a bummer of a village. The Madowell – an estate turned lunatic. And what about Howdone? This last one sounds like a question asked by the waiter when you order a fillet steak.

Custodians of orthography (good word eh? I just learnt it – it means proper spelling), step forward!

Finally this week, the protective metal fencing erected round the rubble that was once the Bay Hotel, Cullercoats, has been torn down. This is an act of vandalism and should be condemned.

A much larger, and farther reaching act of vandalism was the pulling down of the Bay Hotel itself. I'm left to wonder which set of vandals the legal authorities will be pursuing more.

Why me and Polly the dog failed to make Royal Ascot

23rd June 2005

APOLOGIES FOR this column's non-appearance last week. Regular readers (hi there, mum!) will know such absences are rare – only two in fact over more than two years, for my dedication in inflicting the Mortimer perspective on the North Tyneside public is total.

I was holed up in a hotel room in deepest Northumberland. Just me, my trusty Hermes typewriter and Polly the dog – tapping away all day long to meet the deadline on an overdue play. It was me tapping, you understand, not Polly the dog.

Polly belongs (can dogs belong?) to my partner Kitty, but is mine for a month during her absence. How would the pooch survive with a locked-away writer? Not bad at all.

And somehow the world went on without me. Ascot came to York. The word Ascot has always suggested to me less a posh race meeting, more an old-fashioned gas wall water heater that terrified you when it exploded into life. I accept for most people the associations are silly hats and shameless consumptive excess.

First let me confess a prejudice. Horse racing has always seemed less a sport, more an investment manoeuvre. Remove gambling from horse racing and the whole thing would simply collapse. This is not so for football, cricket, athletics or real sports enjoyed mainly for their own sake.

The entire northern media genuflected and were condescending in the face of this strange southern ritual. York has already virtually ruined itself as a city due to excessive tourism. Why on earth did it need any more visitors?

Plus which, as a million people prepare to protest against world poverty in Edinburgh, there's something a bit askew about the dozens of hospitality tents welcoming the freeloaders to the smoked salmon and £150 per bottle champagne.

I'd always wondered why corporate hospitality went (a) to those people already on the highest salaries and (b) to the likes of PR and marketing consultants who make no contribution whatsoever to the well-being of the nation.

I'd quite fancy a hospitality tent for street cleaners and hospital orderlies but realise this could be a long wait.

I put my thoughts to Polly who failed to reply. Every day people came to clean the room, and I sent them away as I made a pot of tea on the hour every hour.

And I would go out for long strolls in the unrivalled Northumberland countryside to gather my thoughts. Sometimes Polly would come. Other times she was too lazy. On these latter occasions I left the radio on for her.

Why was this? Dogs have existed for millions of years without the radio. Could I possibly believe that many aeons ago, as they trekked across the frozen tundra in search of food, dogs were contemplating how empty their lives were without a daily dose of *You and Yours*, or as they lay in their primitive lairs, they were yearning for the millennia to pass and allow them access to *Money Box Live?*

One theory is that dogs chose us as companions rather than the other way round, and this ensured their survival. But did they do so in the knowledge that we would inflict upon them years of tinned mush, that we would dress them up in tartan coats, and that for a certain number of them, every year would bring the ridiculous and degrading spectacle of Crufts?

Literature has various famous dogs.

My own favourite is not John Steinbeck's Charlie, nor even White Fang created by Jack London. It is Jumble, the great anarchic canine of that great anarchic anti-hero, Richmal Crompton's William Brown. Jumble resembles a second-hand wire brush, pads with muddy paws through the house, steals pies off window sills and would cause Crufts organisers to faint in disgust.

It rained for most of my stay in Northumberland. Perfect weather for writing. Not so for the other hotel guests, who coincidentally included my friends Dave and Carole Courtnadge and her son Joseph. They took in good spirit the fact that for 90 per cent of each day I ignored them.

It rained at Ascot too. Hats drooped. Most southern celebrities, who rarely venture farther north than Potters Bar, stayed away. Let us be thankful for small favours. The Queen arrived every day, which royalty rarely did for the Blaydon Races. I bet she never gave a thought to me and my play. I bet the fact I was struggling with the male lead never even entered her head. Nor any of those other freeloaders. Still, next year they'll all be safely back in Berkshire. Bye.

Why slices of Satan can turn three into a massive two million

30th June 2005

I HAVE TAKEN to picking up litter. Not mine, you understand. I am far too saintly to drop the stuff. This is the litter of other beings. Not all the time, of course. That would make me look like an eccentric gadgie. But where once I would look down at the discarded Coke can or pizza tray and tut-tut at people's laziness, now occasionally I bend down and pick it up.

This habit began with a curious experience, and has gained momentum the last month during my daily sea-front walks with Polly Dog, who is in my temporary keeping.

The English have a deep-rooted and malevolent desire to drop litter. This is mainly unknown to other races. The English cannot see a clean street or open space but must via some basic instinct despoil it with crisp packets, take-away containers and sweet wrappers. When the place is ankle-deep in the detritus, they can rest easy.

They often discard the litter within inches of a bin. By Cullercoats Metro they regularly toss their fizzy drink containers to bounce off one of the bright new recycling DRINKS CANS bins recently provided by the council.

These new bins are splendid, with the slight drawback that the slot for plastic is just millimetres smaller than the most popular milk container, bringing the regular sight of red-faced locals heaving and straining to effect penetration, if you get my drift.

Let me detail how my new habit began. Some months ago on the square of grass outside Cullercoats Metro station, I witnessed a strange sight. Someone had scattered an entire white sliced loaf. About 30 slices lay pale and soggy, and in no particular pattern. What an awful thing to do I thought, passed on and caught my Metro.

On return the slices were still there, presumably because several hundred other people had reacted identically to me. I went home but the white slices would not go away, as it were.

Finally I returned, gathered them all up and carried the white wobbling pile to the platform litter bin where passengers fixed me with a series of strange looks, as if a man carrying thirty slices of wet white bread was unusual.

And suddenly this small act made me feel better, as did returning to look at the new virginally clean patch of grass. As if I were not simply a passive moaning onlooker, but someone taking action.

This was not the end of it. The sliced white bread returned. Twice. And twice I gathered the slices up as if now I were locked in battle with some unseen adversary. And I would not be denied, each time fortified a little more.

What was behind it? Was this some strange demonic ritual where in the dead of night black cowled acolytes circled the grass, casting the bread and chanting in deep voices, "Slices of Satan! Slices of Satan!"

Was the bread excess to requirements and thrown out on an Easyjet budget flight to Prague (we're on the flight path)?

Whatever, getting rid of it became a matter of pride. You might even say Mother's Pride. And I'd caught the habit.

Now I don't want to get sanctimonious about this. Nor adopt some sort of superior stance. But here is my suggestion. If everyone in the borough were to pick up three items of litter per day – hardly an onerous task – this would amount to 300,000 or more than two million items every week. Imagine – two million fewer litter items on our streets and parks every week, and all for just a few seconds work from each of us! And I can guarantee this small act will leave you feeling better, more fulfilled.

It's called People Power. And it's all very low-key and gentle, and you don't have to storm any barricades, attend any meeting or wear a badge. So go on, pick up that crisp packet. Fight back. Feel better.

Why smoking tobacco could help us stop smoking tobacco…

7th July 2005

IN THE WEEK of Live 8, probably the best event in the history of the world, I spotted a man on Cullercoats cliff tops smoking a pipe. So what, I hear you say. Is that all you have to tell us? Why, you'll next be wasting valuable newsprint informing us a woman was seen leaving a newsagent in Whitley Bay! (*Question: So do you think he's losing it, that Mortimer? Gone off the boil? I mean, a man smoking a pipe....*)

No, no, stay with me. The man was staring out to sea, hands in pockets.

The pipe was clenched in his teeth, and occasionally his mouth would release a small puff of white smoke that elsewhere could see a new Pope elected. I hastily positioned myself downwind of him, the better to savour the aroma.

This small incident filled me with such a sense of well-being and contentment I have been thinking of little else since. I realised civilisation's descent into despair and insecurity probably dates from the decline of pipe smoking.

Most pipe smoking today comes via something called a bong, which is a different matter altogether. At one time everyone had a pipe-smoking uncle. Such species were both calm and magical. They could make coins disappear from their hands and then sneeze them out of their nose.

An uncle lighting a pipe is a never-forgotten memory; the flaked tobacco was packed into the pipe bowl, which had first been cleaned with a thin stainless steel instrument. A match (usually a Swan Vesta's) was then applied to the bowl, the flame sucked down deep into the dark brown flakes which soon became a small glowing furnace as the uncle (and with a bit of luck ourselves) became enveloped in great swirling clouds of smoke.

Life had few shocks so great as my later realisation that the taste of pipe smoke bore little relation to its smell.

This imbued the pipe smoker with even greater status. His (and there are occasional female pipe smokers, but always considered eccentric) was a truly altruistic act. He smoked. We enjoyed.

I remember once hearing a crackling recording of a small gem of a talk given on radio by the writer J B Priestley about smoking a pipe in the bath. Elsewhere the world was rushing pell-mell, getting itself into all sorts of scrapes and conflicts. Meantime Priestley lay back, allowed the pipe smoke and steam to mingle, and was the epitome of contentment.

Which brings me to my problem. Tobacco has become stigmatised. All over North Tyneside and elsewhere people stand shivering in the streets, banned from indulging the habit in their place of work. TV advertisements show the revolting goo which tobacco deposits in your arteries. Restaurants have given it the boot, and many pubs are following suit. We yearn for clean air.

But where does this leave the pipe-smoker? Who can see him as anything other than benevolent? Who ever imagines the pipe smoker goes into histrionics, is issued with an ASBO or is cruel to the goldfish?

While we all hate inhaling other people's cigarette smoke, we yearn to do the same from a pipe. Cigars are on the cusp – an interesting aroma but many cigar smokers just seem to be showing off.

I have only one friend, Paul Miller, who indulges a pipe. I see him rarely. The other pipe-smoking acquaintance lives in Austin, Texas, which means I'm a long way downwind.

But here's a possible solution. The government should subsidise a regular number of pipe smokers to be positioned at strategic locations. They will both calm us all down and allow us to indulge a bit of pleasant passive smoking which (according to my theory) could be sufficient to satisfy the craving of the nicotine junkies thus far unable to give up.

And while a coat stinking of tobacco smoke is rightly considered revolting, the faint aroma of pipe smoke lingering on a garment is far from unpleasant. Thus the enemy (tobacco) could become the ally, while consumption of cigarettes slowly falls to zero.

As for the health of the pipe smokers themselves – just remember, when smoking a pipe, you don't inhale. Strangely enough, you leave that to others.

Summer joy! Boarded – up seafront! The glory that was Whiskey Bends!

21st July 2005

MID-SUMMER and who is that bobbing like a cork off Tynemouth Long Sands? None other than your correspondent, drawn to the briny by the unbearable heat. As I ran down the Long Sands, were those gasps of admiration for my colourful Mario Brothers shorts? Could those cries of "Gosh!" be anything other than astonishment at the purity of this lily-white body?

It is achieved through dedication; years of avoiding tanning parlours and curbing the instinct to stretch semi-naked on towels once the clouds part.

Talking of naked, what to make of the strange affair on Newcastle Quayside at the weekend? Splendid stuff. It was once said kill one person and you were arrested. Kill 100 and you were a national war hero. Similarly it seems, walking unclothed across the Millennium Bridge. On your own, you're in trouble; 1,700 others, no problem.

As I bobbed in the gentle waves, I read a letter from a friend. 'Dear

Mortimer, On Monday, as our lawn slowly turned yellow, they slapped on a hose pipe ban. On Tuesday the river burst its bank and the whole garden is now under three feet of water. Which is the bigger threat, dying of thirst or drowning in our beds?'

I have no answer, except that according to latest predictions, global warming will soon see this country become the holiday capital of Europe. Spain, Greece, Portugal and the like are slowly rising to boiling point, and will soon be uninhabitable except by the likes of scorpions and cockroaches. Neither animal is a particular big spender in the leisure and holiday industry.

Thus we anticipate the invasion. But is Whitley Bay ready? What exactly does it have to offer? For one, it can boast a much larger range of boarded-up seafront properties than any other resort. You may be depressed by this. Don't be. We employ lateral thinking and turn what could be seen as a drawback into an advantage.

Why should our empty abandoned buildings not be marketed like the Acropolis in Athens, or the Colosseum in Rome? Let us celebrate Whitley Bay's great historical ruins.

The echo of a noble age at The High Point! The glory that was Whiskey Bends! The tangible sense of history as we stand and stare at the crumbling piles of The Avenue!

And surely trippers will want to traipse around in the rubble that was once The Bay Hotel Cullercoats in search of some old artefact buried in the dust – a Fosters beer mat maybe, a discarded roasted peanut?

Upstairs at The Dome, trippers could close their eyes and evoke the sounds of those bands that played at Fast Eddie's, in the wondrously decayed splendour of what once was the Spanish City.

The present council have got it wrong. Why bother drawing up endless development plans which never get anywhere? Why bother inviting the public to respond and then simply ignoring all responses?

It doesn't have to be like this! Forget the fatuous (and false) comments that 'we are moving forward'. Who expects the Acropolis to move forward? Or the Parthenon?

Holidaymakers have a strange instinct to stumble around in old stone, and increasingly we can tap into this market. Like Rome, Whitley has screwed up. Stagnated, crumbled, decayed. OK, let's make something of it!

And those holidaymakers who do want something modern can always go across the water to South Shields which, unlike Whitley Bay, took the decision not to rot away.

Let's put those highly paid marketing whizz-kids to work. 'Step back in time in Whitley Bay...', 'Relive a forgotten age...', that kind of thing.

How cheered I am by such thoughts as I bob on in the North Sea, and wonder if the holidaymakers are ready for another glimpse of these Mario Brothers shorts. And the North Sea is, I tell myself, for the first time in living memory, slightly warmer than numbing temperature. What is that bobbing next to me? Surely it couldn't be a scorpion?

The rise and fall of the snurgle; why Cumbria is a nocturnal option

4th August 2005

MY SUBJECT matter this week, dear readers, is the snurgle. Never heard of it? Of course not! I only invented the word two months ago.

In those two months the snurgle has come to dominate my life. It wakes me in the small hours to engage in feverish searches. The snurgle was supposed to be my salvation. It has become my downfall.

Here's a clue. The snurgle is to do with snoring. For sexual attraction snoring ranks just below cold porridge. No-one has ever seductively whispered into a shell-like ear: "I snore a lot."

But I'm afraid I do. And my snoring is stentorian (a word I've always wanted to use in this column – just a posh way of saying loud). Night-time ships approaching the River Tyne have been known to mistake my snores for the Miss Fenwick fog horn. Some have changed course and ended up in Madagascar.

I have no personal experience of my snoring's high decibel count, of course. One great mystery of snoring is that the snorer him or herself hears not a thing. I have never known why this is. You're pretty close to the noise after all. If someone dropped a tin tray on the floor, you'd hear that.

I don't hear my snoring but others do. On the nights I'm with my partner Kitty she is driven at times to wrapping her head in swathes of cotton wool, reciting aloud the Highway Code or in extreme cases leaving the bed to sleep somewhere out of earshot. Like Cumbria.

Her basic good nature is severely tested, but two months ago she handed me a small plastic container and said, "Try this."

Inside was a little object of flexible purple plastic rather like a tiny pair of crab claws. Its claim was that it stopped you snoring. The official name in the Snore-Eezy, but I quickly renamed it the snurgle to imitate the sound it was trying to prevent.

The 'claws' are gently hinged and rounded to prevent discomfort. You hang the snurgle from the inner bridge of your nose, like a dewdrop. Honestly.

It is said to open the windpipes in your hooter, ease breathing, and hence reduce the din.

And it becomes yet one more item that the modern human either adds or takes away when retiring to sleep. Some add slices of cucumber to their eyes, coat their faces in a white goo, or don an eye mask. More likely they take something away: this could be the toupee they hang on the end of the bed, the dentures plonked into a glass, the contact lenses floating in their small container, the wooden leg propped by the wardrobe, the glass eye in the ashtray.

Of mature years though I am, I have previously needed to indulge neither addition or subtraction at bedtime. I am the same person as in waking hours. Until now.

On the first night I attached the snurgle, it felt like some small timid creature hanging on to me. I eventually fell asleep, and woke at 4am to find the snurgle missing. Now the irony of it was the snurgle had done its job and Kitty had slept peacefully. Until it went missing that is, when I woke her with my desperate searching among the duvet.

And the pattern was established. No matter how hard I tried, every night I pulled the snurgle off, woke up, and engaged in an instinctive desperate search to locate it.

Nor did I ever find it till the next morning, and the missing snurgle left me tossing and turning in restless insecurity, further robbing Kitty of shuteye.

I have been forced to give up on the snurgle. Kitty has been moved to resort to another anti-snoring tactic which is, at the first stentorian rumble, to flip me over like a fish on a slab.

This delays, but does not prevent the habit. Some nights I am flipped over six or seven times, and wake up exhausted.

I have argued to myself that a missing snurgle is no big deal, but it doesn't help. Once it's off, I wake, and search feverishly (and always in vain).

Who knows? In a year or two I may mature enough to affix the snurgle once again. Kitty will need no more trips to Cumbria, and there will be no reports of ships ending up in Madagascar.

Until then, I am unsure what to do with it, where to store it. What exactly IS the best policy for a redundant snurgle?

NY: So good they named it once

11th August 2005

PEOPLE ARE hooting with glee at the news of daily flights between Newcastle and New York. I hear fewer hoots about a new book called *The Long Emergency* by James Howard Kunstler. So what, you may ask? The book predicts a much earlier end to the cheap fossil fuel era than expected, and with it also an end to our indulgent consumptive lifestyles.

Such is our dependency on such fuels, says the author, and they are disappearing at such an alarming rate (air travel being one of the main culprits) that it will all soon come crashing down. Whizzing by air to New York? We're more likely to be pushing a hand-cart to East Sleekburn in the future.

Don't get alarmed. You're probably overdue a visit to East Sleekburn, plus which, those famous global travel destinations are often a let-down.

I'm assured it's impossible to get a decent cup of tea and a rock bun at the Taj Mahal, and when I tried to hire a rowing boat to get a better view of Niagara Falls, they refused flat! A blooming disgrace.

Maybe time for a sea change in our holiday attitudes. I am doing my bit. A few years ago my partner Kitty and I booked into the Grand Hotel, Tynemouth, for a mini-break.

The desk clerk stared at my address in the book. "But you only live up the road!" he said. "Yes" I replied, "we just walked along."

People who think nothing of travelling thousands of miles to trudge round old ruins in temperatures hot enough to boil a cat find the prospect of holidaying at home bizarre.

But we're pretty lucky having North Tyneside anyway. And we all tend to walk round our own locale with eyes shut. Holidaying here opens them.

Here's my suggestion. Instead of hanging round in a congested airport, only to be delayed 24 hours by the traffic controllers, eventually making the plane to be sat next to a 22 stone halitosis sufferer insistent on talking throughout the flight about their cheese label collection, try the following:

A holiday that begins with a gentle bike ride between fields of corn (or is it wheat?) on whose paths beautiful horses are exercising, then a quiet lazy mile along a sleepy rural road.

Sounds nice? No fossil fuels consumed in the bike ride, which will deposit you (via Murton and the riding stables) not in New York, USA, but New York, North Tyneside. Admit it, how long since you've been?

And the first thing you see on your local journey of discovery is The Wheatsheaf pub, where a Thursday quiz night will set you back only a quid (see how little you get for a quid in the Big Apple!) there's a ban on bad language (obligatory on 32nd Street), and you get two meals for six quid.

New York USA might boast some exclusive clubs, but none as exclusive as New York & Murton Social Club, where even President Bush wouldn't get past the doorman without membership (not that they'd want him anyway).

They say New York's the city that never sleeps. OK, try this. Our own New York Co-op opens at 7am, after which the village stays open till midnight (closing time of the pizza kebab and burger bar). Seventeen hours ain't bad.

OK, you're still yearning for the Big Apple. This will help. The burger bar's called The Bronx, opposite is New York Pharmacy (as against the English chemist) and there's a Brookland Terrace, which said quickly sounds very much like Brooklyn.

But why bother? Enjoy New York, North Tyneside, for what it is.

There's a graffiti-free bus shelter, and on the edge of the village is a quaint piece of old England never seen in Times Square, which Americans would drool over. The New York Forge, Farrier and Blacksmith.

So hang fire before you go whizzing off in that jet.

And remember, visiting New York as against New York means you're doing your own little bit to delay the scenario of doom as forecast by James Howard Kunstler, and that hand-cart journey to East Sleekburn.

Though looking at the flabby jellies that same indulgent life-style is turning many of our citizens into, pushing a hand-cart to East Sleekburn might not be a bad calorie-burning idea.

A football too soon, and putting the colour back in Cullercoats

18th August 2005

MID-AUGUST and here comes football gate-crashing our dreamy summer of marvellous cricket. Hey – clear off! You gobble up most of the year as it is!

I was enjoying those fancy dress crowds: the Flintstones, the swathes of nuns, the gangs of convicts. I was wondering why cricket crowds managed to drink beer all day without ripping up seats and attacking opposition fans. Why the players often smiled and chatted to one another.

But then suddenly there it was; the premature return of the scowling footballers, the sourness of Souness, and for the first time in the Premiership, some Newcastle United FC season tickets going begging.

Has the cow been overmilked? Does spending £400 on a new washing machine suddenly seem more sensible than investing in another season of grey dross?

Should Freddie Shepherd learn something from Freddie Flintstone?

Channel 4 cricket coverage – wonderful! Billy Bowden the umpire – beautifully bonkers! Only one drawback; the cost of keeping Sky at bay means an incessant barrage of advertisements, mainly for cars, mainly showing glamorous people speeding along empty roads in exotic climes when we know the reality is a fume-choked grid-locked frustration, a nose-to-tail, artery thickening horn-hooting daily nightmare while, for various reasons, the air turns blue.

The ultimate irony is that *The Age of Aquarius,* that song from *Hair* which symbolised the 60s counter-culture, and promised our free-thinking generation a heady alternative to greed and materialism, is now used to flog Ford cars, and thus the capitalist system embraces what once would bring it down.

But look! Here in Cullercoats a bay window proudly displays a pair of trousered dummy legs, upside down. How splendid they look! They cheer me up!

While in Eleanor Street, and on Burnside Terrace I notice several people have painted their brickwork in bright colours. This cheers me up too. As does my newly repainted front door, which thanks to artist Faye Oliver now contains a dozen large-eyed, dreamy female faces staring out at passers-by and commuters. Up the street another artist's house has become an entire statement in purple.

But most remarkable in Cullercoats is the quiet artistic revolution that has taken place over the last year in Norma Crescent out there on the cliff tops.

This is down to some Gallic flair, namely the French fisherman and artist Bernard Harscoet who has lived in the village more than eight years, but recently decided to adorn his house front with a large puffin painted in relief on plywood.

It looked so good neighbours tentatively asked whether he'd mind doing one for them. Of course. So Bernard did. Then another asked. And another. Norma Crescent now has puffins, salmons, cormorants, dolphins, albatrosses, a sea horse, and a pheasant thrown in for good measure. And how much, in this money-grabbing price-for-everything age, does Bernard charge for his talents? Nothing.

So that to walk up and down this unique crescent, and see the splendid al fresco art, makes you feel good on two counts.

Bernard's behaviour and economics would make no sense to £100,000 a week Rio Ferdinand (even less to his agent), but it makes sense to me. And to Bernard. And to Norma Crescent.

Is this Cullercoats fighting back? The village still boasts too many boarded-up properties in Station Road. It cannot easily recover its village heart being ripped out with the scandalous demolition of The Bay Hotel.

(Incidentally this weed-choked site is slowly becoming a wild jungle. Any day now I expect a veteran Japanese soldier to emerge blinking, unaware World War II has finished.)

But this was the village once known as Little Bohemia because of its artists' colony. The past has gone, and no point blubbing about it. But maybe something remains.

And meantime I glean some small hope from the upside-down trousers, the al fresco cormorant, and wonder will they ever be witnessed or appreciated by the troubled looking Mr Souness?

After the violent deluge, the age of the firewall and the Norton...

8th September 2005

I RETURN from a short break, and what happens? The computer goes wonky and the e-mails pack in for several days – all in the immediate wake of violent storms.

Is this apocryphal? Is nature simply tiring of this troublesome mammal species spoiling its planet?

I am informed it is computer error Ref 328/d/961. How comforting. The lack of e-mails, I realise with alarm, means four days without special offers on Viagra, exclusive financial deals from Nigeria, or heavily discounted Rolex watches. Somehow a man must survive.

For the first time in my life I rise early to ring the broadband helpline. Three recorded messages later an actual human being comes on the line.

"It's the e-mail," I tell him, "It's not working."

"Have you checked your TCP/IP settings?" he asks. I muse on this for several seconds while staring from the window at the scudding clouds.

"A good question," I say, "I'm very glad you asked that question." I know this is what politicians do when they want to stall or have no idea of the answer.

"What's your DHCP Client ID?" he asks further.

"Hang on a mo," I answer. I go into the kitchen to make a bacon sandwich drowned in ketchup. This usually helps at such difficult moments. Still the answer does not present itself. But my man does not give up easily.

"Is your RAM disc turned on?" he asks. I have little idea what a RAM disc is, nor what sexually excites it.

"I'm sure it is," I lie.

"OK, what router address are you using?" It is at this moment I realise the paintwork in this room needs a bit of attention and a spider has built a web in one corner.

I wonder about the individual at the other end, and the life he lives. I wonder if he suffers from spots, has had his heart broken recently or is allergic to cabbage.

"Do you have a firewall?" he asks. Now I do have an open range in the kitchen and it does have a wall behind it which prevents a conflagration on the next door neighbours' premises, so the answer to this one is obvious.

"Yes I do," I reply, mustering confidence.

"Is it Norton?" he asks, Ah – Norton! How long is it since I sat on the back of a Norton Commando and roared through the streets of my native Nottingham. 1967? That distinct misfiring sound hinted it was aware its like was soon to be obliterated by the Japanese.

"If only it were," I reply. "I hear they're collectors' items now."

"It looks like we'll have to reboot," he says.

I have never considered this, never for a moment thought these brand new, sky blue Doc Martens might have an adverse effect on the computer.

"Give me one moment!" I say, and hastily change into a pair of black suede boots with nifty purple laces.

"Done it!"

"What model did you say your computer was?"

This information is right there in front of me on screen.

"A MAC 8.6."

"Did you say a MAC 8.6?"

"Yes I did."

A pause. Then his voice, now directed elsewhere shouts, "There's a geezer here still with a MAC 8.6!"

I could swear I heard in the background a room full of disdainful laughter. My imagination conjured a whole host of computer geeks staring at one another in disbelief.

And suddenly a flicker of activity from the screen

"Hang on," I say, "I think the email's working again."

It was too, I didn't know how. Nor him, I suspect.

I guess it must have been the black suede boots.

And they were back – the special offers on Viagra, exclusive financial deals from Nigeria or heavily discounted Rolex watches. Civilisation had returned to the Mortimer household. Or at least until nature, as is its current global tendency, decides otherwise.

A tale of fish and ping-pong; every golf course is safe in free market

29th September 2005

HURRAH! THE hands on the clock in Whitley Bay centre, highlighted as missing in this column, have been replaced, and we can all now age gracefully.

Meantime, I'm flagged down while on my bike in North Shields by ex-fisherman Ollie Allcock whose photograph appears on the front of my book *The Last of the Hunters* (unavailable from all good book shops now).

"Did you know they're threatening to sell the Mission?" he asks. He refers to the Fish Quay-based Fishermen's Mission which for many years has been a warm haven for mariners who've narrowly escaped octopus tentacles or other perils on the sea, and which also serves canny fish and chips.

Seamen no longer are put up at the Mission (known to the cognoscenti as 'the fishmish') but it still seems an integral part of Fish Quay life and in 2003 we used it to launch the Tom Hadaway Festival, celebrating the life and work of the region's finest playwright, and a man who knew a thing or two about codling.

The news comes close on the heels of the announcement that Whitley Bay YMCA is to be sold. This is the shyest building at the coast. It crouches down so as to be barely visible at the Marden Road/Hillheads Road roundabout, and if you want to surprise it and cause it huge embarrassment, creep up behind it on Grosvenor Drive, and shout "boo!"

It was at this building I introduced my young son Dylan to the virtues of the Japanese pen-holder grip in table tennis. Within the hour he was beating me hollow.

With global warming increasing and water levels rising, I've been fearful for the YMCA for some time and the risk that future table tennis may be sub-aquatic. Now it appears the building won't be there at all.

Both the fishmish and the YMCA have slight airs of dilapidation which I quite like. Both it seems are doomed. Replacements, we are told, will be found, but no details.

Developers will make a fortune from the fishmish. It has uninterrupted views across the Tyne. Uninterrupted of course, unless the phone rings. The YMCA could be bought by some recluse millionaire wanting to enjoy his opulence in isolation and misery. One thing is certain. Neither building will end up as a new library or theatre.

The fact that North Tyneside lacks a single decent modern theatre while luxury flats spring up on every corner is the kind of scandal the tabloids ignore. Please, can we have our own Customs House?

But then economic forces are at work, and we are told the free market rules. This means school playing fields get gobbled up to become supermarkets. Yet somehow golf courses never seem under threat. Readers are invited to send reasons in not more than 300 words.

There are a few stubborn areas still resistant to free market forces, but such resistance can only be temporary. It's hard to justify whole acres being given over to a building where people just lie around in bed all day, contribute nothing to the economy but make huge demands on skilled people and expensive equipment. But at least North Tyneside Hospital has installed a profit-making Burger King (just the stuff to make 'em healthy).

But what about police stations? It's a sneak thief to a corporate swindler that not a single copshop turns a healthy profit, and the same could be said of schools. Show me any school in the borough and I'll show you a site where Netto or Safeway could produce a much healthier rate of return than a load of snotty-nosed kids sitting round behind desks.

Now that private enterprise is being introduced into every aspect of modern life, the vigorous breezes of competition will simply blow away anything that doesn't live up to economic expectations.

The fishmish and the YMCA may struggle along for a while in some form. Maybe a lock-up garage in a back lane? Or, like new post offices, shoved away in the corner of Asda.

Either way, it's bad news for the up-and-coming generation of ping-pong players. And the end of some fine fish and chips.

Poetry in motion – is it just going from bard to worse?

6th October 2005

TODAY (THURSDAY) is National Poetry Day, a day on which we poor versifiers (for I do confess myself among this odd clan), fantasise that the entire nation vibrates with iambic pentameter.

This may not quite be the case. Were I to walk out in the streets of Cullercoats this morning with the photographs of the nation's finest poets, it's unlikely they would be recognised by one person in a hundred. About the same ratio may be able to quote me a line of modern poetry, even though eighty two per cent would recognise the line up for the previous edition of *The X Factor*.

All the people who are involved in modern poetry could probably (I often tell myself) gather together in a medium-sized room. And then I realise they often do!

People sometimes write to me as an editor saying they wish to pursue a career in poetry. A career in poetry! They may as well seek a career sailing pooh sticks under a bridge, whistling on the top of hills, or biting someone else's toe nails.

"There is no money in poetry," I tell them, to which someone once smartly responded "and there is no poetry in money".

Thus poor poets wrestle with spondees and caesuras (see what I mean? Already you've lost interest), and are ignored.

I once had a launch for a book of poetry to which no-one turned up. Yes, that's right, no-one. Not family, not friends, not the budgie, no casual passersby. I caught the train home with all the unsold books, wondering if poison, slit wrists or a leap off the Tyne Bridge were the preferred option.

Maybe poetry takes itself too seriously. Maybe people don't like it when it doesn't rhyme (which most modern poetry doesn't). Here's a recent Mortimer limerick which has fun with a north east place name.

There was a strict teacher from Ulgham
Who'd box pupils' ears and then cuff 'em
People thought it quite queer
He should act so severe
to which he replied simply, "stuff 'em".

Many 'real' poets look down on the limerick as a somewhat vulgar form and maybe that is part of the problem.

Intellectually this is no great shakes, but it was fun to write, and who knows, one day it may appear somewhere on the streets of that Northumberland village?

Most poetry exists in almost total secrecy. It either languishes in drawers, or if published, is among the pages of an obscure magazine seen by a handful of people, most of whom are desperate to be published themselves. Go to a poetry reading and most of the audience will write poetry whereas hardly anyone in a cinema audience makes films.

Poetry's a marginalised art form, so let's bring it out into public view. I am doing my bit. My *Sausages* poem is in the window of Darling's Butchers in Cullercoats, I have poems carved onto stones on Holy Island, and locals will have been aware of my illuminated roof poem 'Keep both feet/firmly/in the clouds' which blazed away in the night sky for ten years till corrosion meant it threatened to decapitate some unsuspecting passer-by, and I had to have it removed.

I also dream of taking haiku into doctors' waiting rooms. In Whitley Bay Health Centre, the electronic message drearily repeats the same few words about medical procedure whereas it could be offering patients a whole selection of those small gem-like three line poems, and who knows, such poetic exposure could prove better treatment than all those endless drug company pills.

A small anecdote to end: I was once pleasantly surprised to be asked to judge the poetry competition at Lanchester Agricultural Show.

I was even more pleasantly surprised (when I turned up and announced myself) to be made a big fuss of, given a judge's rosette, a cup of tea and cake, and eventually shown into a large tent. Here I was left alone with hundreds of hens and chickens. Some time later an official appeared and asked, "Have you decided yet?"

They'd thought I'd said I was judging the poultry.

Goodbye to curved windows; why we all suffer embarrassment

20th October 2005

INTRODUCING GREAT Slim Volumes of the World, No.43 – *The Architectural Splendours of Whitley Bay*. We don't have many, you see. There's the Spanish City Dome, increasingly sad and isolated, and there's the beautiful curved windows of the distinctive 1926 Belvedere Building at the town's central traffic lights (Nectar Restaurant that was).

Ah – that curved glass! Like a gentle wave in Cullercoats Bay, like the soft shape of a female hip.

Except it's gone. My friend Jim Jeffrey alerted me to its demise: ripped out and dumped into a skip to be replaced by a flat uPVC monstrosity. Truly the barbarians are among us.

Which has nothing to do with spelling and the North Shields Fish Quay shipping grocers of Wm. Wight Ltd. This truly unique emporium, where you are often greeted with a parrot's wolf whistle (?), sells products ranging from wishing wells to black pudding.

You are invited to sit in the lucky Cook's Chair (and donate to charity) for enhanced chances of a lottery win or pregnancy. There's a liar's bell, and there's also the best comic interchanges on Tyneside once you enter this wondrous shop's portals. Bacon and banter.

At noon this Saturday you'll find the French onion man Olivier demonstrating how to string the weepy vegetables together.

Wights will also make you a poker work wooden sign of your own choice. Examples hang above the counter. This proves that the shop's Achilles Heel is spelling. Among the word casualties are 'peaple' and 'happyness.'

Does this matter or are there more important things to think about? Keeping the fish connection, I'm reminded of George Bernard Shaw's idea for a new Initial Teaching Alphabet (ITA) which would simplify the whole illogicalities of English spelling. Shaw demonstrated how the word 'fish' in English could quite easily be spelt 'ghot' (work it out for yourself). His alphabet never caught on.

Spelling drives some people mad, but I'm good at it. I sat down to the latest Star Spell TV quiz show, and had great fun. Quiz shows were once the home of normal people. Now normal people are so busy making reality television, the quiz shows are taken over by celebrities.

I got all the words right, and spelt them quicker than the celebs. I suppose I might have been insufferable (with two 'f's) had anyone been watching with me, but I lead a sad life and was viewing alone.

How splendid to have no difficulties with stationery as against stationary, to walk fearlessly through the minefield of embarrassment, accommodation, adjoin, desperate and separate. Only two words give me regular grief, phenomenon (just looked it up) and prerogative, where I refuse to accept the first 'r'. Such refusal once cost me a ten quid bet in the Queen's Head, Cullercoats.

For 90 years my mother has spelt (and pronounced) rhododendron without the second syllable, and I don't have the heart to stop her now.

Doom-mongers warn of an increasingly illiterate nation, so it's good to see a mainstream TV quiz show making spelling both fun and in vogue.

Often we now leave spelling to computer spell checks. These are American and therefore wont to get things wrong. Just try the likes of 'colour' or 'centre'. The spell check will alter (or is that 'altre'?) them.

Among the celebs, John Parrott showed a special forte (the 'e' is pronounced here by the way, unlike in words such as 'lake' or 'hope') and the late GBS may somewhere be taking heart from this revival in matters spelling. Why not include spelling questions in pub quizzes (that's two 'z's by the way)?

I have only one spelling test for the barbarians who removed the Belvedere window. Think carefully, then spell 'irreplaceable architectural gem.'

Why am I less than totally confident they'll get it right?

The joys of Hallowe'en and praying for the puzzled birds

3rd November 2005

IT WAS Hallowe'en, and in the best traditional spirit I had locked myself in the cupboard under the stairs as the thunderous knocks came to the door.

Someone lifted the flap of the letter box and I heard a gruff voice: "Trick or treat you b****** – we know you're in there!"

To calm myself I tried to think of other matters. But what was that sound?

Was it a ladder being propped against the outside wall? Was a 14 stone hulk in a Jason mask (or is that Friday 13th?) even now scaling up to the bedroom window?

I let my mind drift to the strange habit of putting the hour back (or was it forward?). Each autumn we did it one way, then in the spring the other. Rather like the Grand Old Duke of York. What was it all for? And what was the 'real' time?

I listened hard. They must have scaled the wall in the back lane, because now they were hammering on the rear door.

"Open this ********* door, you *********! It's trick or ********* treat time!"

What a curious celebration Hallowe'en was. The whole affair was loathed and feared by 98 per cent of the population, allowing a small minority to roam the neighbourhood operating a one-night protection racket. The word 'treat' seemed a slight misnomer.

I couldn't understand why we didn't just give the whole sorry affair the boot. Then I read it was worth £120m to the retail trade, and I remembered we were living in a market economy.

Against that figure, what were a few fatal heart attacks of terrified pensioners, or a state of siege endured by the rest of us?

Plus which I remembered that 'celebrating' Hallowe'en was an American import, stimulated by a series of dreadful films bearing the same name.

And I knew we were now all duty-bound to ape everything American, be it a tatty festival, gobbling down artery thickening junk food, or invading poverty-stricken defenceless countries for no reason.

A new noise was now apparent. It was the sound of raw eggs running down a window pane. I needed to cheer myself up, so thought again about the hour going off (on?) and whether it might just confuse, and divert those millions of birds coming to give us their own flu. A small joke follows: "Extra! Extra! Avian flu strikes down entire North Tyneside Council during full meeting at the town hall! Thanksgiving service to be announced soon!"

Hang on though – how come we can suddenly catch flu off birds? For millions of years we've been immune to the migraine of cats, constipated tortoises, or the rheumatism of goldfish. If anybody told you you might catch a cold from a frog, you'd just laugh.

But here we are facing bird flu. It must have been we humans messing on with nature again. How come nobody's told us?

"We'll be back, you *********!" yelled the gruff one, and a few moments later there was silence. Dare I venture out? I did, if only because I knew if I caught that raw egg early enough, it might make a decent omelette. Like I always say, it's an ill wind.......

A quick glance through the curtains revealed gangs of slouching youths going from door to door, and gobbing.

Ah well. My first visitors seemed to have given up.

Now I knew all I had to fear were a few more days of fireworks through the letter box, then a November 5 that would turn all pets to quivering jelly, and allow local yoofs to indulge the relatively new pastime of pelting fire crews with half bricks.

And before we knew where we were, it would be Christmas, and we could all be drunk or broke, or both. Happy days!

Bring on Auto Chill. We have all kneeled at air pumps for too long

17th November 2005

ILLNESS PRODUCES strange behaviour. Stricken by a bug all week, coughing and spluttering like an old British motor bike engine, I rise at 5am to shiver a feverish way through this article's final draft. Ah – dedication! It is what made Cullercoats what it is today!

A new-style car-wash at Brierdene, Whitley Bay sets me thinking. This retro development employs live people to wash your vehicle as against those monstrous circular rollers that snap off car aerials and leave large patches of muck untouched.

Real people? They'll be getting them to answer company phones next, and we may be rid of the most detested short phrase in the language – 'user options'.

Could these new car washes be the start of a garage revolution? Now I am an unlikely champion of the motorist, a species requiring culling if the planet is to be saved. But in this instance, and in their treatment at the hands of garages, or filling stations, I offer them my support.

The scene is a wet and windy night. You drive into the filling station and wriggle out of your warm vehicle. The garage's token roof does nothing to prevent wind and rain whipping in at 45 degrees as you wrestle with the clunky fuel nozzle.

This either clicks off every few seconds, or fills the tank so fast as to spill fuel all over your shoes. No matter how long you wait before removing the nozzle, it dribbles a few drops onto the floor. Say 5p worth. That's more than £125m extra income for those caring sharing oil companies. And you wondered why it dribbled?

Your car needs water. You hunt the forecourt for a can. You need to check the oil. Likewise you hunt for paper towels. Just occasionally such searches may be successful.

In the garage's mini-mart you queue behind 12 people all buying newspapers and Milk Tray. "What number?" asks the assistant. You've no idea. Walking out, you realise you've forgotten the tyres. You queue again, because in garages, that wonderfully free commodity air needs a 30p token.

The air pump is out in the open, and the rain's really set in. Is there a ramp to raise the car to eye-level? No. In the wet and the wind, and no matter you've got arthritis, you need to kneel on the soaking ground, remove the dust caps and secure the air pump to the valves. The pump's a hissing angry snake that resists such coupling, and has soon dropped your pressure to 2 pounds psi. It is on a rubber pipe yanked from its roll only with a Herculean effort, and constantly striving to retract.

By this time you are exhausted, stiff and wet through. The whole experience has cost you probably £30, thus ensuring the oil company shareholders stay happy.

Mortimer's alternative to this nightmare is called *Auto Chill*. You drive your car into a warm enclosed building, fill in a quick form and hand the keys to a polite assistant. The form details your requirements, fuel, oil, water, car wash, valeting. You are shown into a comfortable lounge. Free tea and coffee are available, magazines, newspapers, a choice of CDs.

More advanced centres may even offer the likes of a shave, or reflexology, or a spot of yoga.

You chill out while your vehicle is being attended to, and drive away a contented motorist less given to road rage. While sitting in the lounge you may well chat to other motorists, and laugh at the primitive conditions your kind were forced to endure for so long. You wonder why you all took it so meekly, and conclude that oil companies didn't really give a damn about the welfare of individual customers, though they made a fuss of Arab sheiks.

I offer the *Auto Chill* concept free of charge to any enterprising reader. As a push-bike owner, it will benefit me little, and I'm a mite reluctant to suggest anything that encourages more motorists.

But basically I'm all heart. Even if this week, it feels like I've coughed that heart up onto the carpet several times over.

Cullercoats Charlie, Henrietta Hudleston and Saline Sid ...

8th December 2005

OFF TO THE Saville Exchange, North Shields, to hear a lunchtime recital by the Russian pianist Evgeny Samoilov. In 70 minutes the man speaks three words. One is Tchaikovsky, the second is scherzo, and the third I forget. Three is easily enough!

The man's charisma and fascination come from letting his music speak for him, so much so I have an almost irresistible desire not to hear him on chat shows or have him open up his home for the cameras of *Hello!* Magazine, or indulge in any other demeaning trivia.

Meantime Cullercoats applauds yet another celebrated inhabitant with the news this week that Lucy Ratcliffe has been voted Britain's Next Top Model. The news sent me scurrying off to the history book to unearth just a few of the famous characters who give the village its unique sense. In case you've forgotten, here they are:

Cullercoats Charlie – Charlie was a strong swimmer, escapologist and pastry cook best remembered these days for his heroic rescue of seemingly doomed sailors stranded on the dreaded Black Midden rocks as the tide rose.

Charlie swam out (against a strong current) arranged the 22 sailors pyramid-fashion on his shoulders and swam back, loudly singing *The Water of Tyne* to keep up morale. It was this deed that led to the founding of police motor cyclists formation riding displays at agricultural fairs. Charlie's mutton and thistle pies alas have passed into obscurity.

Winslow Homer – Most people know the famous American painter who lived in Cullercoats for two years. Less known is the fact he was 8ft 6ins tall and would paint with one hand while doing press-ups with the other. Homer's most famous painting is *At The Bar* which shows 23 locals supping pints in the Bay Hotel. For those of short memory the Bay Hotel was until recently the centre of the village till developers decided that a better option was to destroy the building and leave a large and ugly bomb crater in its place.

Henrietta Hudleston – Henrietta's tragic tale has touched generations. She was knitting a new gansey for her fisherman husband and he went to sea and failed to return. For the next 46 years Henrietta lived in the Cullercoats caves, never emerging once, not even for Harbour Day. During daylight hours she would knit the jumper, and unpick it at night swearing never to do the final stitch till he returned. The story was turned into a Hollywood blockbuster with Jennifer Lopez as Henrietta and Tom Cruise as the gansey.

Saline Sid from Simpson Street – Not everyone knows that Cullercoats' original industry was not fish, but salt. This industry's growth was mainly down to Saline Sid who, whatever the weather, would set out from harbour in his small coble carrying only a cheese and pickle sandwich and a bottle of gripe water.

Villagers would gather to wave him off, just as they would congregate to scan the horizon for his eventual return, though Sid would never sail back to shore till he had harpooned and strapped to his boat side a block of salt no smaller than 10ft by 8ft. People would come from far and wide to buy chipped off pieces, and it was this ready supply of salt that led William Routledge to open Bill's Fish Bar.

Delia 'The Dove' – For many years Delia excited the people of Cullercoats and visitors by her amazing tight-rope act. She would walk backwards and on one leg across a wire stretched between the two harbour piers while cooking a large duck egg in a frying pan. Her career was tragically cut short soon after the introduction of bouncing power boats. One such boat bounced so high it severed the wire, and plunged her into the water where she became trapped under the egg and perished, despite desperate attempts to rescue her.

Space hardly allows me to mention Rocket Rizla who tried to launch St George's steeple as a moon shot nor Wild Bill Hiccup who unwisely introduced 12 man-eating tigers to Beaconsfield.

Suffice to say that Lucy Ratcliffe joins a long line of celebrated Cullercoats citizens. And you know, not one of them ever appeared on Parkinson.

I see the future and it's inflatable inspectors and endless opencast

22nd December 2005

THE YEAR 2005 limps to its conclusion, and you ask what the future may hold for North Tyneside. How fortunate that your correspondent knows all.

January – The 286th proposal for the development of Whitley Bay seafront is announced, and the public are invited to view display boards in the library and offer their comments.

February – A mix-up over bookings means that the Farmers Market and the Wild West show take place the same weekend in Whitley Bay centre. Several smelly cheeses are shot dead, and a French peasant farmer breaks his neck trying to fillet the bucking bronco.

March – Increasing violence on the Metro sees Nexus adopt a new tactic. Inflatable inspectors are placed on every train. They are programmed to wag a finger and say, "I wouldn't do that if I were you" at the first sign of trouble. After three days they have all been nicked or punctured, and five trains go missing too.

April – A 30ft prehistoric dinosaur is found in the overgrown bomb site that was once The Bay Hotel, Cullercoats. Luckily it is vegetarian, and a developer comments: "This is an exciting discovery and an extra attraction for our bold new project." Work on the luxury flats is expected to start in time for the 2012 London Olympics.

May – The controversy over the one-time open air pool at Tynemouth is finally settled with the dumping of 300 tons of nuclear waste. A council spokesman says: "This was too good a financial deal to turn down." Local residents are advised to wear protective clothing at all times.

June – The 287th proposal for the development of Whitley Bay seafront is announced. It includes such pioneering landmarks as a tree, and the developers say they're confident the new flats will be spacious and airy, and pets will be encouraged (goldfish only).

July – Opencast mining company submit plans for an ambitious new development stretching from Tynemouth to Burradon. It would mean the demolition of 23,000 houses, 28 roads, 42 schools, 36 pubs and ten old people's homes, plus pollution of the air. A company spokesman comments: "This will mean the creation of 30 new jobs and anyway in 28 years we shall return the landscape to its previous state. And we can categorically state that in no circumstances shall we be working the site more than 24 hours a day."

August – A sizzling August results in a huge upsurge of visitors to the coast, and no fewer than four tourists are spotted in Whitley Bay. After wandering up and down the ruins of the seafront for two days, they cancel the rest of the week and go off to Bognor.

September – 24 hour drinking is made compulsory in Tynemouth Front Street. A spokesman for the brewers comments: "These new liberalised laws have to be given a real chance and we think this is the way forward. With compulsory 24 hour drinking there is no need to rush your pint, or keep an eye on the clock. We expect no trouble as most people will be totally insensible by the time the 24 hours is up."

October – A cod is landed at North Shields Fish Quay. A brass band plays and the fish is blessed by the Fishermen's Mission just before the Mission closes to become a call centre. The authorities are confident of another cod before the year's end.

November – A well known North Tyneside councillor collapses from exhaustion after writing a 38,000 word letter to the *News Guardian*.

December – Proposal number 289 for Whitley Bay seafront is rushed through council. There will be 8,000 luxury flats for rich southerners. The Spanish City dome is sold to a developer to be rebuilt in the Arizona desert. To cater for the town's cultural needs, a busker will play for ten minutes every Saturday outside the ruins of The Avenue.

How will you respond to the delights of my seasonal quiz?

29th December 2005

BY NOW, LIKE everyone else, you're climbing the wall, and wondering just when the whole tedious affair ends. Hosanna! With this in mind, I have set you a seasonal personality quiz – several likely situations and how you might respond. Check your scores at the end to reveal your true inner self. Or something.

1. Putting out the wheelie bin, you notice every family member has thrown away your present, including the false Gazza-style chest you bought for Uncle Eric. Do you (a) make a note to buy him a whoopy cushion next year, (b) wear the chest yourself or (c) pour whisky into the family trifle?

2. By now you are virtually broke. The door bell brings a charity worker collecting for distressed reality TV contestants. Do you (a) hand over your last coins in a splendid sacrificial act, (b) nick his tin, or (c) donate the false chest?

3. You discover Uncle Nakka under the dining room table four days after he was due to return to his Northampton old people's home. Do you (a) adjust his paper hat, (b) revive him with stale turkey or (c) hoover round him?

4. At 3pm on Christmas Day every television set in the street blows up. How do you prevent mass suicide? Do you (a) suggest an impromptu session of arm-wrestling, (b) amuse everyone with your farmyard impressions or (c) decamp en masse to the display window at Dixons?

5. You spill brandy sauce down the ample cleavage of a little-known Christmas guest. Do you (a) set to immediately with a man-size Andrex tissue, (b) ignite it with a match or (c) talk in a very loud voice about the failure of Andrew Flintoff on the Pakistan tour?

6. The woolly striped jumper knitted for you by Aunt Clarissa is 12 sizes too big and has three arms. Do you (a) wear it down the pub with a poloni sausage in the third arm, (b) feed her eight large gins then burn it, (c) feign an attack of St Vitus Dance, preventing you leaving your bedroom till Easter?

7. A homeless down-and-out with BO and halitosis comes calling Christmas Day for food and shelter. Do you, (a) lecture him on the merits of self-sufficiency and the self-righting mechanisms of the market economy, (b) get him to carve the turkey, (c) send him away with Aunt Clarissa's jumper?

8. The new neighbour you invited for Christmas lunch arrives with a pair of knickers on his head but no explanation. Do you (a) ignore the fact throughout the meal, (b) casually enquire if he'd like to hang his knickers anywhere, (c) inadvertently spill white sauce on his head, requiring some action?

9. You inexplicably wake up at 9am on Boxing Day morning in the queue for the MFI sale, wearing only a paper hat. Do you (a) sing a medley of Robbie Williams songs, (b) hide in a white wardrobe, (c) go in search of the best discounts on leather settees?

10. The book on Celebrity Gussets given you by cousin Bill is, you suspect, the very same copy you gave him for Christmas 2004. Do you (a) challenge him during the mince pies (b) post it through the Oxfam letterbox or (c)

Tippex out the greeting in preparation for Christmas 2006?
So how did you score? A scores 5, B scores 7 and C scores 6.
50-59 – Get out more.
60-65 – No hope.
66-70 – Spend less time on idiotic quizzes and take up a hobby.
Happy New Year!

Lilac walls or beige? Importance of basic choice in the new NHS

12th January 2006

A LETTER arrives from a hapless reader who informs me he prefers to remain anonymous. He writes:

Dear Mortimer,

I was knocked down by a car in the centre of Whitley Bay recently and left bleeding in the road until an ambulance arrived and out jumped two medics.

One medic leant over me and said: "Take a look at these please." He pushed into my hand four brightly coloured brochures, each extolling the virtues of a different hospital in the vicinity.

"Please select the hospital of your choice," he said.

I could see my leg was shattered, the bone was sticking out and I was losing a lot of blood. I mentioned this fact and the second medic said: "Ok, why not put him on the fast track choice?"

"Right," said medic one, "to save time reading all the brochures, we'll fill in this tick list. Just answer some simple questions which will guide us to the hospital of your choice."

A dark blood stain was spreading across the tarmac and I felt myself going dizzy.

Medic one asked: "Do you (a) prefer a hospital with south facing wards, (b) one with cotton as against nylon sheets or (c) one which has bacon on the breakfast menu?"

I felt myself slipping into unconsciousness, but medic two shook me back awake.

"Which is more important to you," continued medic one, "(a) a good supply of neuro surgeons, (b) the latest x-ray equipment, or (c) wheelchairs on demand?"

I was making small gasping sounds. I tried moving the leg, and the protruding bone wiggled about.

"I'm a bit worried," said medic one. "He hasn't answered a single question yet."

"It looks a bit serious," said medic two, "maybe we should just whizz him up to North Tyneside."

"Do you realise what you are suggesting?" said medic one. "You are suggesting we deny this patient the basic right under the new NHS – that of choice."

By now a largish crowd had gathered, and an animated discussion began over the merits of patient choice or otherwise. It looked as if an infection was setting in on the leg.

"It's just that it's looking bad," said medic two.

"So your solution is to abandon the basic principle of our new policy just because of some minor blimp? We no longer impose our own choice on NHS patients, remember?"

"I suppose you're right," said medic two, resistance crumbling.

Medic one produced the list again. "Right, some answers this time please if you would. State your preferences in the right order when choosing a hospital, (a) late night cocoa, (b) ward windows cleaned weekly, or (c) a request show on hospital radio."

"I think the customer might be about to pass out," said medic two.

The rest is all a bit hazy to me. I have a dim memory of some angry words from the crowd, and two burly men placing me in the back of their builders van while the medics still argued about the tick boxes.

Then I was being wheeled along a corridor while a man in a smart suit was looking down at me and saying, "On behalf of Whizkid Marketing which now handles this hospital account, may I thank you for choosing this location."

"We would like to keep you informed on our other important activities such as tanning salons and a new range of mobile phones, and unless you tick this box in the next three seconds, we shall assume consent."

It was then I passed out. I am now recovering from the multiple fracture and through your column would like to thank the two builders, and hope I didn't leave too much blood in their van. I have still not filled the forms in. Perhaps you could tell me if this renders me liable for prosecution? Yours sincerely, etc. etc.

On yer bike – for the sake of Cullercoats and the world

26th January 2006

H URRAH FOR North Tyneside Council for supporting the new bike shop in Livingstone View, Tynemouth. But as the borough welcomes one new bike shop, it risks losing another. This is the wondrous Lavericks, of Station Road, Cullercoats, a magnet for those wearing bright tight lycra and a painted tortoise shell on the head.

The location is a strange one. Though Station Road, Cullercoats, is much less busy than Station Road, Whitley Bay, it is about three times as wide.

No-one knows why, just as no-one knows why most people choose to walk in the centre of the road rather than on the pavements.

The road is as wide as a three-lane motorway. Given its short length it is the nearest to a square road we are likely to get. Shops come and go in Station Road, Cullercoats.

Only Lavericks, the bright and cheery electronics shop, and Smithy's, where the smile is as wide as the sandwiches, seem to have staying power. Oh and of course, the corner bookmakers.

Bob the Barbers closed to become (guess what?) flats. A second barber has just closed, and though for 100 years the road had a TSB bank, I no sooner opened an account for my (then) wee son, than it closed its doors.

As a man who had long favoured bikes against cars, I am in and out of Lavericks regularly. I savour its smells of gear oil and saddles, its bikes hanging off walls and ceilings, its thousands of scattered accessories whose every location somehow Angus and Marge know.

I have bought three or four bikes at Lavericks, which also repairs them when needed.

The experience of picking up the repaired bike is somewhat different to collecting a repaired car from a garage. In the latter case a mechanic will shake his head slowly, suck in his breath, list 12 extra unexpected faults, and present you with a bill about the size of Chad's GNP.

I'm hard put to spend £25 a year on bike repairs (or 50p a week), and have been known to argue for a bigger bill. And the customers look more relaxed.

Like me, once they're in the shop, they like to hang around, like to glimpse the Dickensian clutter of the rear workshop where sometimes a 'patient' is racked up for treatment. Who likes to hang around a garage?

Radio 4 listeners recently voted the bike as the world's best invention. The panel of scientists wanted something more hi-tec. They were wrong. A bicycle is a magic contraption. It comes alive only with the application of human energy, and in return will propel that human at a greater velocity than is possible on foot, but still slow enough to appreciate the world around.

The bike/human partnership is unique, and much more interesting (and benign) than that of human and internal combustion engine. It is a partnership in harmony.

The bike is a safe, silent, clean energy source that helps prevent practitioners becoming fat slobs, and does its bit not to plunder the planet's rapidly vanishing oil reserves.

And now Lavericks, a mainstay of Station Road, part of the lifeblood of Cullercoats village, is up for sale.

Word is that a few of the interested buyers might keep it as a bike shop, but that many more are already counting the potential shekels to be made from turning it into flats.

Yes, dear readers, more flats! And yet more of them about to spring up on the site of the Bay Hotel.

I am considering robbing a bank, buying Lavericks, and installing in it a mate who likes nothing better than tinkering on with bike parts. Or maybe if you're one of those people sitting on fat reserves, you could do the same. Or maybe North Tyneside Council could find a way of ensuring the great emporium of Lavericks does not bite the dust.

Bikers of the world unite! You have nothing to lose but your chains.

Vacancy at St James' Park and the sound of Cullercoats' future

9th February 2006

A BRIGHT SHARP Saturday morning in Cullercoats, with the sea glistening like a tray of diamonds beneath a winter sun; the waves, which sometimes are wild roaring beasts, on this day were tame dogs lapping at the shore.

Suddenly a deafening noise rent the air. On the site of the former Bay Hotel, several 30ft girders were being hammered into the ground. This would only take an hour or so, during which time several flocks of seagulls fled in terror, six gadgies in the Crescent Club wrapped their mufflers round their ears, and on the beach three dogs pooed in fright.

As I stopped to watch Cullercoats' future taking shape, a passer-by paused.

"I assume," he yelled "that the good folk of Cullercoats are highly excited to see this brand new development."

"They can scarcely contain themselves," I bellowed back above the thunderous din. "I hardly know a person in the village who wasn't just yearning for the historic Bay to be pulled down to make way for more luxury flats."

"Were there any sentimentalists around," screeched the man, "you know, people who were against the march of progress?"

"Always a few of them," I roared in return. "There was a group of them forty years ago as well when they pulled down half the ancient village."

"I suppose some people never learn," said the man cupping his hands to his mouth for greater volume.

"That's true enough," I yelled back.

As the next girder was hammered home, the man asked, "Did you get a letter asking you to apply for the manager's job at Newcastle United?"

I was aghast.

"How did you know that?" I asked.

"Well, everyone did," retorted the man at 120 decibels.

My letter stressed what an exciting, glamorous prospect it was, managing a group of talented young men who'd lay down their lives for the club – at least till a better offer from Feyenoord came along. There was a sentence about the chance of travel to Europe, though this had been scratched out; another promising trips to Manchester United and Arsenal, where someone had written by hand, 'or possibly Crewe Alexandra'.

"So how many of these letters did the club send out?" I asked.

"About 100,000," shouted back the man. I looked at the letter again. A series of bullet points said, 'Be seen on TV every week! Ride around in a large car! Watch matches close to the touchline protected by a plastic dug-out from hurled burgers!'.

No drawbacks were mentioned. But I realised you might have to face eight minute long tedious questions from Garth Crooks on Football Focus, and sometimes your players, seething with frustration at having to live on only £40,000 a week for an activity thousands happily did for free, would beat each other up in front of 50,000 fans.

And of course, you would have to deal with the chairman. By now ten girders were in place and the workmen took a break, leaving a welcome soft cushion of silence like when your mother would switch off the Hoover.

"I think it would be a great job," said the man, "I mean just look how many people have tried it over the last ten years. Not like Manchester United. No one ever bothers to apply there."

By now the thunderous din had restarted and a kittiwake was attempting to burrow under the sand.

"Are you certain you want to be part of that awful world?" I yelled.

Suddenly his confidence fell away. "No, I'm not certain at all," he confessed, "but it's about the only job whose salary would allow me to buy one of these new flats."

I left him staring as another girder was hammered deep into the ground.

North Tyneside tourist delights the copy writers failed to notice

23rd February 2006

I SEE THE North Shields born director Adrian Moat has made a swanky new commercial promoting the region. Good luck, I say. The trouble with these things is the predictability of the material: Durham Cathedral, Holy Island, Hadrian's Wall, Bamburgh Castle – stop me if you've heard this one.

Doing tourist promo stuff, however glossy, is hack work. I know. I did it for a while. Pick up a tourist brochure and you'll find it well-sprinkled with such lazy words as 'timeless', 'sun-kissed' or 'idyllic'.

Small towns tend to 'nestle', and the greatest boast is that a place or area is 'unspoilt', the irony being that this very same brochure is doing its bit to ensure such a state doesn't last long.

Not that tourists inhabit the same world as locals. How many Athenians ever clamber up to the Acropolis? About the same number as the coastal residents who traipse round Tynemouth Priory.

I realised the time has come for *Mortimer's Alternative Tourist Guide to North Tyneside*. Few of the following are likely to feature in a glossy brochure but for me, each has an idiosyncratic appeal.

Shortest coastal journey on public transport

The 325 bus turns onto the sea front at John Street, Cullercoats, then 100 yards or so later turns off again up Mast Lane. This could be marketed as the Coastal Photo Challenge, with only a few seconds for tourists to get their seascape snaps.

Largest bowl of soup

Castaways cafe and bric-a-brac shop, tucked away at Seaton Sluice, offers two soup sizes. 'Normal' is sufficient to satisfy all appetites and is in fact large. The 'large' is oceanic, and the finishing of the same could be a tourist challenge.

Farthest apart toilets in a public house

The Quarry, Cullercoats, has the men's at one end of the pub, and the women's at the other. The long walk between involves two right angles. The pub could be persuaded to employ experienced guides for the benefit of tourists likely to get lost.

Quickest shop queue

Tom Owen's greengrocers in Whitley Bay often has a queue of a dozen or more customers. But this is the only queue which moves at normal walking speed and before you have time to think, your satsumas are being lifted out the basket.

The most bizarre shop queue

Tourists could be invited to experience the Co-op, Cullercoats, phenomenon. Enter the shop at a quiet time, stroll round the empty aisles. By the time you reach the check-out, 13 customers have mysteriously materialised and formed a long queue. No one can explain this.

Miracle ice-cream
A small cafe/shop in unfashionable Seaton Delaval, which never has to advertise, attracts constant queues for an ice-cream that is unlike any other. The appeal of this product can be gauged by the fact that on my latest visit, the queue contained an African chieftain, a Venutian, and an aardvark (an aardvark is the first living creature mentioned in the dictionary).

Biggest bloomer
Give tourists a laugh by taking them to see the Lord Collingwood monument at Tynemouth.

The good Lord was supposed to gaze, symbolically, out to sea, but through some cock-up was positioned wrongly, and now will spend eternity looking across at South Shields.

Strangest sign
Alas, this has now been removed, but the Tourist Board could urge for its replacement. The sign was on Cullercoats seafront, and a single arrow indicated 'Beach and Metro', which are in opposite directions.

There may be more and readers are encouraged to get in touch with suggestions. Only one stipulation – I want nothing that is timeless, idyllic, or which has a tendency to nestle.

The rise of the machine and the importance of the spontaneous

2nd March 2006

THIS WEEK saw the announcement of more record profits for banks and oil companies – as high as six billion quid in some cases. That's billions by the way, not mere millions.

At the same time comes news of cash-strapped small post offices throughout the country threatened with closure, and a funding crisis likely to bring extinction to four out of six North Tyneside Citizen Advice Bureaux offices. It's a funny old world.

Meantime your correspondent whizzes to London. It is essential these days to buy a train ticket in advance, or risk paying a price the equivalent of the GNP of a small African nation.

Even so, every rail journey has 28 different prices, and getting a favourable one may depend on how much the phone operator's bunion is playing up.

At least this part of the transaction involves a human being. "Your ticket will be waiting for you at The Fast Ticket Machine in the station," she told me.

Why did this news fill me with apprehension? Why did I travel into Newcastle that morning clutching the eight digit code number, in a state of anxiety? I later confessed same anxiety to three different people to discover they all felt the same when faced with the ordeal of said machines, be they for rail or plane tickets.

It was 7.15am, and six people were queuing for the three Fast Ticket Machines. The left hand machine had broken down and an operative fiddled with its innards. The right hand machine was behaving itself, but the centre machine was having a bad hair day. I offered it my credit card for identification, but it was having none of it. A member of the station staff hovered close by.

"Give your card a good wipe," she said, so I attempted this hi-tech solution. No good.

"You'll need to join the normal queue, and give the reference number to the assistant," she added. I did this. This 'normal queue' assistant did not malfunction and managed to produce the ticket without needing a good wipe.

There had now been three people involved in making work the Fast Ticket Machine. I remembered the joke about the machine that did the work of six people but took seven people to work it.

I don't like the Fast Ticket Machine. I suspect no-one does. I don't know why it's there. I have nothing against machines in principle. Machines help manufacture lots of things more easily, and as engines, whiz us round the world. I love my washing machine, and, on a smaller scale, my electric toothbrush which has saved my gums from a Napoleonic retreat.

What I don't want is machines that replace interhuman activity. I don't want an automated answering service. I don't want to travel a Metro system devoid of staff. I don't much want the impersonality of shopping on the internet where a mouse offers few creature comforts.

I want more, not fewer people in my life, often in small insignificant ways. Such people don't have to express undying love, life-long friendship or wish to discuss great philosophical problems. I may swap a few words with them on the weather, Saturday's match, or the price of fish. My small exchanges with such people make me feel more of the great human fabric.

When future historians look back at our age (should we survive long enough) they will pinpoint the main social disaster, the factor that helped produce more loneliness and isolation, as being the insane, the ludicrous, the disastrous and damaging policy of replacing in increasing numbers, human-to-human interactions, with those of human-to-machine. End of sermon!

Except to say, on the same train, somewhere near York, an announcement came over the Tannoy. Not an apology for the journey being three weeks late, nor news of the buffet closing for stocktaking; the man's voice said: "We would like to wish nine-year-old Charlotte, who is travelling for a day out in London, a very happy birthday!"

The carriage broke out into spontaneous applause, even though none of us knew or had ever met Charlotte. I don't know why, but this small moment seemed an important antidote to the machine culture.

The enigma of buses and where do we go from here?

9th March 2006

THIS WEEK, dear readers, we are looking at buses. Surely you remember buses? They were part of all our childhoods. We would run around the streets playing at buses; we would make engine revving noises, and, as drivers, turn imaginary steering wheels.

And when we got to travel on real buses, we would rush upstairs for the front seat. This was a special kind of magic; it was like a fairground ride. As if airborne, we looked down on the world from three sides.

The bus seemed capable of squeezing through impossibly small gaps; it tilted and wobbled in turning corners, which both thrilled and scared us.

Buses had conductors with heavy leather bags in which the shaken change made a slightly duller sound than normal chinked money. These conductors also had, strapped across the other shoulder, a ticket machine.

You handed over your money, the conductor clicked in certain co-ordinates, turned a handle, and a tongue of white paper with dark blue printed details emerged from a narrow aperture. You wanted to own one of these mysterious machines more than anything in the world, but no shop sold them. No matter; when you grew up you would be a bus conductor, or maybe a bus driver.

I have lately been observing buses at the coast. You can spot me on the corner of Mast Lane, Cullercoats, on Whitley Road, sometimes in Tynemouth. I cut a rather sad figure, I agree, but there you are.

I ask myself what is it that unites all these buses, what is the common denominator? They are different colours, some single, some double decker. Since Margaret Thatcher's deregulation in the early 90s, they sport many different company names and logos.

Yet there is a unifying feature. What is common to all these buses, regardless of colour, company, or height, is that they are all empty.

I say empty, though to be fair, I spot the occasional gadgy, or the odd elderly woman sat on the front seat for fear of excessive acceleration or braking throwing her around the aisle.

And I did see a bus the other day with five passengers. But by and large, for argument's purposes these buses are trundling round North Tyneside and Newcastle virtually empty – often with a seating capacity of 50 plus.

And this at a time when our roads are rapidly moving to gridlock from the excess of single occupancy cars.

Were this column possessed of great resources, and a team of researchers, I would even now be studying statistics and graphs, and talking to a whole swathe of transport experts.

As it is, I'm stood on the corner of John St, Cullercoats, observing another 325 trundle past full of empty seats (if that is not a logically impossible phrase).

Questions that suggest themselves include the following: has no-one else noticed?

Is there not somewhere in a bus company office, some bright executive who will look up from a sheet of facts and figures and comment, "Hey, you know all these buses we buy at more than £100,000 apiece, all those drivers we employ, all those mechanics, all those people to plan routes and timetables, all those bus shelters we erect along the route, all those big depots we build to house the buses overnight, well you see, I'm just wondering if it's all worthwhile because – well, the thing is – all the buses are empty. Yes, that's right, driving round and round all day. Empty."

And will there not be another bright executive who will ponder this and say,

"You know, you have a point there. How come no-one else spotted it?"

And then two factions will break out.

On one side, the accountants who say withdraw all bus services for lack of demand.

On the other someone appealing for the vision to attract people back to a form of transport that has become marginalised and associated with losers.

Maybe we should have singers and dancers on the buses. Maybe we should bring back conductors. Maybe all bus journeys should be free. Maybe smiling stewards and stewardesses should dispense hot drinks.

Otherwise the accountants will win. And the day will come when children, far from fantasising about this form of transport, will turn to their parents and ask, "Mummy, what was a bus?" Just at the moment cars are choking us all to death.

Wayne's World, Mortimer's World and question of 6 figure advance

16th March 2006

THE NEWS that Wayne Rooney is to receive £5m for a five-part autobiography has taken the literary world by storm. I'm reminded of a recent comment by a literary critic when asked if he thought a celebrity model had herself written a single word of her recent autobiography.

"Not only has she not written a word of it," he replied, "she hasn't read a word of it either."

For the confused reader I should point out the difference between a biography and an autobiography. The former is a person's life story, the latter is the life story of someone who's also a car driver (auto – gettit?).

And while famous footballers and other celebrities are often invited to become part of the literary world, the reverse is rarely true.

The chances I will be asked to turn out for England at football are pretty slim, even though I would be more than willing to provide a 'ghost' player, a cunningly disguised replacement on the pitch itself, while I sat in the stands and took all the praise.

Plus which a life story should be just that – the story of a whole life. Meaning you could only write it when you were dead.

Wayne Rooney has thus far lived only 20 years, many of which I suspect were dedicated to eating steak pies. This activity may be stretched a bit thin when described over the course of 100,000 words, though apparently one of the highlights of the Alan Shearer autobiography, *My Story So Far* was when, after winning a championship medal with Blackburn Rovers, he went home to creosote the garden fence.

Such an activity is not to be dismissed lightly. Would you rather have Big Al smashing up hotel rooms or engaging in mass orgies with wide-eyed bimbos? Of course not.

That fence remains well-creosoted to this day, and should Shearer in this, his final season, take home an FA Cup winner's medal, I look forward to him applying another coat within hours.

Naturally your correspondent has been under enormous pressure from various sources to pen his own autobiography. Why do I resist the daily six figure offers via phone calls, emails, and post, you enquire?

Am I uncomfortable with what I'd call the 'autobiographical conceit', that expectation that people are interested in the moment you squeezed your first pimple? Or do I secretly believe that if any writer's life were that interesting, he or she would not need to invent a fictional one via their books and plays?

Clive James had the right idea. In his autobiography he confessed some of the book was true and some of it made up. And who was to know exactly which was which?

Thus what follows are a few snippets from *The Life of Mortimer*, a work which may or may not eventually find its way into print. See if you can tell what is fact and what is made up.

1) Peter Mortimer's first job was as a trainee false teeth salesman.

2) His grandmother often used to move house without telling anyone.

3) At the age of 10, he boxed 15 three minute rounds against his older brother for the world heavyweight championship and was knocked out in the final round.

4) He fell through the ice of a Siberian river and was nearly swept away.

5) He rode a horse from Moscow to New York.

6) If he goes near marzipan he suffers projectile vomiting.

7) He has owed Joe Cocker five pounds for 35 years.

8) He has never set foot on King Edward's Bay.

9) He recently filled his partner's diesel car with petrol.
All these in fact are true. Re: no.5 – Moscow is a small farm near Gilsland, Cumbria, and New York of course is up the road near Murton.
But the above is probably a long enough account of the *Life of Mortimer*. The world is already awash with vacuous life stories. I think I'll try to write another play. And I might just creosote the fence.

Oh to be in Marden Quarry now the giant sausage has arrived

30th March 2006

SPRING HAS sprung, and here is your man trogging off to savour the delights of Marden Quarry in Whitley Bay. I am armed with my new weapon – a bird spotter's guide from my partner Kitty.

I have spent my life woefully ignorant about matters avian, a state of affairs only partly redeemed through working six months on fishing boats, and spending an entire winter on Holy Island (bird population, about six trillion).

But I am developing a childlike delight in now not being confused by the more simple species (coot or curlew? No problem!), and I excitedly anticipate the time when I can point a finger and say, "Ah, a black eared wheatear if I'm not mistaken", or unfussily remark, "Hmm, unusual to spot a red crested pochard hereabouts."

Walking round Marden Quarry has a liberating effect on the human soul. It frees up the brain and imagination in a way that reality television only ensnares it.

I've concluded that an individual never gets a brilliant idea while watching reality television, though as it's less disruptive for the government for us not to think up new ideas, they're happy to see the form flourish.

Here's a new idea. I have these last few years come up with various brilliant concepts in this column, united by the fact they have all been totally ignored. The realistic side of me suggests this one will suffer no better fate.

It's time for a Marden Quarry Festival. Yes, yes, I know we have other festivals. The Wild West Festival in Whitley Bay for instance. But at this particular time do we really want to ape gun-crazy America? Fish Quay Festival?

Gone, and with a replacement (Mouth of the Tyne?) no one can quite define or identify.

Whitley Bay Jazz Festival? Might be better if it took place in Whitley Bay. Cullercoats Harbour Day? Homely, but as it makes hardly any use of the rocks, the sand or the sea, it loses an opportunity.

For many, Marden Quarry and lake are a hidden secret, so here's a sense of discovery to start with. Fishermen use it a lot, and an angling competition should be involved. There are said to be one million fishermen in England, though the number of spectators is about six. Get the fishermen to wear fancy dress and give them jokes to tell onlookers. And encourage that unknown species, the fisherwoman.

Throughout the day people could race round the lake for the Marden Trophy. Contestants would run against the clock, in pairs, three-legged style, many of the pairs made up of opposing North Tyneside councillors, which may prevent them writing interminably long letters against one another to this newspaper. The six fastest pairs would race again in the evening final.

There would be no alcohol. The top car park could include a few stalls, on the bottom grassy area, a stage for jugglers, musicians and conjurors, and a bouncy castle area reserved for adults, for while many of us have become childish, we've forgotten how to be childlike.

Rowing boats would take people out to the lake's small islands. Here they could stay for 30 minutes doing absolutely nothing except being quiet with nature, after which they would be rowed back.

As the lead-up to the festival, local communities would be encouraged to create something special. This could be a scarf knitted long enough to stretch round the lake, though more practical might be the world's longest sausage to do the same task. This could be eaten in the evening barbecue.

If vegetarians are aghast, part of it could be meat-free.

The quarry has only two entrances, so entry could easily be organised, and though lumpen lager louts might try disruption, who knows, they might even discover an alternative form of enjoyment.

I shall be there of course. It's forgotten that I once came third in a three-legged heat at my primary school. Plus which I shall be eagle-eyed throughout. I might just spot an icterine warbler.

Dead swan on a beach and a house full of feathers...

13th April 2006

WHAT A WEEK, dear readers! I walked into the bar of The Queens Head, Cullercoats. Sat in the corner, staring miserably into their pints of draught Bass, were Gordon Brown and Prince Charles.

"Why the long faces?" I enquired.

"He'll never stand down," said Brown, "all this waiting and waiting."

"I think she'll just go on forever," moaned Chuck. They both nodded gloomily. At that moment a local rushed in and exclaimed, "Dead swan found on Cullercoats beach! It's the end of civilisation as we know it!"

We all hurried out to find the bird lying at the bottom of the north slope, but then noticed, further along the beach, a well-known tourist campaigner taking another dead swan from a large bag which he dropped onto the sand. We immediately tackled him on this strange behaviour.

"That Scottish resort where they found the dead swan – pictures of the place all over the media worldwide in hours – what exposure!"

"You mean," I said, "you're deliberately causing this avian flu scare by dropping dead birds on the beach?"

"No such thing as bad publicity!" he exclaimed. "By tonight the world will be talking about Cullercoats and Whitley Bay!"

"A funny thing, publicity," I said. "Fewer than 200 people worldwide have died of bird flu. I suspect more people die each year of ingrowing toenails. No publicity about that."

Chuck and Gordon were looking on, both still disconsolate.

"This is just what HE wants," said Gordon. "A scare like this, Dunkirk spirit, rally round the leader etc."

"A dead swan!" said Chuck. "They're Royal birds. She'll get all the sympathy."

A small crowd had gathered and someone at the back shouted, "We're all doomed!"

"You've more chance of winning the lottery than catching bird flu," I said, and immediately regretted the comparison. For millions of poor souls, life was only made bearable by the thought (however remote) of such a windfall.

A functionary approached and handed me a buff form.

"Sign here, please," she said.

"What is it?" I asked, and she replied, "You'll find out when you get home."

I signed and said to the sad duo, "Why don't you both come round my house for a cup of tea? Cheer you up."

Another strange scene awaited outside my home. A large lorry had drawn up and various people in white protection suits and paper masks were coming in and out, and spraying everything in sight.

"What gives?" I enquired.

"Your house has been requisitioned," said one in muffled tones.

"Requisitioned?"

"One dead swan means a 1000 sq mile exclusion zone, with three million chickens needing to be kept indoors."

"So?"

"You're taking 50,000 of them. We've left you one spare room for basic needs."

"You mean I've got a house full of chickens?" I asked, but already he'd gone, and I could see a flurry of feathers at an upstairs window.

"Maybe we should go to The Copper Kettle for that cup of tea," I said, because neither Gordon nor Chuck had cheered up one iota, and hey, it wasn't their houses that were bursting with chickens!

Over a rock bun, Chuck said, "Why can't she give a chap a decent chance? I mean, who wants a coronation at the age of 80?"

"It seems years since I bought that new anglepoise for the desk at Number Ten," said Gordon glumly, "I don't think it will ever get used."

In all this furore over bird flu, I had never even considered the impact on our two pretenders, and their chances of a decent job.

Through the window I could see more and more large white vans arriving and sticking up their large satellite dishes. A local jumped out of a car with a load of Asda crab sticks which they promptly stuck on a makeshift stall bearing the words 'Freshly Caught Off Cullercoats'.

Already the Copper Kettle was filling up with media folk, and curious visitors. But I'm not sure either of my two distinguished fellow tea drinkers even noticed. Each in his way felt he'd been well and truly given the bird.

Ice cold in Cullercoats – this way for a short sharp shock...

20th April 2006

THE FIRST bank holiday of the year, and look! One brave soul has ventured into the North Sea, turned the colour of Wedgwood pottery and been carried out by his friends as stiff as a plank (him, not his friends).

I too shall venture into that briny before long. Why? Because, as mountaineers put it, it is there. What better reason? I have already indulged a small Easter paddle, the water temperature inflicting the kind of foot pain I'd have thought possible only from the Spanish Inquisition.

Courage! For the last year I have been indulging the kind of masochism that prepared me for that sea. This is the morning cold shower, a perversity made popular in English public schools, as the young bloods were readied for the task of conquering foreign climes.

Is it an enjoyable experience? Of course not. The enjoyment, as with head banging, comes when you stop. Cold showers are said to be good for both the heart and circulatory system, and a quick check reveals both operating satisfactorily.

The cold shower has never been fully marketed or exploited by the admen, maybe because its money-making opportunities are few. The one-time Wimbledon FC would have a cold shower before every game, an eccentricity that helped that band of misfits from one of football's barren areas to beat Liverpool in the FA Cup Final. It's hard to think of their successors, the bland MK Dons FC, achieving such an oddity.

There are different techniques to taking a cold shower. Some people opt for the Gradualist School: this favours slowly turning the control dial from hot to cold in the belief it lessens the pain. To my mind it only prolongs the agony, and I advise the short sharp shock.

First indulge yourself in hot soapy water, shampoo, gel, generous latherings of the nether regions. Sing a little. After such pleasantries, pull the electric cord. There is a few seconds hiatus while the remaining hot water clears itself through the pipes. Then suddenly it is cold.

The effect is so drastic that the showeree involuntarily indulges a whole series of gasps and verbal ejaculations.

"Oooh! Aaaaah! Eeeeeeh! Oh! Weeeeeh!"
Anyone outside the bathroom at this moment may suspect that some kind of sexual ecstasy is being achieved within. For this reason, if showering in anyone else's house, I place one hand over the mouth during this time. This results in merely a few muffled yelps.

Once the water is fully cold, I count to 100. This I do aloud in a shivery jerky voice (more fun for any eavesdroppers). By number 90, I am like a frozen cod fillet and cursing the whole dreadful affair. Come 100 I mercifully turn off the shower, step out, take a towel and experience a kind of nirvana or bliss. Every inch of my body zizzes and tingles, and I am ready to climb Everest, swim up the Amazon, and traverse the North Pole before breakfast.

At such moments I think of those unfortunates who fall out of bed, have a quick splash, then a half-awake exit, whereafter they sit in an artery thickening traffic jam coughing on the day's first tab. My own shower unit is fairly old, a gentle spray blossom. More modern ones are powerful enough for riot police, and to blast away the coalface in deep shaft mines.

My partner Kitty indulges the daily cold shower habit, and son Dylan too.

On one level, it is ridiculous, on another a kind of morning purge, an expunging of the guilt of being an indulgent Westerner in a deprived world. Or maybe it's just the preparation for that first North Sea dip.

A sad footnote this week, the death of Sam, the faithful King Charles spaniel, and my travelling companion in 1998 for a penniless 500 mile trudge through the UK to write my book, *Broke Through Britain*. Sam died a few days short of his 15th birthday at the Whitley Bay home of his owner Sarah Davidson. For most of that strange and exhausting journey, he was my soul mate.

Blotting paper, beetles and the mixed pleasures of a travel pass

11th May 2006

DISPARATE EVENTS combine to strange effect. What can it all mean? Firstly, in Cullercoats Post Office a man approaches the counter to enquire, "Do you sell blotting paper?"

These days blotting paper is about as common as a back yard mangle.

Nobody needs it because liquid ink has disappeared. Ink now comes sealed in a cartridge that slots into your printer. I am one of the few people whose study contains different coloured bottles of Parker's Quink.

None of these colours is green. It is well-known that people who write in green ink (usually on lined paper) are prone to such oddities as shouting at custard or falling in love with a house brick.

I have a delicate Waterman fountain pen, bought for me years ago by my friend Pat Riddell. It has documented several of my travels. I love filling it, and love writing with it. After a fountain pen, a ballpoint is a vulgar object, and a spoiler of the fine art of hand writing.

Event number two: at a jumble sale at Holy Saviour's Church, Tynemouth, I pick up a box marked Beetle Drive. Said aloud, this may sound like the paving leading up to Ringo Starr's house, yet it predates the Fab Four by many years.

Beetle Drive is a game, the object of which is to draw a beetle on a preprinted sheet, different parts of the beetle are linked to different dice numbers, and contestants keep throwing the dice till someone has drawn the complete insect, at which time they shout "beetle!" and you start all over again. The skill factor is minimal.

Post-war, beetle drives were hugely popular and would fill community halls from which the word "beetle!" could be heard ringing out at regular intervals.

What have either of these two incidents to do with this Metro travel pass in my hand? I am now of an age where for £8 I can ride the Metro and buses free for a whole year after 9.30am.

This comes via the Gold Card. Remove the first letter of the word Gold and what are you left with? Exactly.

My emotions are mixed. I use (and criticise) Metro frequently, and the card will save me in excess of £600, hurrah. Yet when it arrived, I felt it must belong to someone else. Just as when, on those rare occasions I'm asked to produce it by an inspector, I expect a reaction of "Oh, but sir, this is a pass for the over 60s. Some mistake surely?" As it is, they simply glance, nod, and move on.

How can I be in possession of such a card? It was only yesterday I first went into a pub for a nervous underage drink. My leather trousers still hang on a rail, and I haven't yet got round to cutting my hair to a sensible length.

Seeking solace, I tell myself I'm the same age as Mick Jagger. But then it's just possible I'm also the same age as that gadgie in sagging beige trousers hobbling along the street.

Growing old is the new taboo. For the Victorians it was sex, later it became death, now we're in denial over age, rushing in our thousands for botox and plastic surgery to help us live a lie.

The old become invisible. How many old people are used in advertisements? And when the media do give them a chance to air their opinions, it's with such mocking programme titles as *Grumpy Old Men*.

What has all this to do with blotting paper and beetle drives? Only this. The mention of blotting paper made me nostalgic for another age, and I almost fell into the same trap with beetle drives.

Except I now remember beetle drives were pretty pointless. A much better communal activity in the 21st century is the pub quiz, a contemporary phenomenon unheard of all those years ago.

You're growing old when you constantly yearn for the past. The present is the only time really worth yearning for. Some things were better in those days, some worse, but they've all gone!

Coming to terms with this makes a travel pass more acceptable. And puts blotting paper and beetle drives into context. And next week, our theatre company starts an ambitious nine-month community venture creating and then staging a new full-length play. But to take part you have to be 60 or over. Ageist? Of course – in the best possible way!

The strange tale of Pirate Pete and the relieved student...

25th May 2006

THIS WEEK'S column has only one ambition – to cheer up Cullercoats Bay. Of the four North Tyneside beaches, only Cullercoats failed to secure the coveted Blue Flag Award in last week's announcements.

There's dancing on the sands at King Edwards, Tynemouth Long Sands, and Whitley Bay. What can be the reason for the Cullercoats omission?

Was errant dog poo found out of season? Was it the beach's political sand writing, as exclusively reported in this column last week?

Is it born of jealousy among the other beaches? Cullercoats is the only beach to host a wee festival (Cullercoats Harbour Day), and while the other three cannot boast of a single accessible cave between them, Cullercoats has legions, some of which in smuggling days were said to lead up into the big houses on Beverley Terrace.

Which allows me to recount the tale of Roger, who once emerged via these cave tunnels into a fine lady's bathroom. The lady was, let us say, in a state of déshabillée.

Roger was clutching a load of contraband at the time, while the lady was soon clutching a towel as she ran screaming from her bath, and kept running till she reached Seaton Sluice, unfortunately dropping the towel just past St Mary's Lighthouse.

There is now a small plaque marking the exact place where the towel was dropped, and there are plans to film the tale with Angelina Jolie as the surprised lady, and the smuggler still to be cast, though as he's likely to have a beard and a big belly, the favoured money's on Brian Blessed.

I invented all that of course (to help cheer up Cullercoats), but not the following, which is as true as a straight arrow.

I was once a pirate in Cullercoats Bay with Dodgy Clutch Theatre Company. A group of children was despatched beachwards, and told that somewhere in the caves they'd find Pirate Pete with his buried treasure map. I secreted myself at the back of the largest cave in time for their planned 3pm arrival.

I was wearing a striped top, a red bandana, eye-patch, sword, sandals, rag-patch trousers and my skin was covered in gravy browning.

The children were late, but at 3.10pm a group of geology students arrived with their lecturer to examine the cave rocks as part of their field work. They all clutched clipboards and looked very earnest, and they came ever closer to the back of the cave where I was dressed as a pirate and liberally smeared with Burdalls gravy salt.

I crouched behind a rock while the lecturer explained the likes of fissures and petrological formations and everyone scribbled notes. I scarcely dared breathe as he seemed to drone on for centuries, but eventually he led them out the cave and away. I stood up with great relief only to find someone else experiencing great relief too. One male student had stayed behind for a pee.

I shall never be certain which of us was the more embarrassed as we stared at one another, him caught mid-act, or me emerging from the rear of the Cullercoats caves on a Wednesday afternoon in 1986 dressed as a Caribbean pirate. I thought of some easy explanation, but realised none was possible. Not a word was spoken. He adjusted himself and hurried from the cave to the safety of daylight. Who knows how he recounted the tale? Who knows in what unknown student common room they talk still in hushed terms of the Cullercoats ghost pirate?

Can Whitley Bay, King Edwards or the Long Sands boast such a tale? And while King Edwards has the legend of Jingling Geordie (soon to be a Pageant play), long-term it may not be able to compete with the growing myth of Pirate Pete. Hurrah for Cullercoats.

From the barren lands of the SE, a heartfelt plea for help

1st June 2006

AND SO NEXUS supremo Mike Parker is to stand down (see this column January 19, February 16). Will a new age dawn for Metro? Will those put-upon travellers finally give a thumbs-up to the (mainly useless) CCTV cameras?

Meantime, North Tyneside Council is to be chaired by a Mortimer. No relation, though a brace of us at large in the borough may be excessive.

Did you see a drought order has been issued in the Sutton and East Cheam areas of leafy Surrey? On Radio Snore, a golf club official was bewailing the catastrophic effect on the greens (no, not the Sunday lunch vegetables), so it's perhaps not surprising I received the following letter from the secretary of the Affiliated Home Counties Golf Clubs.

Dear Mortimer,

May I, through your vast numbers of intelligent readers, make an appeal on behalf of our members who have fallen on hard times. We have been forbidden to water our greens and I cannot even begin to convey the misery this is causing.

Cracks are appearing in the carefully manicured grass, which is becoming powdery. Accurate putting is all but impossible and yesterday a leading local estate agent missed a three foot putt.

Two days ago, a group of entrepreneurs, who play at least four times a week gave up in frustration and ordered their chauffeurs to drive them away, and I personally know of the MD of a large motor chain who left the course in a state of some exasperation, and spent the next three hours sinking expense account G and Ts in the club house.

You will appreciate just how valuable a round of golf is to the modern businessman, and the potential effect on the economy of these extreme conditions – I say 'businessman', though there are talks about possible lady members.

But what, I hear you ask, can you people up there in the north east do to help? Firstly I know that traditionally many of you chappies are without gainful employment, and therefore are blessed with free time. Secondly we read that your region has abundant water supplies thanks to the Kielder reservoir, built to supply a Teesside steel industry that rapidly collapsed.

I'm also aware you're used to long distance walking.

Didn't a group of you from Jarrow walk down here some years ago? Weren't you led by someone called Howard Wilkinson, the football coach? Sorry if I'm a bit hazy on the facts.

Anyway my suggestion is this: that several thousand of you equip yourselves with decent footwear and each pull one of those stand-by water containers down the A1 and into Surrey. I estimate 5,000 containers would hold enough water to restore the greens, get our members putting happily, and put the economy back on course.

After all, when one region is suffering, it is the common duty of another region to come to its aid. How many times has the south east come to the aid of the north east over the years? Why, there was – that is, I could mention – what I mean to say is – well, the actual details escape me for the moment, but you get the picture.

We would of course give you brave chappies a fine welcome on arrival.

Alas, as non-members, you would not actually be allowed on the golf club premises, but I'm sure some of our splendid ladies could knock you up a warm plate of food in the village hall to prepare you for your return journey (I assume black pudding would be alright?), by which time of course the containers will be empty and easier to pull.

As you stride out on this historic journey, your every step will be fortified by the knowledge that once again business executives in the south-east are back on the golf course, and a potential crisis in the corporate world has been avoided.

I thank you in anticipation of your speedy co-operation ... etc. ... etc.

Why a tealess train has us ducking under the table

8th June 2006

EVEN NEXT door's tortoise is getting excited over the World Cup, and here's a strange incident that occurred as I was travelling from Tyneside to Rotherham in order to see the aged mater.

Over the Tannoy came one of those ding-dong noises followed by the deadpan announcement, "Attention train crew, disability toilet alarm activated."

Over the course of ten minutes this same announcement was repeated several times. What does it mean? What are we passengers supposed to do about it?

Is this the same disability toilet alarm activated several times over, or is there a trainful of disabled people activating different alarms for reasons as yet unclear?

Do the train crew take any notice? Or are they too busy with the serious business of buffet car stocktaking?

This second announcement came as I stood up to make the journey for a cup of tea. "The buffet car is now closed for stocktaking." Each train journey this stocktaking is carefully planned to begin at the exact moment your taste buds are salivating for hot liquid. It lasts for a full hour.

I imagined the ritual. One member of the train crew holds aloft each item and declaims, "One Mars Bar – giant size!" A second member repeats, "One Mars Bar – giant size!" and records same in a large ledger with a scratchy quill pen.

"One breakfast ciabatta with mushroom!"

"One breakfast ciabatta with mushroom!" (scratch, scratch)

"One chocolate muffin!" And so on.

I resigned myself to a tealess state as the man sat next to me turned to ask, "So what do you think about John Prescott then?"

This being England, I gave the kind of noncommittal grunt which could cover every possible response.

"I think," continued the man, "he should go to Germany in place of Wayne Rooney."

This was an unexpected idea. Firstly, given Prescott's occasionally garbled linguistics, I could see him having great problems in the pre-match line-up singing *God Save The Queen*.

He'd end up with one of those strange wobbly mouths opening and closing like a goldfish out of water.

Didn't it happen once to John Redwood?

Secondly, Prescott's acceleration off the ball wasn't what it once was, and despite his reputation, I wasn't certain he could score.

"He was very impressive on that croquet lawn," continued the man, "let's have him in the full squad." He paused and added, "I took my wife to see the latest England game."

"Jamaica?" I enquired, and he replied, "Not at all, she was very keen to go."

We travelled on and I fantasised about thin white plastic tea stirrers. The man said, "I'd been hoping to get to the other friendly."

"Hungary?" I enquired.

"I certainly am," he answered. "A pity the buffet car's closed."

Onwards we journeyed, on our tealess train of activated disability toilet alarms.

The man turned to ask, "Which of the England players do you feel is the most improved?"

There could be only one answer.

"Crouch!" I said enthusiastically, and the next minute he'd ducked under the table, peering out with a look to suggest he expected a flying beer can hurled by some florid-faced miscreant.

When he re-emerged, I said to him, "So, same old problems with the England team, eh? Metatarsal."

"Actually," replied the man. "I've got all their albums, though I do think they've gone off a bit since *Dustbins of the Damned*."

I didn't comment. The train was pulling into Doncaster, where I had to change. I stood up, and bid farewell.

Along the platform I glanced into the window of the buffet car. A member of the train crew was holding aloft a tuna and cucumber roll while a second was scratching something into a big book.

My only thought was, come on England.

What to do when asked for your great granny's maiden name by an unlaughing policeman

15th June 2006

WE WERE JUST settling down to England's first World Cup comedy of errors when the front door bell rang. I answered it to find 250 police officers outside.

"Freeze!" said the lead officer.

"Freeze?" I replied, "but it's 27 degrees centigrade today."

The man was wearing designer riot gear, smelt of Macho aftershave and was pointing at me a weapon that looked capable of taking out a Sherman tank. I noticed that 80 of the officers had begun scaling the side of my house.

"Watch out for the pointing!" I said, though I'm not sure they heard. "So what's all this about?" I asked the officer.

"Information received!" he barked, as he waved a hand and yelled, "Go! Go! Go!" This brought another wave of officers up the street.

"What information?" I asked. There were only a few minutes before kick-off, and I was looking forward to my Peter Crouch Long Lollipop, 6ft 7ins in length and guaranteed to last the full 90 minutes.

"Did you or did you not write this?" he asked and shoved under my nose a copy of *Mortimer at Large* from May 23, 2003, which included the sentence, 'The world has been stunned by the news that weapons of mass destruction have been found in a Cullercoats litter bin.'

"My little joke," I said.

"It's potential evidence!" he replied.

"Potential evidence of what?"

The man looked slightly unsure. "Potential evidence of – " he paused a moment and then, "potential evidence of potential evidence."

All these police officers just for me! This must have been a great time to commit a burglary, rob an old lady or set fire to your least favourite school.

I cocked an ear to the TV in the lounge. Luckily Garth Crookes was still only half way through an 18 minute question to Sven, so kick-off might be delayed.

At this moment the neighbour's dog ambled up the street.

"Freeze!" yelled the officer, but the errant pooch failed to respond and 28 officers opened fire.

For some reason I found myself thinking about The Laughing Policeman. His name was Charles Penrose, he was making 'laughing' records pre World War One, and was still acting in panto post World War Two. As well as his famous song, I also have vinyl recordings of him singing *Laughing Policeman's Baby* and *Coppers on Parade*.

An officer scooped up the dead dog, waved his other hand and barked (barked – gettit?) "Search the house!"

"Will you be finished by half time?" I enquired.

"It could take a week," he answered.

"Two hundred and fifty officers a whole week to search a small terraced house?" I asked, "Are you looking for a lost molecule?"

By this time a cordon had been set up round Cullercoats and people getting off the Metro were asked to give their great grandmother's maiden name, and then frisked.

"I must admit," I mused, "given overstretched police resources, we do seem slightly in the realms of overkill here – in the case of the dog, quite literally."

"Acting on information received," repeated the officer.

"Hmm," I said, "so suppose for sake of argument, I said to you that a bloke in John Street had 15 cruise missiles in his back yard –"

I never got time to finish my sentence.

"Regroup! Regroup! Regroup!" shouted the officer. "Operation John Street! Go! Go! Go!"

A few seconds later the vast swarm of officers, their weapons and their Macho aftershave had disappeared round the corner, leaving a few metal hooks stuck in my brickwork.

I went back to the TV set, where the kick-off had been further delayed with Garth Crookes still not having finished his question to Sven. Plenty of time to get stuck into my Peter Crouch Long Lolly.

Man in the elephant's head proves why cricket losers are winners

29th June 2006

WITH THE World Cup in full swing, it was off to the Riverside, Chester-le-Street, for the latest one-day cricket international. England predictably got tonked by the Sri Lankans who batted with such ease they could still be at the crease now.

In part cricket has succumbed to the same marketing philosophy as football, so that when wickets fall or boundaries are struck, macho tunes are played very loudly, though I've yet to meet a spectator who likes such nonsense.

The banking insurance sponsors stick their logos all over, along with their strange slogan, 'Protection is our Game', which suggests if you don't play along with that game, you could end up at the bottom of the River Wear wearing concrete feet.

And though Durham CCC have worked miracles, they might have a quiet word with the transport officials; few buses, and with 16,000 people trying to get to a 10.30am start, you're stuck with two Newcastle-Chester-le-Street trains – one leaving at 8am, the second at 11.22am.

Large signs at the entrance state, 'No alcohol to be brought into the ground', a piece of rank hypocrisy which fails to add, 'Because we want to make a fortune selling our own'. Beer and lager stalls are in profusion (£3 a pint) as are the swarms of peripatetic booze sellers, spacemen-type packs on their back. I found only one stall dedicated to tea and coffee (which no-one stops you bringing in).

Despite the vast booze consumption, there's a relaxed atmosphere suggesting sports hooliganism is to do with more than alcohol. This sense of carnival is in contrast to the often edgy or confrontational feel in football grounds, where winning is often considered a matter of life and death, or on which one's entire future happiness depends.

Cricket fans are a knowing lot, and keen to see their side win, but without the belief that defeat will bring the cosmos to an end, and when England were obviously heading for a heavy loss, the crowd manifested strange, and not unwelcome behaviour.

A conga dance attracted a large following including one man sporting an elephant's head and another wearing a coconut shell bra. Elsewhere in the crowd a horned red devil was lifted on high and carried past a man dressed as a priest to loud cheers.

Suddenly we saw a great bendy snake rise up from the crowd. This twisty-turny creature was made up of several hundred plastic glasses. A few moments later a second snake was seen rising up some distance away, and making its way towards snake one, presumably with sexual congress in mind.

As one conga dance finished, a second was started and led by two dozen Elvis figures, complete with white rhinestone outfits and quiffs. All day they'd been serenading us with The King's greatest hits. Meantime Sri Lanka were moving inexorably towards England's total, their small band of supporters rising up in colourful explosion at every boundary.

We England supporters had other entertainment. Step forward a great lard factory of a man (and curiously, all the entertainment was male), who pulled his T-shirt over his head, and slapped his massive rolls of fat into all manner of quivering shapes; his great pendulous breasts shook this way and that, and his huge sagging belly wobbled like some giant blown bubble. He took his bow to more applause than his team had been able to attract all afternoon.

And of course the Mexican wave, which begins sluggishly, the kind of spluttering yes-no of a damp car engine, but then for maybe ten minutes moves its irresistible way round the entire ground, except for the hospitality free-loaders in the corporate boxes who sip their free booze on the balconies, and mainly decline to indulge.

Come Saturday we'll all be in front of the telly watching England and Portugal. Why will it be a tortuous, rather than an enjoyable experience (especially if we lose)? And is there any point to me suggesting that should we suffer defeat, we should all get out into the street and dance the conga?

I must go down to the fair again, the arms that reach up to the sky

6th July 2006

SUNSHINE AT The Hoppings? The two are incompatible. Where is the thick Somme-like mud of yesteryear? I am a Nottingham lad who grew up secure in the knowledge the annual Goose Fair was the biggest of its kind in Europe. My belief was challenged on Tyneside with similar claims for The Hoppings. Tynesiders also scoffed when I claimed Notts County were the true Magpies. It's a wonder I stayed here.

Goose Fair was more influential in my education than any schooling. As a spotty adolescent I would stand fascinated at the Waltzer, staring at the fairground lads who took the money.

They were rakish, tattooed, gypsy like, a roll-up often dangling from their lips. They had a look of utter disdain as they walked those wooden boards whose momentum would have put most of us on our backs.

They took your money without speaking a word, often declining to look at you. You handed over a note and panicked when they walked away, but they always returned with the change, by which time the Waltzer was often at high speed. They were the surfers of the fairground, totally fearless.

I wanted to be one of them, ride the boards of the Waltzer and look fascinating. Career teachers were pushing under my nose glossy brochures about Barclays Bank, the Civil Service and ICI. I wanted to work on the Waltzer.

The ambition remained unfulfilled, but the Waltzer lads are still there – and were once here at Whitley Bay until our fairground was pulled down to make way for obfuscation.

Fear is one draw of fairgrounds. We live in a compensation culture where you're afraid to lend a neighbour a ladder in case he falls off and sues. Yet we flock to the fairs to put ourselves in terrifying situations.

The rides are monstrous and beautiful, scary works of art infinitely more impressive than much modern sculpture. And why has no-one ever put into a gallery the fantastic artwork of the ghost train and its like?

And what of the crystal balls? Exotic women in caravans of beautiful gilt, each woman claiming to be a relation of Gypsy Rose Lee, offering fortune telling and palm reading. Long queues form, hoping the promise of a tall dark stranger doesn't mean a mugger or traffic warden.

The fortune tellers are all female, so too their customers. This is a world free of male cynicism and scoffing.

But where now is the Ron Taylor Boxing Booth? This ran for decades, a throw back to another age. As a youngster I longed to pit my boxing skills (I was Nottingham schoolboy champion, if you must know) against the likes of Battling Bill from Beeston, to be part of that primeval bear pit, globs of spit and blood flying from the ring into the baying audience. Another unfulfilled ambition.

Thus, haunted by memory, I walk almost ghost-like round the Hoppings, where you can pay 50p to go into the Rotor but a ride on the Sling Shot would set you back a tenner. For this you are put into an open 'ball' and hurled at great speed into the air.

What a bargain!

Small stalls still offer ludicrous enticements (Four Darts! Score More than Three to Win!), and many people stagger round with their prizes of eight foot pandas or clutching giant inflatable hammers, whose novelty will wear off in minutes, and which are doomed to slowly fall into deflated neglect in a house corner.

Why was I inevitably drawn to the Waltzers (only two remaining)? The music was deafening, the lights flashing, female screams whirred past as the cars whizzed round in a circling blur. From the central control box a voice yelled through the PA 'Hold tight now! Here we go!' A siren sounded, dry ice billowed forth, the cars rose and fell, and there, walking across the undulating wooden boards, as if several decades had never happened, were the youths, as footsure, upright, and disdainful as ever.

They took no notice of anyone. Without a glance they took the money. Theirs was a world removed, a microcosmic circling world in which they were supreme, and I was as fascinated with it at The Hoppings in 2006 as I had been all those years ago at Nottingham Goose Fair.

I trudged off to the Metro, ignoring stall holders' shouts to chuck balls into a bucket, or throw darts at playing cards whose hidden metal backs made scoring impossible.

I would never work on the Waltzer. I would never knock out Battling Bill. But at least, to look on the bright side, I was unburdened by an eight foot panda, or a slowly deflating hammer.

How we are failing screen test, and impossibility of TV-free pint

13th July 2006

WHY, ON A SUNNY Friday afternoon could your correspondent be seen clambering onto his trusty push-bike to visit no fewer than eight coastal hostelries?

Is this any way for a scribbler of a certain age to deport himself, and indeed by pub eight, was he capable of any deportment at all?

Rest assured, my motives as always were the enlightenment and education of you, dear readers. My journey was alcohol-free.

I'd been thinking of tellies in pubs and George Orwell's great novel 1984 in which giant telly screens are both omnipresent and continually switched on – in fact they have no 'off' switch. And while in 1984 you couldn't escape the telly (usually the massive face of Big Brother with a sound track of state propaganda) the telly's function was also to watch you.

My own house boasts only one small telly and is therefore becoming an historical curiosity. Most households now have a telly in every room, some with screens the size of football pitches. These are about as tasteful as a stretch limo, but just in case you find yourself in a corridor which is telly-free, you can always watch on your mobile.

With this relentless TV onslaught, and 20,000 channels, some with the intellectual challenge of a damp shoelace, you might think that the great British institution, the public house would be a haven away from the flickering screen, a small oasis, an escape where people could sit and talk, and daydream and generally do nothing much at all.

You could be wrong. As my thoughts and deeply scientific research prove, not only has almost every public house surrendered itself to the telly, almost every set is tuned to the same subject matter.

We are turning into a nation of Sky Sports junkies. We now walk into our rapidly changing public houses to see giant screens offering us underwater badminton, white water rafting on live buffalo or some other ludicrous sport that has no relevance to our lives.

But now here's a curious fact. Although this army of tellies flicker away from opening time to last orders, though they are now located in every pub's every nook and cranny, for the most part, they are totally silent.

So that even if your curiosity did stretch to learning more about underwater badminton, your chances are slim. And every day, in every pub it is someone's task to switch on the tellies, and ensure the volume is turned down to zero. Do these people ever stop to ask themselves the meaning of life?

Naturally on big sporting occasions, such as England boring the pants off us in the World Cup, the sound comes back on, and for these times most pubs roll down a giant screen roughly the size of Belgium.

Let me whizz you through my random tour in search of the telly-free pub. **Last Orders** in Whitley Bay (previously The Railway) had five medium size screens, one 42 inch plasma, the occasional monster. They're all continually tuned to Sky Sports, except occasionally at weekends a music channel. The pub does not allow kids or baseball caps, and definitely no kids actually wearing baseball caps.

In the **Monkseaton Arms**, two 42 inch plasma screens, three normal, one occasional monster. In the **Dolphin**, Tynemouth Road, one big plasma in the front bar, but at 3.33pm it was actually switched off. The back room's telly-free.

Two plasma and one normal flicker away silently in the **Cumberland Arms**, Tynemouth. Would they consider showing anything other than Sky Sports – drama or documentary, say? No.

In the small bar of **The Ballarat**, North Shields, a single 42 inch plasma will soon be joined by a second to keep it from loneliness. I looked in vain for a telly in **The Beacon**, West Monkseaton. but it's there. A recent addition, it's hidden away behind an abstract painting and brought out 'on special occasions'.

And so my biggest hopes: **The Magnesia Bank** in North Shields where never once had I stared at a screen. Telly has now secured its first small foothold, a giant screen up in the Bank Suite for the World Cup. And what of **The Fire Station**, Whitley Bay, and Wetherspoon's much publicised no-telly, no juke-box policy?

Alas, telly-creep is here too. It's only small, it's only terrestrial, but it's arrived. Step forward please, the North Tyneside pub that will have no truck with telly whatsoever. Should it exist, I will both visit and praise it, though, despite my inherent optimism, I fear my search may be a hopeless one.

Note: I was later informed both the Tynemouth Lodge and Prince of Wales, North Shields are telly-free

Let us dance round mighty mast and sing its high-tech praises!

3rd August 2006

PRESENTING UNIQUELY for your education this week, Mortimer's one dozen good reasons why they should erect the proposed giant phone mast at Cullercoats Metro Station.

1. It is almost six hours since I sat on public transport and heard someone yelling into their mobile, "I'm on the train!" One more new mast will increase mobile availability, and ensure such time lags are much less likely.

2. At the moment, Cullercoats Station has nothing remotely approaching 14.7ms, (that's more than 40ft). Even the station bridge is less than half this height. So let's think big, let's walk tall!

3. We're always being accused of slavishly aping America these days. Well – here's a chance to prove the critics wrong! The USA have banned such masts near schools or in residential areas (as have NZ and Australia). Let's show our independence by allowing them!

4. The quicker we can get new phone masts the quicker the phone firms can introduce gambling onto our mobiles. As we're assured the new generation of giant casinos will lead to regional regeneration, surely mobile gambling will lead to individual regrowth!

5. It is alarmist talk to say the mast is close to houses. Percy Avenue and Marden Terrace are yards away! And the thousands of daily commuters passing by will be in close proximity only for short periods – surely not enough time to contract some awful disease!

6. The people making the application have written to local residents to say, "Our site team has carried out an extensive survey of the area and have highlighted this location as the best option for development." By this I assume they mean 'best option' for residents, so that's fine by me!

7. This applicant says in the same letter, "Our client recognises that developments of this nature have sometimes caused concern with regards to public health and impact on the environment." See how sensitive and caring they are?

8. Surely this proposed mast is only responding to public demand (which is what our market economy is all about)? I can't be the only person regularly to have noticed groups of pickets outside Cullercoats Station waving such

banners as WE DEMAND A 40ft PHONE MAST! Have I not also heard them chanting "What do we want?" "A giant phone mast!" "When do we want it?" "Now! Now! Now!" Or is all this merely hallucination brought on by the great heat?

9. Even allowing for the fact that there is a small chance of contracting cancer or leukaemia from being near such a mast, is that not a small price to pay if it makes it easier for us to view the latest digital video clips?

10. Let's think positively. The mast could become a great tourist attraction, with the Monkseaton Morris Men annually doing a Maypole dance round its base. We could give them protective clothing as extra precaution against contagion.

11. As objections to such masts almost always fail (though heaven forbid the procedures should be called a sham), and as we do need to conserve energy in this great heat, why not simply forget any protests and go to sleep on the couch in front of *Celebrity Nose Picking*?

12. That previously mentioned letter from Stappard Howes (catch line – 'Building Communications') includes the phrase, 'We trust this will not cause you inconvenience,' and I for one feel old-fashioned politeness like this can go a long way!

There may be some stroppy types among you determined to stand in the way of progress, and in the pursuit of objectivity I feel duty bound to inform such folk that objections should be sent to Stappard Howes, 122 Dundyvan Road, Coatbridge, ML5 1DE.

But hey – if you ask me, you're better off snoring in front of *Celebrity Nose Picking*. Less trouble all round.

Note: The phone mast proposal was eventually thrown out

Don't fret pet, chilling out at the coast is the latest thing

10th August 2006

PEOPLE ADAPT to the freakishly hot weather in different ways. One friend has set up Tar Busters, a service freeing people trapped in sticky hot Tarmac. His ancillary firm sells you hamburgers, TV *Quick*, or a rapid haircut while you're awaiting rescue.

It cannot be long before reality TV comes and points its camera at such folk – maybe with the title *Tar Very Much*.

Other people moan that the North Sea is becoming almost hospitable, thereby denying the bather the necessary masochism. The latest novel by the North Shields writer Debbie Taylor, *Hungry Ghosts*, includes the unusual acknowledgement to 'Sirkka-Liisa Konttinen for introducing me to the delights of cold water swimming'. This may soon be an anachronism.

My own latest dip resulted in initial yelps of pain for only five seconds, whereas previously 15 was the norm. And ten minutes into bobbing about, I had still not turned into a Birds Eye product, which is disturbing.

Global warming is slowly changing the sun from our friend into our enemy. Fashionable dwellings of the future will face north and have a minimum of direct sunlight. Tanning parlours will become as rare here as in Zimbabwe, as we gasp for air, dab our sweat-soaked brows, and fantasise about spending several hours inside a Mr Whippy machine.

But do not despair! I awoke the other morning to the sonorous tones of the foghorn, Miss Fenwick. I opened the curtains to be greeted with that grey blanket which is the unique sea fret of our coastline. I had seen the future, and it worked!

Here is a possible salvation for our coast, salvation which the authorities have singularly failed to deliver during 20 years of relentless decline. Could Whitley Bay be saved not by bungling and procrastinating politicians, but by a cold grey blanket?

Admittedly the fret is unpredictable; it arrives and leaves at its own bidding. At present its arrival is still greeted with long anguished moans from hundreds of heliolaters (a posh word for sun worshippers), pouring off the Metro for a day of supine indulgence. Such moans could change to hurrahs if our coastline becomes one of the few places in the UK to keep cool, a refuge for poor souls suffering endless sweaty armpits, and desperately seeking escape from the 30°C hellhole our lives have become.

Let the cool arms of the fret embrace you! Let its cloak protect you from the incessant sun! Lie on the beach without fear of burning or skin cancer, and experience the rare delight of goose pimples! Pale people will be viewed enviously by onlookers who will remark, "She must have holidayed in Whitley Bay!"

Tourist board slogans will include, 'Chill in Cullercoats!', 'Stay Tynemouth Cool!' or 'Whitley Bay? No Sweat!'

On the Greek Islands, along the Costa del Sol and Costa Brava, locals will form long queues hoping their planes due for the haven that is North Tyneside can take off without getting stuck on the runway Tarmac. Such folk are dreaming of the luxury of an ice-cream that won't melt before they can eat it! They are fantasising about a holiday that is not inside a hi-powered oven!

The unpredictability of the sea fret is, I concede, a slight problem.

I was tempted to suggest expensive research to enable us the better to control and predict the phenomenon, until I realised it was this very same arrogance and messing about with natural forces that got us into this mess in the first place.

If we hadn't thought we could do as we pleased with our precious planet, we wouldn't now be ringing every shop in a 20 mile area in a fruitless search for the last available electric fan. No, we must let the fret come and go as it pleases. Treat the whole thing like a gamble, like the National Lottery. No-one seems worried about odds of 14 million to one there.

The chances of getting a fret-day are much higher. Hope springs eternal, and if this means we must get used to day-trippers shaking their fists in fury at the blazing sun as they miss out once again, so be it. Who knows, tomorrow they might just strike lucky?

Why the cucumber must be set free – a moral tale for our times...

17th August 2006

CONSIDER THE cucumber. When holding said vegetable I am often tempted to administer a small tap to someone's head. Don't ask me why.

Cucumbers are considered cool in the way, say, a turnip never is. As cool as a turnip? No-one would dream of saying it. Cucumber sandwiches are quite posh, and if the bread is cut into small triangles, and the crust removed, they're positively upper-class.

The cucumber I have in my hand is encased in a plastic film, and I have spent several hours wondering why. Over thousands of years the vegetable has evolved a perfectly efficient skin, or rind. It discourages insects taking a nibble, and those same posh people cut the rind off when eating same sandwiches, thereby (they claim) reducing risks of indigestion.

All vegetables and fruits have a skin, or rind. Yet for some reason we would not dream of encasing a single tomato, apple, grapefruit or banana in a tight plastic film.

(Banana skins by the way are so revolting it cannot be long before reality TV happens on the programme *Celebrities Try to Eat Banana Skins*).

Back to my cucumber. I stare at it and wonder about the effort, time and labour expended in adding this plastic film. Every morning people have to drag themselves from their beds, drive through heavy traffic to the small production unit, and spend eight hours engaged in this totally useless task. Should I meet such a person I shall first ask them, "And what do you do for a living?" When they reply, "I wrap cucumbers in a tight plastic film," I shall ask further, "And why do you do that exactly?"

It is at this moment they will realise their working lives are useless and futile. I shall try to console them with the fact that many occupations – i.e. financial consultants, PR people, and lecturers in media studies – fall into the same category, but this may not be sufficient compensation.

Let us move away from the production to the consumption side. The first requirement when faced with such a cucumber is the removal of the same tight plastic film, for it is impossible to slice the vegetable with the film in situ.

Removing the cling film is not easy. You need to insert a knife between film and cucumber, then wriggle it around until some kind of incision is made into the film, which then can somehow be peeled off, and the resultant crinkly shrunken mess thrown away to make its own small contribution to our recycling problems.

Add together the time, energy and money expended at the production end, plus the time expended at the consumption end, and you'll see this is considerable. And the achievement? To have in your hand a cucumber in the very same natural state it should have been in all along.

Plus which my cucumber can now breathe, whereas previously it was suffocating.

Am I perhaps highlighting this as a small example on the insanities of the modern world and technology?

Do we wrap cucumbers in a thin plastic film, simply because we know we can?

Was the cucumber wrapping machine invented by accident, but once invented, could not be ignored?

I have no answers.

I have toyed with the idea of parading outside my local Cullercoats greengrocers with a banner FREE THE CUCUMBER! but feel such a protest may be seen as low priority when faced with such issues as the Iraq War or the problems in Lebanon.

I put my faith in the simple, but harmless delusion that this column exerts any influence over anyone, and that all greengrocers, having read my 700 words will exclaim, "Mortimer is dead right!" and immediately refuse to take delivery of any imprisoned cucumbers.

By this small act, a small group of workers somewhere in the world will be freed up to do something useful, and slicing a cucumber will no longer be a needlessly arduous task.

And thus Utopia grows a bit nearer.

A society in denial, the shame it's convenient to forget

12th April 2007

FOR THE FIRST TIME, my mother doesn't know who I am. This is less disconcerting than you might think. I walk into her old people's home, and she offers up the kind of smile you give a stranger.
"Do you know who I am?" I ask. She knits her brow. "I might do," she says.
"I'm your son." I reply.
"Alex?"
"No, your other son, Peter," I say.
"Oh, yes," she says.

In the lounge, the old people sit round the perimeter, some silently staring into the room's empty centre, some mumbling, some sleeping with slumped heads. They are positioned in a way that makes human interaction as difficult as possible.

In one corner a TV set is blaring out the inanities of daytime telly. No-one is watching. The television, in true Orwellian fashion, is always on.

No matter what day or time of day I visit, the scene is identical. These people have been dumped. And we have dumped them.

Many of the home's carers are young females, who can have little concept of or empathy with their patients' long history, and what has brought them to this point. To the youngsters they are simply the old who have always been old, just as they themselves are the young, who will always be young.

Ironically, the carers speak to the inmates as you would speak to a child, except louder.

None of these old people has any voice. They have no influence, or political clout.

Politicians conveniently forget them. There's no mileage in them. They are the huge silent scandal deep within our society. Probably millions are living like this. They are invisible.

Old age is the last taboo of a narcissistic hedonistic youth-obsessed society in denial. If we ignore old age, it might go away. Close your eyes and it doesn't exist. Visit the plastic surgeon.

In the future (I hope) we will look back on this shame, as we now look back on slavery. How could we shovel people away into such places and still think ourselves a civilised society?

Sometimes my mother grasps my wrist with her painfully thin hand and says, "I just want to die." As she speaks, she looks around furtively in case she's overheard by the authorities.

I have little idea how to respond; sometimes I adopt a breezy and unconvincing bluster about things not being that bad, sometimes I kiss her on the forehead, sometimes I give her a silent hug, scared in case I crush her fragile brittle bones.

If I stay too long in the home I suffocate. The suffocation is partly my own guilt, that I have helped bring things to this.

I push my mum out the front door in her wheelchair, whiz her up the hill, breathe deeply the free air outside, watch the wind play in her white hair.

And now she fails to recognise her own son. I should be devastated. Yet strangely there's also a relief.

Her new mental state blocks out much of the awfulness of her institution.

My mother has shrunk back into some fantastical make-believe world, as if in self-protection

Her nonsensical words, her repeating of the same question ten times in one minute, her occasional belief she is back on the Irish farm of her childhood, or that people long dead are in the room, all these somehow cushion the reality of where she is.

Others are not so 'lucky'. One old woman I'd never spoken to grasped my hand and in the feeblest of voices pleaded, "Get me out, please."

Where is the imagination that could make such homes more bearable, less grimly Victorian?

Why not have computers in old people's homes, let the inmates surf the web, send out emails? Why not encourage babies to come and crawl about? Why not fill the homes with cats and dogs and parrots and goldfish? Every time I take in Polly the dog, my mum cheers up. Yet the practice is frowned upon by the authorities. Pets are forbidden.

We spend billions on immoral wars, or futile macho weapon systems, while we allow our old people to rot.

Why are we not more ashamed?

My mum died on January 15, 2008

Importance of rubbish, placing of bins & relevance of cardboard

26th April 2007

I AM WORRIED about the bin men. I say 'men' because for no apparent reason it seems an occupation curiously unpopulated by the female of the species.

In days gone by I could understand this. The bin man strode into your backyard, picked up and slung over his shoulder the heavy bin. Pausing only to give you a wink through the kitchen window, he'd break out into an Alfred Doolittle song from *My Fair Lady* (remember Stanley Holloway?) and lug the bin to the waiting cart. The task needed a bit of male beef. Not so much now.

Plus which at Christmas you gave the bin man a tip. Now you rarely see him, but I'm still worried about bin men. Are they becoming confused? Here's why I ask. Where once there was a single set of bin men, now there are two.

One group calls weekly to the back lane to pick up the wheelie bin. This is lidded and large enough both to contain and secrete an average sized person. In fact I once wrote a play in which I did secrete an average sized person in a wheelie bin, the joke being the character was Osama Bin Laden. Some saw it as bad taste.

The wheelie bin is placed onto the whirring slightly menacing machine that tips it into the belly of the great Rubbish God. Your bin is then returned somewhere within two square miles of your back gate.

The second set of bin men call fortnightly to your front gate to pick up the plastic recycling box. This is much smaller, open, and would probably only hold a small pig, though why anyone would want to keep a small pig in a plastic box is beyond me.

Time was you'd put very little into the plastic box while the wheelie bin was stacked full. Often I would have to get into the wheelie and leap up and down to make more room. This exertion produced curious looks from neighbours. Times have changed. We're becoming ecologically educated.

More stuff is recycled. Much of what once went into the wheelie bin now goes in the plastic box. Two weeks' newspapers alone from this house more than fill the box, even if much of these are comprised of useless supplements which, for all they are read, may as well be written in Mandarin.

Large plastic milk containers cause a problem. Even if bagged these form a pile unstable enough to be blown to Seaton Sluice at the slightest wind. Or charvers may choose to kick 'em around. Empty tins attract nosey dogs, even when washed, and wine bottles always seem prey to that strange species given to smashing glass at every opportunity.

Meantime in the back lane I trundle out a wheelie bin that often contains only one plastic sack of refuse. If I open the lid and shout in, there's an echo. Given the present accommodation crisis, I'm thinking of renting this large space out. I feel I am short-changing the bin men. Should I leave them an apologetic note for bothering them with such paltry pickings?

Thus one container is wildly overfull and collected each fortnight. The second container is half empty and collected every week.

This curiosity probably ranks small on the scale of changes to our life brought about by global warming. It is unlikely the North Tyneside Refuse Bin problem will feature largely in the pending G8 summit.

But it cannot continue indefinitely. Any suggestions, readers?

Here's one to go on with. Why not banish those small open plastic containers entirely? They are impractical, too small, generally useless. Let's send them to a local piggery.

Meantime I leave you with one of humankind's great troubling questions. If like me, you find your plastic box emptied save for a single Weetabix packet or egg box, do you wonder exactly what the recycling folk have against cardboard?

The glass ceiling for Whitley Bay FC and the trouble with Harry

3rd May 2007

TO DURHAM City FC, and ecstatic scenes as Whitley Bay won the Northern League championship for the first time since 1966, a year usually noted for other football triumphs.

What a wondrous team Whitley are! Yet to win the league and not be promoted – what's that about? For though Whitley should now go up to the Unibond League, financial reality, and travel costs make this impossible.

Step forward some great benefactor please!

I was still pondering this lunacy when the doorbell rang. It was Prince Harry, disguised as Long John Silver.

"I have to travel incognito, Mortimer," he said.

"Come in," I said, offering him a cup of tea and a Rington's ginger biscuit. Not many Royals call these days. King Faisal of Iraq once knocked for a cup of sugar; on one occasion King Leopold (I think) kipped on the floor after a Bruce Springsteen gig.

Harry put down the inflatable parrot and laid the wooden leg to one side.

"It's all this damned Iraqi business," he said, "it's driving me bonkers."

I'd read the reports: controversy over sending off to the war zone the third in line to the throne. A fine gesture to stiffen the sinews of our brave lads (and lasses), or a stupid move likely to see his head blown off?

"They say you're very keen to go Hal," I said, gently reminding him not to dunk too long. "In fact they say you'll leave the army if they don't send you."

"Hm" he replied. "It's deuced difficult, old sport."

"Tell me about it Hal," I replied, "I mean, everyone knows how much you love the army."

"Yeeeees, well" he said, adjusting the eye patch, "I was jolly excited at the start, rubbing boot polish on the old cheeks, crawling along nets, firing off big guns, driving tanks – it beats talking to those crusty old devils in the palace anytime, if you know what I mean."

I reminded him my entire experience in uniform was three weeks in the cub scouts, so I was hardly in a position to comment.

He was devouring the ginger biscuits somewhat rapidly, with the look of a ravenous, hunted individual.

"So surely nothing has happened to change your mind?" I asked.

"Two things," he replied. "Firstly, all that business with those marines getting captured, and showing themselves up to be utter berks, rushing to sell their stories."

"What's that got to do with your situation, Hal," I asked.

"It's obvious," he said. "From now on every clothhead in the armed services will be flogging some tale to the tabloids. I wouldn't be able to scratch a buttock without it being sensationalised as front page news. My life would be hell."

"You've got a point there," I conceded. "What's the other thing?"

"It's this Iraq war Mortimer," he said, tilting his three cornered hat.

"What about it?"

"It suddenly struck me. It's a senseless waste of time."

"So if you feel like that Hal," I said, "why insist they send you?"

He paused for a moment as if about to reveal some great truth. I realised he was trying to locate the over-dunked and now separated biscuit.

"My plan was this: I'd threaten to leave the army if they didn't send me. I calculated they'd never dare risk sending someone like me over there. I'd be able to get out and the public would still see me as a hero."

"Pretty ingenious Hal," I said, "but it didn't pay off, eh?"

"The reality Mortimer," he said, "is that there's so few people willing to serve over there, they can't afford to turn anyone down. So now they've called my bluff and I'll soon be bound to that mad hellhole! Unless I could get someone to replace me of course." He paused and gave me a long look: "What are you like at driving a tank?"

"A good try, Hal," I answered, "a bit long in the tooth though. And I'm in the Briar Dene quiz next week."

It was my turn to give him a long look.

"Are you much of a goalscorer, Hal?" I asked.

It was a long shot. Sign him up for Whitley to replace Lee Kerr, a bit of loot and influence behind him. It might keep him out the army, and we might yet get into the Unibond. Watch this space.

The art of the street; how wheelie bins could get things rolling

10th May 2007

A MORNING stroll along Newton Avenue, Cullercoats took me past a serried row of wheelie bins stretching several hundred yards. Their stoic appearance revealed few signs of being items at the centre of a controversy.

One bin had painted upon it a smiling face. Admittedly this was from the primitive school of art – three curved lines, three dots – but it gave off a sense of simple pleasure that made me feel good, and almost moved me to whistle.

It also put into my head a bold new idea to chuck into the great wheelie bin debate.

I've long thought we should make more use of our visual artists, and also those art students who are locked away in colleges before emerging with their degrees to design pizza cartons and corporate logos.

Some time ago, during this region's Visual Year of the Arts, I wrote to the visual arts officer of the then Northern Arts suggesting some innovations. One involved those grim grey steel shutters that come down on so many urban shop fronts at night.

Far from making any area feel safer and more secure, the effect is to turn same areas into forbidding ghettos through which we hurry nervously. Why not recruit the art students to paint all these shutters in imaginative bright and vibrant colours, creating an atmosphere less that of Alcatraz, more like a carnival? I never received a reply from the esteemed officer.

Another suggestion for using artists came via this column when I proposed that St Mary's Lighthouse could serve as the focus for a national graffiti festival.

Scaffolding could be erected, and hundreds of graffiti artists encouraged to decorate the lighthouse's entire surface. The artwork would be on display for two weeks, fully documented for a future photographic exhibition, then the same artists, by agreement, would return the tower to pristine white.

The project would attract huge publicity, bring in many visitors, and constructively harness rather than marginalise the creative power of the graffiti merchants.

To my utter and total amazement the idea remains thus far unacted upon. But lo, another 'art idea' now presents itself.

Once a week (for the present time at least), those bins are trundled out into serried rows for collection throughout the borough. Imagine if each bin had on one side a vivid and original painting/design from an arts student.

Hey presto, as if by magic, a 300 yard long al fresco art exhibition would appear at 8am!

Imagine 100 streets in the borough taking part. Details could be given out about which exhibitions would be on which street on which day, so that people could visit – either individually, or as part of a tour. Two streets a week would mean we could spend a whole year visiting these outdoor exhibitions.

You'd need to be prompt. Turn up late and the exhibition would have melted away, each bin trundled off back through the gate. This sense of ephemera would invest the 'exhibition' with a real urgency.

And it might get us to visit streets we never knew existed, thus proving the Mortimer maxim that truly exciting journeys can often be on our own doorstep.

Judges could select the most impressive bin per street for an end-of-year exhibition. This could be at The Baltic, should there be room among all that obscure installation art from Scandinavia.

The idea would make art presenters and curators of all of us, for without hundreds of individuals bringing out the bins, there would be no show. It would also, in a society of increasing alienation, bring an unusual link between neighbours.

And each year, another 100 streets, another group of arts students, another full programme of instant exhibitions.

As usual, Mortimer the Optimist awaits the first move from the powers-that-be.

Can it be long in coming?

The Metro guards' stag parties, and kicks of the young wrinklies

17th May 2007

HOW FLATTERED I was last week upon approaching the Metro turnstiles at Haymarket, to find an inspectors' guard of honour. I assumed the ten-strong phalanx was to commemorate my recent 200th column in this newspaper. A lump came to the throat (actually, it was a badly chewed piece of Granny Smiths).

Would this splendid reception committee break out into spontaneous applause?

Would they hold an archway of *News Guardians* above my head while singing 'For He's a Jolly Good Fellow'?

I thanked each one in turn, an act which drew strange looks, and brought a verbal response from only the final checkie, who said "Tickets and passes please."

Ah well. I flashed my Gold Card. At such times I secretly hope for the response, "Oh come now, surely you're not old enough for one of these!" Instead, the checkie merely nodded.

Later that day my partner Kitty told me of an incident at roughly the same hour on a Metro. Two 'young wrinklies', those feral youths old and bitter before their time, walked up and down the carriage blasting out loud music on their radio, and offering obscenities to all and sundry.

At Walkergate Station the female driver eventually emerged and asked them to get off. The ferals refused, but the driver bravely stood her ground while passengers lowered their eyes.

More radio and obscenities later, and with the threat of police arrival, the ferals left the carriage. As the Metro pulled away, they delivered a series of strong kicks (and more obscenities) at the windows.

Like most of us, my brain splits into Jekyll and Hyde when told of such incidents. Dr Jekyll is deeply disturbed and wants to understand and alter the nihilism, the futile black anger of such a lost unhappy generation.

Then up jumps Mr Hyde, blood rushing to the head. Mr Hyde longs to squash flat with a giant mallet such ugly pondlife.

And while this second reaction is fully understandable, especially at the flashpoint moment, long term it doesn't get us far.

The point m'lud, is this. Everyone knows how common such incidents are on Metro. And delightful though it was to have my guard of honour at Haymarket, the checkies might just have been better employed split into pairs, and riding the trains. For reasons that are beyond me, this rarely happens. And despite the evidence to the contrary, Nexus continue to make complacent statements about both reduced levels of crime, and the efficiency of the three trillion CCTV cameras.

Two observations: the high level of Metro anti-social behaviour is not officially recorded and therefore shows up in no crime statistics, nor is there a single incident of a CCTV camera stepping in to prevent such anti-social behaviour.

Readers may remember your correspondent making such points in an open letter to the then Nexus chief Mike Parker in January 2006 in a column that produced wide response and support. Parker huffed and puffed an unconvincing reply. He has now gone.

With his successor Bernard Garner, we have swathes of guards, like some strange stag party outing, piling onto the train for a few stops, disembarking, then not seen again for several weeks or months. Sometimes they check tickets. Other times they huddle together in conversation and ignore us all.

My impressive grasp of higher mathematics has worked out that if you divide ten checkies into twos, they can travel on five times as many trains! Readers wanting the full algebraic theory, please get in touch.

It really is simple, but here it is again for the benefit of the needy.

The more inspectors you have on trains, the safer we all feel, the more people will return to the system, and the greater its income. Unpleasant they may be, but these kids aren't really a threat to civilisation as we know it, and are easily discouraged by the presence of checkies.

In Mortimer's ideal world, the Nexus authorities now leap up, shout "Of course!", and immediately do something about it.

Until that happy occurrence, put your hand up if one of your first acts when the Metro pulls in is to check the carriages for signs of feral youth? Thank you. You can put all those hands down now.

Happy travelling!

Back in the Summer of Love, with a little help from my friends...

24th May 2007

THE RENAISSANCE of singer Joe Cocker – a new album, a tour, and much media exposure including last week's Jools Holland show – reminds me I own the rights on his first record, and that for 40 years I've owed him a fiver.

It was 1967, and the Summer of Love had just happened. At Sheffield University for reasons never quite understood, I was studying economics. I was chairman of Sheffield Students Rag, where we decided to cut a fundraising record.

Local bands were cajoled into playing free at the city's Mojo Club, run by a certain Pete Stringfellow, who now owns half the world's night clubs. Even then a certain notoriety attached to Stringfellow. After my dealings with him I was interviewed by the police, which made me feel scandalously important.

Rag Goes Mad at the Mojo was that almost forgotten form, the EP, its glossy cover design psychedelically aping the recent Beatles LP, *Revolver;* we recorded four hours of material.

Three of the bands have been swallowed by rock's great black hole of obscurity. The fourth was Joe Cocker's Grease Band (he was then unknown, and a gas fitter in the city). To go upmarket he dropped the 'Grease' in favour of 'Blues'. Later, in the editing room it became clear Joe Cocker had star quality while the other bands were – well, just other bands, so we put three on one side, and filled the other side with Joe.

His was the last act on stage, way past midnight, by which time much of the audience had drifted away. We remaining few stamped and yelled in the background in an attempt to disguise lack of numbers. The singer invested his finale, *Saved,* a great Lieber and Stoller classic, with some rude words of his own, and you can clearly hear my mate bellowing "Filth!"

The EP – on Action Records, a label we specially created for the purpose – sold a few hundred copies round the city and raised some loot for charity. My own purple-prose sleeve notes include the following: 'Mr Pete Stringfellow introduced the boys to the stomping cheering hand-clapping audience, and just how much sweat was lost during this fantastic recording is a matter of conjecture. What is certain is that to relive the experience requires only the playing of this disc. It's all here – as it happened.'

Quite.

Over the years, I often thought of sending this collector's item to John Peel, but as I own just a single copy, I desisted. For all I know the disc is worth several grand, and somewhere along the line, as director of Action Records, I own the rights, something I'm unlikely ever to do much about.

During that same Rag Week in '67, Joe Cocker played at a Rag Dance in the students' union. We were paying him a fiver. The other band failed to turn up and I asked Joe if he'd do another set to get us out of a fix. He looked whacked, but agreed, because he was a pretty accommodating guy. He asked for no loot, but I said I'd give him an extra five quid.

At the night's end, the band packed up the gear, loaded the van, and drove off, no doubt Joe thinking of the next day's gas fitting. I totally forgot that extra fiver, and it remains unpaid to this day. I never met him again.

Joe Cocker went on to become one of the great white soul singers with a voice like a rusty saw. Strangely enough, the other claimant to that title, Tyneside's Eric Burdon, was also on the Jools Holland show the same week.

My own career as a record producer was to prove short-lived. I eventually graduated with a BA (Econ.) Honours, which logically should have seen me pursuing some well-paid career in industry or banking, but a need to scribble words led me down a less lucrative, but more interesting path.

Does Joe Cocker ever recall these incidents? Probably. Artists often find that fame proves false, an anti-climax, while the formative years become the most real, an exciting memory life-long.

Having said which, he's never written for his fiver.

The reasons we have been going round in circles for 100 years

31st May 2007

SIGN OF the week; on the approach to North Tyneside Hospital, the following is on view – 'Dental Clinic (Vehicles Only)'. A filling station presumably?

Meantime little attention is being paid to the recent 100th anniversary of the roundabout. Where are the spin doctors pushing to give this landmark a high profile?

Perhaps a historical mini-series with J-Lo's bottom as the roundabout itself? Or a commemorative magazine in 342 editions (edition one half-price!), complete with self-assembling roundabout kit (built in the comfort of your own home!)?

The first roundabout was the Etoile encircling the Arc de Triomphe in Paris. It was the brainchild of French architect Eugene Hernard with the brilliantly simple idea that if all traffic flowed anti-clockwise (read clockwise for we Brits), and allowed entry from the right, it would keep moving.

An American called William Phelps Eno also claimed to have made the same invention. His claim was dismissed, and from thereon out of spite the Yanks referred to roundabouts as traffic islands, a ridiculous title that suggests traffic lives on them.

Come to that, I've often fantasised about living on a roundabout *(Oh no! Not another Mortimer book coming on! – Ed)*. There's a big roundabout in Gateshead just above the Metro interchange, where a person could lose his or herself in the undisturbed flora and fauna. A small tent and gas stove – perfect!

Several roundabouts near the coast have enough trees or shrubs to guarantee solitude. Thousands of vehicles roar round them hourly, but a human foot rarely steps upon them. When did you last walk on a roundabout? Exactly.

Roundabouts are the eye of the storm, a calm surrounded by swirling turmoil. I have been known to lie down on a secluded roundabout centre and stare at the sky. How comforting it is. Thus far no men in white coats have arrived.

And 100 years on, roundabouts still work, and are respected. If we discount the modern mini-version – mere pimples in the road – few motorists drive round the wrong way or fail to accede to traffic from the right. We have not yet taken out our modern malaise on roundabouts.

There have been changes. Some roundabouts now display advertisements. This is because adverts break out like a rash wherever people are forced to pause for more than a few seconds: bus stops, post office queues, doctors' waiting rooms, and now roundabouts.

And while we ban US style hoardings alongside motorways (where we're driving in a straight line), we allow adverts at roundabouts, where maximum concentration is required.

I await the first court case where, accused of causing a roundabout accident, the defendant claims, "But I was just reading the advert for Smithwicks sausages, m'lud!"

Another recent trend is placing traffic lights at roundabouts. This is like mixing custard with gravy.

Were Monsieur Hernard to witness traffic lights at roundabouts he would turn in his grave (anti-clockwise, naturally). He would realise that overall this signifies we have lost the battle against the car, (a fact all politicians and planners know, but are terrified to come clean about), for roundabouts on their own are perfectly capable of dealing with any sane level of traffic and only when we face the madness of gridlock does his beautiful invention risk breaking down.

Meantime my mind turns to a story plotline in which the central character drives endlessly round the same roundabout. This would be a simple allegory about the modern human condition and our ability to travel great distances without actually getting anywhere.

The person's futile act would be a cry for help, yet in the huge thronging mass of traffic, the fact that the vehicle hour after hour simply repeats the same small circular journey, would pass unnoticed.

Except by the story's second character, peeping out from the roundabout's foliage. He spots the futile circler, and somehow saves him/her.

They spend the rest of their days together, unnoticed in the island's seclusion. They have merely a small tent and a gas stove, and a mad world encircles them. But they survive and find a new meaning to life. Hollywood may even film the story. Probably with the title, Traffic Island.

Metro's advertising – what is it to do with marinated chicken?

7th June 2007

TRAVELLERS USING Cullercoats Metro of late have experienced a strange phenomenon *(a phenomenon is by definition strange, therefore your statement is a tautology. Less verbal slackness please – Ed)*.

For several weeks, at intervals of not more than one minute, the PA system announced, "This is a –".

There the announcement would end. Passengers would exchange puzzled glances. What could it mean?

Was it a competition, complete the sentence in not more than 12 words, with the most original answer receiving the prize – possibly an entire 30 minute Metro journey with no-one swearing out loud?

I sent in my clever entry which read, "This is an incomplete sentence, but not now." I heard nothing.

Was it news of national importance that had somehow been sabotaged? Perhaps England had recalled Tom Finney for their important European cup games? Perhaps Tony Blair had cancelled his farewell tour of West Allotment? Perhaps the new owner of Newcastle United had made his first ever visit to St James' Park?

After a few weeks, the message grew to, "This is a Northumbria Police announcement. Please be aware that the consumption of alcohol –".

Again the ending was abrupt. This was some improvement but not much. I began to wonder if this was subliminal advertising, the kind where they slowly drip feed us morsels of information so that by the end of the campaign, when the product name is eventually revealed, we are all gagging to buy it (this is the theory – there again, advertising people tend to live in a world of their own). I concluded the explanation must be more mundane.

I pressed the platform's help button. I lead a sad life and often do this. I imagine the person at the other end (it's usually a male), sat in the bowels of some vast windowless building, a half-eaten beetroot sandwich at his side, skin formed on his forgotten cup of tea, a small pimple on his cheek. He dreams of those out in the sun and fresh air, his only contact being via this intercom.

Secretly he envies them the freedom, which is why he is rarely jocular. I put my question.

"Were you aware the Northumbria Police announcement at Cullercoats Station is incomplete?"

"Our engineers are aware of that, yes."

"I wonder when it is likely to be fixed?"

"Our engineers are working on it."

At this point I realised our relationship would be fleeting and almost entirely unmemorable. Should I attempt to prolong it? I could ask him if he'd read the latest Martin Amis novel, had he heard the new Nick Cave album *Grinderman,* and did he realise that marinating chicken in lemon juice before casseroling gave it an extra kick? I did none of these things.

"Thank you very much. Goodbye."

A slight feeling of emptiness follows such conversations; I am left staring at the help point grill.

I would need to complete the announcement myself. I came up with the following options, (oh no! Not that accursed phrase 'the following options'!)

ONE: "Please be aware that the consumption of alcohol is exciting, dangerous, sexy, and should be encouraged at all times. This message is brought to you in conjunction with the Licensed Victuallers Association."

TWO: "Please be aware that the consumption of alcohol is best achieved by the same alcohol being poured into the mouth and then swallowed. Use of any other body orifice for this task is strongly discouraged. This message is in conjunction with the Department of Health."

THREE: "Please be aware that the consumption of alcohol dates back to such civilisations as ancient Egypt, and that the Greek God of wine, Bacchus, was considered one of the most important deities. This message is funded by the Open University. Please check our web site for a whole range of

mind-expanding courses."
Readers can provide their own version.
Then it came to me! The incomplete message was punishment for my article of May 17 criticising Metro for failing to tackle anti-social behaviour! Instead of publicly replying to the criticism, Metro chief Bernard Garner chooses to rebuke me via information deprivation! Will it work? We'll see.

STOP PRESS: The message has now returned to, "This is a – ".

Ten million years of evolution, and the invasion of the e-mails

14th June 2007

UNTIL THAT moment, it was a normal day. At Cullercoats the tide came in bang on time. I failed to watch Big Brother. Newcastle United promised 'a new beginning'. The hedge remained uncut.

And then this. E-mails began arriving. Lots of them. Just under 1,000, in less than 20 minutes. As the e-mails marched up the screen like an invading army of ants, my jaw dropped ('kindly pick that jaw up, if you don't mind'). 600, 700, 800, 850 – at 902 they stopped. Or were they merely taking a breather?

Who had sent them, and to what purpose? Surely not that bloke in Seaton Sluice who said the column was rubbish?

Somewhere on my computer was a mechanism for simultaneous deletion. I had no idea where it was. I began deleting them individually.

As I click-click-clicked the delete button time over, there was a macabre if crazed sense of satisfaction. I was the mad soldier with the machine gun, screaming "die!" as he mows down the advancing enemy waves.

Hang on though. The e-mails began again. I broke out into a cold sweat (I prefer a warm sweat, but it's been chilly of late). This was the end.

More and more e-mails would swarm in, ten thousand, a million, a billion, five trillion. The computer would eventually blow up, and the e-mails would swarm onto the floor.

They would begin to devour the furniture, the walls, myself, then march off to meet the other trillions of swarming e-mails which had invaded every other computer, and were now uniting to ensure our total destruction. The day of judgement had arrived, Armageddon...

I pulled myself together (firstly picking up my jaw). I rang my friend Kate who understands the reasons for computers better than I.

She gave me a helpline number. A man with an Indian accent thicker than molasses answered. I managed to make out one word in ten. Something about disconnect the modem?

"And what about when I reconnect it? Won't all the new e-mails just be queuing up?"

We were growing irritated with one another and he said, "I will give you another helpline number to ring."

An instinct caused me to enquire how much this would cost. The answer was £1 a minute. I found myself wondering what the weather was like in Bombay.

I declined to ring helpline number two. I rang off, and disconnected the modem. I stared at the blank screen, knowing the computer was simply biding its time.

As I paced the room, my friend Meriel rang. "The same thing happened to me last week," she said, "I had 2,000 e-mails arrive before they stopped."

I took small comfort from this, at least they had ceased. For several hours I was hopelessly indecisive, casting furtive glances at the blank screen. Modern technology suddenly seemed baffling, hostile, and out of control.

"What's it all about?" I yelled to no one in particular. "What's the point?"

The swarming e-mails served no purpose, except irritation. They were of the 'failed message returned' school, from addresses unknown to me.

The mischief maker was not trying to sell me Viagra, shares in a Nigerian company, a new range of pills, soft porn or anything else. The exercise was futile.

I paced on. Had ten million years of evolution come to this? I grew nostalgic for benevolent inventions, such as the wheel, or the vacuum cleaner. No one had ever been invaded by vacuum cleaners.

I knew there was no alternative. Eventually I had to reconnect the cursed modem.

I did so, and rogue e-mails began to swarm once more onto the screen.

It was clearly the end of civilisation. So be it. It was our own fault. We had

self destructed.
Hang on though, a few dozen e-mails in, the invasion ceased. It ended as inexplicably as it had begun.
But the experience has left its mark. I now view the computer with deep suspicion. Is it sent to destroy us? Is it biding its time? Are we totally defenceless against its scheming?
As I plan a less stressful, less hi-tec future, I suddenly realise I am hugging close the vacuum cleaner.

Some fail to recognise Bambi, for others the problems are different

21st June 2007

CAN IT REALLY be September 2003 since this column last addressed the topic of pub quizzes? The popularity of quizzes, despite a few anomalies, remains undimmed. Such anomalies include the occasional deliberately unanswerable jackpot question.

How many freckles does Mel Gibson have (exact answer only wins), or how many breaths will the average vole take in a lifetime?

My own Achilles Heel remains the picture round, where I am likely to enquire, "not sure – is it Fidel Castro?", only to be told that it's Bambi.

Some quizzes lay on feasts of food, others eschew even a crisp. Running quizzes is exclusively male – I have yet to come across a female quizmaster (or mistress).

I prefer home-grown quizzes to the ubiquitous Quizgo, a kind of quiz bingo originally bought in to thwart the growing number of hustlers attracted by the soaring prize money.

In an increasingly alienated and lonely world, pub quizzes remain essential social glue, yet some geeks still scuttle off to the loo to seek answers on their mobile phones. They just don't get it.

My most frequented quiz venue of late has been the Briar Dene on Whitley Bay seafront (an accepted alternative spelling is Brier Dene).

It's an intelligent, well-thought through individualised quiz not over reliant on soaps or reality TV. The MC Harry brings the right mixture of gravitas and humour, and the participants' loyalty can see up to 30 teams taking part, some of whom have been so doing for 15 years. This year the Briar Dene celebrates its 1,000th quiz.

People donate prizes from their holiday trips, and Harry takes a keen interest in the teams' make-up, often highlighting a new group from Sunderland, or recently, (even more exotic), California, who presumably chartered a special flight to be there.

As with all quizzes, some answers are in dispute. Our own team's answer to the question, "What type of people lived on the island of Lilliputt?" was "The Lilliputians" (Gulliver's Travels being one of my favourite books) whereas the only accepted answer was "small".

Two aspects of the quiz are odd. Teams are given numbers rather than selecting their own name, which both denies them individuality, and robs participants of the chance of some topical creativity.

In the days when quizzes took place at The Queens Head, Cullercoats, a friendly rivalry developed between teams eager to find the name with the best contemporary humour. Thus, 'Erickson's Eunuchs' would be popular during the World Cup. There was also a certain pride to hear your team name announced among the front runners. Not quite the same when you're announced as "team fourteen."

The other oddity is this. No doubt prompted by motives of hospitality and fairness, the Briar Dene has a policy of highlighting certain teams as 'disadvantaged.' These are marked out for special prizes.

The first disadvantaged category is where there's only two people per team. As several teams include six or seven, this is a welcome helping hand for the occasional brace huddled in a corner.

The other disadvantaged category is if your team contains – wait for it – only females.

Yes, you did read that right. If your quiz team is wretchedly unlucky enough not to contain a single male of the species at the Briar Dene quiz, then you rank among the disadvantaged.

As far as I can tell, this rule has applied throughout the quiz's life, and, even in Britain of 2007, where sexual equality has been fought over, and in a great number of instances won, it goes unchallenged.

Now the news is out via this column, two possible consequences suggest themselves. One is a placard-bearing all-female team descending on the Briar Dene next week, demanding to be treated as equals.

Just as intriguing is the prospect of the same behaviour being manifested by an all-male team, demanding an equal 'disadvantaged' status, hence bigger chance of prizes. Or maybe nothing will happen at all, and maybe every Tuesday the loyal customers will trek to the pub quiz as usual, and not raise an eyebrow at the confirmation that to be born female is to be intellectually disadvantaged. As they say, only in the north east.

Monolith that stares at the North Sea, & silence that surrounds it...

28th June 2007

ROB WINGATE gets in touch about last week's column. He informs me that a female pub quiz master (or mistress) DOES exist hereabouts, albeit across the water.

The pub is the New Ship, in Cleadon, the quiz inquisitor is Janet. Her roots are in Cullercoats, and the quiz is each Tuesday.

Meantime the next Mortimer competition is in the 'I Remember When' category.

Readers of mature years are invited to send in their long-distant memories of Whitley Bay Station before the main exit was closed, and passengers could still walk straight out onto Station Road.

Such a luxury is deep in the mists of time, but have a go!

There's also a prize for any photograph depicting one or more human beings working on the new station flooring. Be patient, photographers – and you may get that rare snap!

This lack of human beings has been troubling me. I notice it round the new blocks of luxury flats that are spreading like a rash through our borough.

The common factor about such places is the lack of people. No kids are playing games, no-one is sitting out. No windows are open to reveal men in white vests singing along to Italian opera arias.

Are the residents glumly locked away watching more dreadful reality TV while their souls shrivel?

Can they relate to the world only via Google? Do they return from stressful jobs bearing Marks & Spencer meals for one, then lock the doors?

Such buildings suck the life from their surroundings. Take that recent arrival, the controversial Winslow Court on Cullercoats sea front.

This unappealing block of flats squats in the middle of our traditional seaside fishing village like some unwelcome guest at a party who no-one knows how to remove.

With its lack of balance, (four storeys on two sides, three on the other two), plus its zimmer frame balconies, it has all the aesthetic appeal of sour milk.

Already the TO LET signs are beginning to appear in the windows, indication that the buy-to-rent merchants are about their business. The odd lit window apart, there are no signs of life.

I long to see someone scurrying in and out with shopping bags, people sat outside in the warm weather with drinks and nibbles, children playing hopscotch. I long for the place to become at least partly human, and in some way redeem itself for replacing the very heart of the village – The Bay Hotel.

The building is a mausoleum in Cullercoats centre. It is a black hole. It is the dead zone. It is a loveless monument to the investors and speculators who have created it for their own financial gain.

Should you attempt to measure the heartbeat of this building, the ECG would flatline. The building stares out to sea with blank eyes. It is a cold behemoth.

We do not know why it is here. Yet here it is. Who in Cullercoats welcomed it? Thus, our democracy.

Sometimes I walk from my house to the seafront, momentarily forget the building's presence, then turn the corner. And shucks, there it is.

Who will ever speak warmly of it? Who will ever mention it, like the Watch House, Cliff House, or the old lifeboat station, as part of Cullercoats heritage? The Bay Hotel was.

Ironically, the block is both immovable and temporary. For while the solid Victorian grandeur of the Bay Hotel may have lasted another 500 years, modern buildings such as Winslow Court have no such aspirations to longevity. The Long Term is not a fashionable phrase. Ask any builder

Unfortunately, the monolith will not crumble away next week. It has plonked itself down like some alien spacecraft.

What happens when a building does not belong? When it is out of sync?

We can't ask it to leave. We can't change it like a jacket that isn't right. We can't send it back to the shop.

No doubt Cullercoats asked itself the same questions forty years ago, the

time of a similar blight. *Plus ca change.*
How do the Winslow Court residents feel?
If only I could find one, I'd ask.
Alas, they're as elusive as those Whitley Bay Station floor-layers.

No smoking in pubs and it's raining cats and dogs

5th July 2007

FIRSTLY, A small step for man, a larger step for womankind. News comes through from the Briar Dene pub, Whitley Bay (see this column June 21) that all-women teams will no longer be classed as disadvantaged. Hurrah!

Meantime, I found my friend Billy Bonkers in nostalgic mood. He was sat in the middle of his flooded living room in a large pair of wellies, a fishing rod in his hand.

"Caught anything, Billy?" I asked and he replied, "flu."

"How long ago those halcyon days seem now, Mortimer," he said.

"And what days would they be exactly, Billy?" I asked scooping up a cupful of water to throw out the window, a somewhat futile gesture as it was coming in through the open door.

"Surely you remember, the summers of hosepipe bans?" he said. "Water was so short we used to queue at the standpipes at the end of the street – that was a community spirit if ever I saw one! – and the newspapers were full of photographs of cracked and dried river beds."

"Sometimes I think those days were overrated," I replied, "Let's face it, it wasn't all fun."

"More fun than this lot," he said, "Did you go down to the Hoppings last week?"

"I would have done," I said, "but they'd let out all the motorised dinghies."

"They're still looking for the big wheel," said Billy. "Sank without trace."

I wondered what sinking with trace involved, but said nothing. Instead I commented, "Well Billy, it's all down to global warming. We've mucked about with, and exploited the planet so long, now we're paying the price."

"Balderdash!" he spluttered. There was a slight tug on his line. In excitement he played his adversary for a short time, then after a sharp yank came up with a damp Tetley tea bag on the hook.

"Do I take it Billy," I asked, "that you are one of the – admittedly dwindling – band of global warming sceptics?"

"What else has happened of late, Mortimer?" he asked.

My guesses included the sale of Newcastle United, Gordon Brown's coronation, and the comeback of The Spice Girls. Billy poo-pooed all three.

"It's obvious," he said, "it's the ban on smoking in public places."

"Yes," I said tentatively, "but I fail to see what that has got to do with you sitting in your wellies in a flooded living room."

"Stands to reason!" he boomed. "People are now being forced out of doors to smoke where normally they would have done so in nicotine choked rooms."

"Agreed," I said, still not quite getting his direction.

"The point being, Mortimer," he said, "the natural home for all that tobacco smoke is the small confined spaces of bars, offices, and other places of work, and now we are going against nature."

"Surely, Billy," I said, "you don't mean a few people standing outside smoking is causing this second age of the flood?"

"That's what I mean exactly," he said. He leant over and threw me an old cardie.

"Smell that!" he said. It stunk of tobacco and nicotine.

"Now smell this one I've worn in the pub since the ban," he said and chucked over a second. It smelt as fresh as a mountain breeze.

"So tell me this, all that tobacco that should be soaked into my second cardie, and millions of others like it, where is it now?" asked Billy.

"Well, I –"

"Released into the atmosphere that's where, and with the disastrous consequences we are seeing all around us. There are millions of people throughout the land, Mortimer, puffing away outside, when they should be puffing inside, and all that second-hand smoke that should be going into other people's lungs and impregnating clothes and the wallpaper – well, it's simply escaping into the air. Calamitous!"

It was not a theory that I'd heard expounded in higher scientific circles. I realised that while Billy was wearing wellies, I was not, and the damp by now had crept up to crotch level.

I began sloshing my way towards the door, while he stared in crazed fashion at the small bobbing hook, anticipating the excitement of another landed tea bag.

Best way to prepare yourself for a begrutten costermonger

12th July 2007

BEST EXAMPLE of self-destructive advertising this week? Tucked away behind Eldon Garden in Newcastle is a shop sign, 'R *Ormerod, Watch and Clock Repairs*' and next to it, the firm's own large clock. It's broken.

Meantime, I am approached in the Tynemouth Lodge pub by a fellow with the following query: "What is a costermonger?"

The Tynemouth Lodge is a watering hole I inadvertently failed to mention in my column of July 13, 2006, when I went off on my North Tyneside pushbike odyssey in search of that haven – a telly-free pub.

For the record, the Lodge is unencumbered by a single screen, plasma or otherwise, and unusual, even extreme behaviour is required by customers, i.e. real conversation.

The costermonger query was the second literary request of the week. I was also called upon to provide my favourite word, of which more in a moment.

Costermonger – one of those annoying words you've heard before but without much idea what it might be.

No-one else in the Lodge knew the answer. The man returned 15 minutes later to say Wickipedia defined a costermonger as a man (a sexist assumption surely?) who sells things from a street barrow.

My own check later was slightly less high-tech – I looked it up in volume one of the Shorter Oxford Dictionary – and revealed Shakespeare also uses the word in Henry IV, and that it can be a term of abuse.

I imagine a heated domestic row; as she loses her patience, the woman screams, "Get out! I never want to see you again, you monster, you insect, you unspeakable creature, – you – you – costermonger!"

Secondly, an e-mail enquiry from the splendid charity Education Action

International, compiling for fundraising purposes a selection of writers' favourite words.

Many people's vocabulary is now said to be limited, some using only a few hundred words from the half million or so knocking about.

A pity because spending the odd hour flicking through the pages of the OED in search of the wondrous and the obscure is fascinating stuff, albeit unlikely to replace watching Big Brother as a leading leisure pursuit.

One word for which I've always had an affection is 'sepulchral' meaning dismal, gloomy, melancholy, (happily my own character is none of these). Whenever I am about my travels, and there's somewhere or thing with even a hint of melancholia, be it a church or a mangy cat, I'm in like Flynn scribbling down 'sepulchral'.

It is not only the meaning of words that attracts, but also the sound, the phonetics, (itself quite a nice word).

This attraction is often for unlikely reasons; I'm intrigued by the rare word 'begrutten'. Phonetically it's a bit of an ugly duckling, hunched up in the corner. Matters don't improve much with the meaning. Begrutten means swollen in face by much weeping. I have to accept that 99.99 per cent of the population will go through their lives without once uttering or writing this word, even if confronted by a whole assembly of people whose unifying feature is being swollen in face by much weeping.

The response is more likely to be "Blimey – look at that lot!"

Which is why I ask you to speak it out loud, wherever you are, let it feel it has some small part to play in the linguistic life of our nation.

Ready?

"Begrutten."

Thank you.

And so to my chosen word. It is rather grandiose and with a sense of its own importance, but has a certain presence. It demands to be enunciated properly, without slurring. This word cannot sit in a sentence anonymously. It also feels very tall.

The word is 'stentorian'. It refers to the human voice, and means very loud and far reaching. My affection for it is perhaps explained by my own voice being very loud and far reaching (when Miss Fenwick fog horn fails down the coast, I am first choice replacement).

'Stentorian' has now made the pages of the *News Guardian*. This could be its liberation.

And rare words can be liberated, or dragged from obscurity. How many people a few years ago had ever heard of 'arachnophobia', or had much clue about 'Jurassic'? Then suddenly they were all over the place.
Dig up your own favourite (neglected) word today. And send it to me.

Football 'O' factor; every question is answered 'yes, that's right'

19th July 2007

MY APPEAL for cherished, if neglected words brings from Noreen Rees the following: ormolu (gold leaf gilding, a kind of bling substitute she suggests) and imbroglio (a confused heap – a state she sympathises with).

A card signed merely 'Joyce' says her English master, complaining of purple prose would employ 'grandiloquence' and 'bombast' – pompous or inflated language. Splendid words all.

Meantime, the press now call the Sunderland manager Keano. There is a long tradition of this. Newcastle's Peter Beardsley was tagged Beardo, which gave the impression he was well endowed with facial hair.

Footballers don't grow beards, though one hirsute specimen, (name of Dennis Mortimer incidentally), did play for Aston Villa.

Back to the 'O' factor. Is it merely for abbreviation? Possibly, except Keano has twice as many syllables as Keane.

Previous generations of footballers had more elaborate monickers. The press nicknamed Nat Lofthouse 'The Lion of Vienna' because of his onetime heroic exploits against Austria.

But did Nat ever walk into his local Bolton pub to be greeted with "Good morning Lion of Vienna – a pint of the usual today, is it?" Or did his nearest and dearest lean over the table and say, "Pass the brown sauce please, Lion of Vienna?"

Doubtful.

The media is also obsessed with tagging managers as 'big'. Newcastle United now have Big Sam Allardyce, and once there was talk of Big Ron Atkinson taking over. Being described as 'big' means you have a loud voice and are taller than 5ft 2ins (excuse my non-metric measurements, like many others I simply can't shake off feet and inches).

Rather than the ubiquitous 'big', most football managers would suit the adjective 'ugly'. This is because their faces could have been sketched by Goya. The features of any football manager, no matter how aesthetically pleasing and attractive on the onset of the career, slowly metamorphose into a gargoyle with the intolerable pressures of the job. Many look on the point of explosion.

Nicknames are given to sports people, but rarely attach themselves to chartered accountants. Why is this?

Because sports people are high profile, and required to be a source of endless news, gossip and feature items, the requirement is to make them media celebrities. This can be difficult when, outside their sports ability, they are often totally colourless.

One (misguided) tactic is the interminable post-match Saturday football interviews on BBC One, which employ the 'Yes, that's right' principle of reply. Listen closely to these interviews. Each question put to these overpaid, morose premier stars has a self-contained answer, and any sense this is a two-way conversation is mere illusion.

Example "Would you say David, that United today showed a great team spirit, and reminded us why they should not yet be written off in the title race?"

Superstar David pauses for a moment and replies "Yes, that's right."

Another piercing question follows on rapidly.

"Now then David, would you agree that the signing of Mel Custard from Barcelona has given a much-needed balance to your midfield which was probably lacking during the first half of the season?"

David pauses. He takes a swig from his high energy drink (£100 every time it appears on screen), adjusts his cap to make sure the sponsors' logo is well in view (£500), and with a small nod of the head replies "Yes, that's right."

The interview itself will have earned him an extra grand. He does not donate this to charity.

Interviewers are primed by their producers never to ask a question which does not fit the 'Yes, that's right' formula response, nor which is remotely provocative. Should any interviewer stray from this diktat he or she (almost always a 'he') would be sacked.

Thus you will never hear on Football Round-up the likes of, "Well, why did you break that full-back's leg with that appalling foul tackle?" or "Perhaps you could explain exactly why you need four Alfa Romeos, three Jaguars and a Porsche, especially after your three month ban for drunken driving?"

If they simply did away with these fatuous interviews, we'd have time for an extra Tom and Jerry cartoon. I rest my case.

See you next week. This is Big Morto signing off. Yes, that's right.

Lost on Metro – true significance of stuffed dogs and false legs

26th July 2007

METRO HELD a lost property auction last week, as they do every year. The auction took place in South Shields Market Place, and among the items auctioned were a paddling pool, a garden fork, a bag of grass seed and a bicycle.

Previous items that have come under the hammer include several wigs, a stuffed dog, a false leg and a kitchen sink.

You couldn't make this kind of thing up, but as a playwright with a penchant for the theatre of the absurd, I may as well have a go.

THE SCENE IS A DOMESTIC INTERIOR, ENTER MAN
MAN: I'm home, beloved.
WOM: You're late.
MAN: Oh, delays on the Metro, you know the kind of thing.
WOM: Hang on – look at you!
MAN: What do you mean?
WOM: Well, just look at you, you're as bald as a coot!
MAN: What? Oh damn! Must have lost the wig when I fell asleep. It was so hot.
WOM: Tell me about it! Me and little Tootsie have been waiting all day to jump into that paddling pool (ENTER TOOTSIE, EXCITED)
TOOT: Paddly, paddly, paddly!
WOM: Left it in the garden, did you?
MAN: What?
WOM: You did buy one of those special offer paddling pools from B&Q?

MAN: Oh, yes, of course!
TOOT: Paddly, paddly, paddly!
WOM: So where is it?
MAN: Damn! I knew I shouldn't have put it down to help that old lady off at Howdon! (TOOTSIE BURSTS INTO TEARS)
WOM: Now see what you've done. Well, your tea's in the oven, but probably dried up by now. It'll be caked on the plate, which will be terribly hard to wash. Thank goodness for that new kitchen sink. I can't believe you broke the last one trying to clean your 1000cc Yamaha in it.
MAN: I didn't realise motorbikes were so heavy.
WOM: So where is the new sink?
MAN: Hang on, I know it was still there when I last looked at Walkergate...
WOM: You left it on the Metro, didn't you? Along with the wig!
TOOT: Paddly! Paddly! Paddly! (STARTS BITING FATHER'S LEG. ENTER YOUNG SON DIRK WITH FOOTBALL)
DIRK: Hi dad! Time for penalties!
WOM: I told you Dirk, your father needs to sow that new lawn first. But he did promise to do it this evening, so the grass should be sprouting up pretty soon, and you can shoot all the penalties you want.
DIRK: Bend it like Dirk! Bend it like Dirk! (GETS VERY EXCITED)
MAN: Erm – well, you see, the thing is this, son –
WOM: You do have the bag of grass seed?
MAN: I put it down for a moment to ward off this gang of charvers and –
WOM: Oh my God, I don't believe it! (DIRK STARTS BAWLING AND BEATS THE EASY CHAIR WITH HIS FISTS)
DIRK: Dirk want penalties! Dirk want penalties!
TOOT: Paddly! Paddly! Paddly! (BITES HIS OTHER LEG)
WOM: You lost your wig, you forgot the paddling pool, you mislaid the grass seed, is there anything else you failed to bring home?
MAN: (FIGHTING OFF HIS DAUGHTER AND RESTRAINING HIS SON) Of course not – just who do you think I am?
WOM: The salmonella sausage?
MAN: Got it!
WOM: The cod liver oil cookies?
MAN: Right here!
WOM: The boil-in-the-bag lettuce?

MAN: Safe and sound!
WOM: (CALMING DOWN SLIGHTLY) Well, at least that's something. At least you're not totally and utterly useless.
MAN: Thank you dear. I'll just go and freshen up (WALKS OUT OF ROOM)
WOM: Wait a minute, why are you hopping? Why is your right trouser leg flapping like a flag? And why only one shoe?
MAN: Oh, no! I never noticed, I mean I thought my left leg was getting a bit tired, but –
WOM: I don't believe it – you've left your false leg on the Metro!
MAN: I only unscrewed it for a minute to scratch my back, I must have –
WOM: Pathetic! And how on earth will a one-legged man take penalties with his son? Or play with his daughter without a paddling pool?
(CHILDREN START BAWLING AND BITING AGAIN)
Get out! Do you hear me – out! (MAN HOPS OFF)
END OF PLAY

How I discovered time travel between kitchen and living room...

2nd August 2007

FAVOURED NEGLECTED words continue to arrive from readers. An anonymous note suggests 'mugwump', which was once a craft shop in Durham City, but means an independent in politics.

The word is said to derive from the US Republican in 1884 who refused to support the official candidate.

George (no surname) puts forward 'proctoheliosis', with a photocopied dictionary entry showing the root as 'procto', the lower bowel, and 'helios', the sun, hence a condition of someone believing the sun shines from their backside.

Nice attempt George, and for *Ingenious Hoax of the Week,* a box of liquorice allsorts is winging its way to you.

Meantime, the new No Smoking law brings a curious situation. On the odd fine day of late, I've sat down outside various coastal watering holes, the better to enjoy the sunshine, but such is the excess of al fresco fumigators, I've been driven indoors in search of fresh air!

Another curio presents itself. I am a self-confessed radio addict with a set in every room. No sooner do I enter any room than I switch on the radio. My favourite station is *Radio 4,* unkindly described last week as the sound of old ladies knitting. I also like *Planet Rock,* despite its tendency to wallow in a fictitious rock Golden Age.

I exercise to *Radio 3,* vastly superior to the easy-on-the-ear tosh of *Classic FM;* there's nothing like a blast of Hindemith to aid the stretching.

Regular *Radio 4* listeners will know the anomalies between Medium Wave and FM. For some reason, though *Radio 4* is not a sport channel, and an identical service is available on *Five Live,* the Medium Wave surrenders itself to test match cricket for five days at a time.

The two frequencies split for other programmes too: morning service, shipping forecast, yesterday in Parliament etc. But for most of the time, they're identical – or are they?

Try this small experiment. In adjacent rooms, and when the programme is the same on both frequencies, have one radio on *Radio 4* FM, and one on *Radio 4,* Medium Wave.

Move speedily between rooms. What do you notice? Yes, that's right, FM is about two seconds ahead of MW.

It is perfectly possible to move from the FM room into the MW room and catch the same words a second time.

By now you are concluding that your correspondent has a pretty sad life if his main social activity is moving between rooms to hear the same programme. But indulge me!

There is one sacrosanct moment on *Radio 4,* and it is the pips, the time signal that to the nano-second fixes the hour as that of Greenwich Mean Time (GMT). GMT is Holy Writ. It was to Greenwich that the entire world looked as the new millennium approached. All other world times are based on the Greenwich Meridian.

We may now be a second-rate nation, full of obese sullen neurotics addicted to anti-depressants, we may be brain-dead through an endless succession of reality television shows, our children may be shooting at each other with large guns, half of us may be paying impossibly high mortgages on houses under four feet of water, and Sunderland may well be about to eclipse Newcastle United.

But we can still be proud of GMT and the pips! And there is never a delay in sounding the pips. I have known an errant programme, over-running its time, to be faded out to allow the pips to sound.

Highly sensitive equipment is involved in accurately fixing GMT. It is an exact science.

But where does this FM/MW anomaly leave us?

If the pips can sound in one room, then slightly later in another, what is the real time? Is it the one? Or is it the other? Or somewhere in between? Does anybody know?

Why is there a time lag between FM and Medium Wave in the first place? Do the staggered pips mean the end of civilisation as we know it? Is it all relative? Would Einstein have anything to say?

Confusion reigns. And I await enlightenment. Some time or another.

Fringe benefits of coming to terms with disaster as the show goes on

9th August 2007

MINNEAPOLIS, Tuesday

IMAGINE THE Tyne Bridge suddenly plunging into the river. Yet post-bridge disaster, life goes on in Minneapolis, as somehow it goes on post-disaster anywhere.

Fans flock to the *Twins* baseball game, and also to the banks of the Mississippi to get glimpses of the tangled wreckage of their once-great bridge. Here, ice-cream sellers do good business, because that's how things are.

Our Somali taxi driver is discreetly chewing the stimulant leaf, qat. He's intrigued I know about qat from my time spent travelling in Yemen, and straightaway makes me a business proposition.

If I bring in two suitcases of qat at a time via London, all expenses will be paid, and I'll earn $1,500 dollars per trip.

I work out that six trips would provide enough dosh to bring our theatre company Cloud Nine over for the Minnesota Fringe Theatre Festival (which is what son Dylan and I have travelled to see). Or maybe not.

But life goes on. This is the biggest fringe in the USA, ten days, 162 shows, 850 performances in 22 venues; still small compared to Edinburgh, but with a warmer heart. And all these people busting a gut to entertain us, somehow seems the right kind of celebratory response to what's happened.

So we walk and bike round the city, gobbling down four shows a day.

Before the al fresco performance of *Queene Margaret,* three Shakespeare history plays condensed into an hour, and staged in a busy open car park against a background of police sirens and trains, audience members who've travelled via bus, bike or foot are given two dollars apiece for their green credentials.

When the rain comes down, free brollies are handed out and post-show the audience is invited into the Bedlam theatre building for warming – and also free – tea and coffee.

Every fringe show costs $12 (just over £6), none lasts more than an hour, and a pass for the entire festival is $140 – seventy-five quid, which you might blow in a day of theatre-going in Edinburgh.

An army of volunteers backs up the professional admin, and while participants (and audiences) are still predominantly white in this increasingly multicultural city, and there's too little activity out on the streets, this is still a fringe dedicated to theatre, unlike Edinburgh which has sold out to the mammons of stand-up.

Minneapolis, a city as flat as a pool table, and with huge seasonal weather extremes, abounds with theatres, in posh districts and poor districts, often imaginatively converted from old warehouses and flour mills, with such names as Mixed Blood, The Soap Factory, Jungle, Bedlam, Joe's Garage, Circle of Discipline.

The impressive Theatre de La Jeune Lune recently won a coveted Tony Award, while The Playwrights Centre declares itself 'scent-free' for the festival – (no deodorants or after-shave), and Bryant-Lake has a bowling alley attached. More people go to theatre per capita in Minneapolis than any US city other than New York.

British perceptions of the USA sometimes conjure Eastern and Western seaboards populated by talented, interesting and affluent people, but between the two, a great lump of land in which dwell the rednecks and the hicks.

Minneapolis, a vibrant cultural city full of parks and lakes, belies this. While the adjacent twin city St Paul is the state capital, Minneapolis has the larger population, and even in these dazed post-disaster days seems a laid-back community at ease with itself.

Dylan and I are festival spectators, not participants, but such is the curiosity generated by his Geordie accent, he could stage a street corner one-man show just by spouting out loud. Hadaway, Dylan man.

There are few good vantage points to see the collapsed 35W bridge, previously the city's main artery across the Mississippi, (which we tend to think of as a Southern states river, but is already big and wide up here near the Canadian border).

One busy spot is the strange protruding appendage up high on the massive new temple to the city's theatre life, The Guthrie Complex.

Called the Never-Ending Bridge, this sticks out maybe 70 metres from the main building. People stand on the extremity of this artificial bridge that ends in mid-air, to view the wreckage of another bridge that now, tragically and accidentally, does exactly the same thing.

And meantime, elsewhere throughout the city, the shows must go on.

Seduced by showmanship as Newcastle prepare to save world...

16th August 2007

I RETURN FROM Minneapolis to a backlog of readers' letters numbering at least two. John Morgan writes to say that that the 'time shift', happens not only between different radio stations but also between analogue and digital TV.

Plus which, it occurs on the internet says John, where it is impossible to get your computer time to marry up with Big Ben or the pips. He tells of a computer company which abandoned a major contract because the various systems involved failed to agree what time it was. Ah, technology!

Meantime, my column on obscure words (July 12) continues to draw a response.

North Tyneside activist and stalwart Ylana First discovers in the 1980 Penguin edition of Roget's Thesaurus the word 'lyophilize', meaning to refrigerate. It is not in my own edition of Thesaurus, nor my two volume OED, and this may well be the rare bird's first-ever outing in a periodical, which makes me tempted to write it again. Lyophilize.

I also return home to Newcastle United's winning start to the season, a victory that has caused several local pundits to predict them winning the Premier League by at least 12 points, followed next year by the European Cup, and soon thereafter their solving of global warming.

Such optimism I put down to the departure of Freddie Shepherd. The man was clearly overweight, and obviously ran out of puff well before 90 minutes were up.

Whizzing across the Atlantic twice in ten days not only leaves a carbon footprint as big as the Yeti's (my air flights are severely limited these days dear reader), but also turns the brain into a damp cloth. For 18 hours I was able to utter only the word 'glung' (not to be found in the OED).

My own recent anti-American sentiments, bred by a corrupt fool of a president and an outrageous immoral war, were tempered by Minneapolis, a cultured, pleasant and courteous city.

One memory is of their open and friendly exchanges, both on a personal level and in shops and stores, where staff seem imbued with an almost childlike delight to be of assistance.

Contrast this with our own outlets where customers are often met with a sullen indifference, a shrugged reluctance to be of any real help, a glazed and bored look, often from young and pimply staff for whom the work seems to be nine levels of torture invented by Dante.

Why the contrast? Have our own management deliberately chosen the least experienced (and therefore cheapest) work force, invested them with no training (which costs money) and provided them with dreadful working conditions?

And if so, should we really be surprised that the staff take it out on the customers?

Be advised oh retail giants, it is a false economy! If the staff loathe their employers, they will not love those they are supposed to serve. Who in time will go elsewhere.

Meantime, and for no particular relevance, I mention one Minneapolis image that stays in the mind.

In the Calhoun district on a street corner pavement (sidewalk in their lingo), sat a beggar, a vagrant, a tramp, a vagabond a bum, a hobo, a loafer, a cadger, a borrower, a mendicant, a schnorrer (sorry, the Thesaurus was still on the desk).

His hat was in front of him he held a piece of cardboard on which were neatly written the words, 'Why Lie? It's for Drink.'

This was a touch of brio (nice word), a cheekiness which I guess only the Americans could carry off. He did not seem a defeated victim.

Yet either the man was lying, in which case he had no right to ask for loot, or he was telling the truth, in which case he was wanting the public to feed what may have been an addiction.

He smiled at passers-by so disarmingly, and those same passers-by (including Dylan and myself) were so amused, that we laughed, exchanged a few words, then tossed coins into the hat without a second thought.

Only later did I think it was maybe this same sense of showmanship that seduced Blair, and caused him so uncritically to throw coins into Bush's hat, when objectively it was such a bad idea.

Figures in a landscape; how Whitley flags up its own idea

23rd August 2007

THE FINAL WORD (literally) in the obscure/interesting words saga. John Morgan offers 'syzygy' (yoke, pair), no vowels, and from six letters three are 'y'. Good 'un. Meantime, the world's media, plus the public, flock to Newbiggin-by-the-Sea to observe Sean Henry's new large offshore sculpture, Couple.

It's the first of its kind in the country. Newbiggin has not had such publicity since a goat ran amok in the High Street (I just made that up). We need something similar in Whitley Bay. The sculpture that is, not the goat.

Such events bring a buzz to a place. Recent plans for our own fair town rely not on creative artists but commercial developers.

Commercial developers rarely set the pulses racing when they put their blueprints on the table. This is possibly because their main motivation (unlike creative artists) is profit.

Not all public works of art set the heart beating. North Tyneside commissioned the crane sculpture Tyne Anew which stands on the river bank.

It's pretty pathetic, and rendered insignificant by the real shipyard cranes it is meant to celebrate. Soon, Tyne Anew will be the only crane left, so maybe we'll all notice it more then.

So where is the coast's big bold piece of public art? The area is a haven for creative artists; someone should be getting them out of bed to build something to stir our blood.

Something like the Angel of the North, which, incredibly, has now been with us a decade, and which, along with The Sage, Baltic, and Millennium Bridge, made people sit up and take Gateshead seriously. Previously the town was a joke, an eyesore festering on the wrong side of the river to the 'real' Tyneside, its only well-known monument being Brendan Foster.

Admittedly, in a poll last week the angel was voted the second least satisfactory tourist attraction in the country. But this is tosh. Significantly, this poll was run by a travel company. Now one attraction of the Angel is that it remains gloriously uncommercialised: no cafe and gift shop attached, no night-time floodlights, no guided tours. It's just there, so go and see it if you want. There's not much profit in this for a travel firm.

(Readers at this juncture are referred to my own poem celebrating the Gateshead icon, titled *I Married the Angel of the North*. 'A tour de force' – Pig Breeders' Weekly.)

Not that Whitley Bay is without new structures. Bang in the town centre, attached to the Coliseum, two new flag poles have appeared. What is their purpose? Will said poles soon sport the distinctive Northumbrian red and yellow flag, affirmation that Whitley Bay is indeed part of the historic county of Northumberland, thereby banishing to deserved oblivion the functional sounding 'Tyne and Wear'?

(Think of all the haunting music and poetry that includes the word Northumberland. Now name anything similar which embraces the three words Tyne and Wear.)

Or will the first fluttering cloth be the Union, or St George's flag? Thus far, no flags. And if you stand waiting for the first flag to be hoisted on these (admittedly short) poles, your wait may be a long one. There won't be any. These are not flag poles, but mobile phone masts. Admittedly, they do not look like mobile phone masts. Which, I suggest, m'lud, is the point of the exercise.

Consider if you will, the recent history of mobile phone masts at the coast. Cullercoats Action Group launched a vigorous and eventually successful campaign to prevent T-Mobile erecting a mast outside the Metro Station. The company have now turned their attention to Tynemouth, but this grassroots democracy business is proving costly and bothersome for them.

So what do O2 do? Construct smaller masts exempt from normal legal restrictions, (no messy petitions) and for good measure make them resemble flag poles. Who on earth ever objected to a flagpole?

Thus creative thinking of a sort is in evidence at the coast, and, like Newbiggin, we have two new structures on public display.

But whether the world's media (or public) will flock to celebrate phone masts disguised as flag poles is another matter.

This course can change your life as autumn approaches!

30th August 2007

AUTUMN APPROACHES, and with it the wonders of adult education. In those dark hours when we feel it's all up with the world, consolation comes from knowing thousands of people are signing up for flower arranging, dog grooming or Etruscan for Beginners.

All of which must be better (as Janis Joplin put it) than sitting in some goddam chair, watching television.

Thus I find myself browsing through the *News Guardian* for courses offered in Seaton Valley.

Choices include Level 2 Cake Decorating (a two-tier cake presumably?) plus Emergency Aid for Appointed Person. What happens if emergency aid is required for a non-appointed person?

"Quick, this man's leg is virtually severed and pumping blood! Emergency aid immediately!"

"Hang on, is he an appointed person?"

"Afraid not."

"Then tell him to hop off."

Courses are run at Seaton Valley Community Education Centre, and those signing up get a free buffet.

My favourite course (and you couldn't make this up) is called Ladies Non-Swimming Club. This spans ten weeks and costs £23. Sessions last

45 minutes.

Since reading this, despite matters elsewhere of great importance, I have been able to think of little else. Were I the right sex, I would be enrolling immediately.

As it is, I have to be content with the imagination...

(ENTER COURSE LEADER)

C.L: Right – everyone here? Good. First of all, has anyone done any non-swimming before?

(VERA'S HAND GOES UP)

VERA: I once went to Bamburgh for a day and reclined on the golden sands.

C.L: But you didn't actually go in the sea to swim?

VERA: No. I had a beetroot sandwich and a rock bun, and came home at 4pm.

C.L: Hmm, anyone with a more committed experience of non-swimming?

(ANN'S HAND GOES UP)

ANN: I went to Tynemouth baths, changed into my cossie, fitted my snorkel and stayed in the changing cubicle for two hours.

C.L: Much more positive!

(JANE'S HAND)

JANE: I'm a bit confused. Does non-swimming involve going in the water or not?

C.L: Good question. Probably easier if not. Once in the water, any movement could be classed as swimming, and disqualify you. Read the leaflet *Non Swimming in Ten Easy Lessons*. In theory a woman could just walk down the street and say, "Hey, I'm non-swimming!" Another could be simply lying in bed with a mug of cocoa, and claim, "Look at me, I'm non-swimming!" But it's best be in the proximity of water at least.

JANE: Now I'm even more confused.

VERA: Perhaps you could give us an example to make it all clearer?

C.L: Of course. Take the case of Mrs Thelma Fudge, who is probably the most celebrated non-swimmer in the UK. I wouldn't be here today without the inspiration of Thelma Fudge, a pioneer, an advanced thinker, a free spirit, an adventurer, a –

ANN: So what did she do?

C.L: Thelma Fudge travelled down to Dover beach, donned her specially designed cossie, coated herself from head to toe in goose grease, put on her close fitting goggles and bathing cap, turned to the waiting cameras to give the thumbs-up sign, turned back to face the hostile sea, walked boldly towards that unforgiving element –

ANN: And?

C.L: And a few feet from the water's edge she stopped. Already over in Calais they were making preparations to welcome this brave cross-channel swimmer.

But Thelma Fudge was even braver than they imagined.

JANE: She never went in the water!

C.L: Exactly! For ten hours Thelma Fudge stood there, adjusting her position only slightly to accommodate the changing tide. And thereby became the highest profile non-cross-channel swimmer there has ever been.

VERA: That kind of level must take training and dedication.

C.L: Of course. Nothing comes without discipline.

JANE: How can non-swimming help us in our everyday lives?

C.L: Good question. Firstly, socially; non-swimmers tend to mix with other non-swimmers. And the Civil Service now recognises HDNS as a valuable qualification.

ANN: HDNS?

C.L: Higher Diploma for Non-Swimming.

VERA: Is it a disadvantage if you once actually learned to swim?

C.L: It makes it harder naturally, but not impossible.

JANE: Will my previous course be of any use?

C.L: What was it?

JANE: Non-basket-weaving.

C.L: Every little helps. Now, if we could just fill in the register?

The string theory of the universe ensures a well-trimmed lawn

6th September 2007

I WAS DOING a spot of gardening. This is rare. The previous occasion was the same day I'd watched Bobby Moore lift the World Cup for England. Gardening is a wonderful zen-like activity, both physical and mental, a oneness with nature that nurtures soil and soul.

Except I hardly ever get round to it. Nor know much about it. "That species there, is it a hydrangea?" I asked a neighbour recently.

"That's your drainpipe," he replied.

Last year, in a fit of commitment, I bought a pair of gardening gloves. One has gone missing.

My garden is little larger than a postage stamp, my lawn so small that for two people to sunbathe they need to take turns.

Strangely enough, other Mortimers have green fingers, (it's all those mushy peas they eat by hand). A childhood memory is the comforting noise of the lawnmower pushed back and forth of a balmy evening by some family member.

How reassuring this was! I would take a deep breath and sing in resonant tones, "There'll always be an England," at which point neighbours would throw a bucket of water on me.

Manual mowers have mainly disappeared, that same laziness that has made the TV remote the norm. Some people have motor mowers; more popular is the strimmer.

Strimmer sounds like the name of a punk rock hero. I have just co-purchased one with partner Kitty, whose own lawn is equally minuscule.

Examining the strimmer's underbelly I was amazed to see it consisted basically of a revolving circular centre piece from which dangled a short length of wire, or plastic covered string. No blades, no sharp edges.

How can a piece of string cut the grass? Yet it does. The strimmer decapitated every blade of grass in no time.

Unlike an old-fashioned mower, whose flashing circling blades throw up green arcs of grass, the strimmer operates in secret, whirring away within its plastic cover. Yet the principle is obvious. The string/wire whizzes around, and the grass is cut.

I wanted to know how it worked. I cut myself a length of string and began flailing the grass with it. The grass merely bent backwards, then righted itself soon after.

I tried thicker string, wire, even a short length of rope. The grass was unimpressed, and, more relevantly, undecapitated.

In desperation I took a piece of string, tied it round a single blade of grass, and pulled the knot tight. It failed to decapitate the grass.

I found myself wondering how Mr Strimmer first came upon the invention. Was he sitting one day on his lawn with a cup of tea when lateral thinking took over?

"You know Mrs Strimmer," he would have shouted through the open window, "I think a piece of string would cut the lawn much quicker than a conventional mower."

A large anguished groan would be heard from inside the house. Eliza Strimmer was a long sufferer of her husband's madcap inventions, all of which thus far had failed to lift them from their two-up two-down in the more rundown part of Girdle Bassett.

How could Eliza forget her husband's anti-gravity ice-cream, designed to prevent dollops accidentally falling from cones? Or the boomerang hat, said to return of its own accord if blown off the head in a gale? He had genuinely believed his tins of striped paint would be a winner, but no.

Nor was there much more success for his edible furniture which you simply ate when you wanted a decor change.

"Isambard," she would have replied patiently, if a little wearily, "it is a common law of science that to cut, to incise, or to sever requires the services of metal, and sharp metal at that."

A lesser man would have left it there, concluded that his inventions were charming if useless, and dedicated his life to something unremarkable such as wage clerking. Not so Isambard Strimmer.

He broke the mould. He dispensed with metal and sharp blades. In future grass would be cut with a dangly bit.

So revolutionary was this, that Isambard Strimmer's name is now spoken in hushed tones in every branch of B&Q – at least it is if you can find a sales assistant to speak it to.

In the footsteps of Orwell, without malfunctioning bulb

13th September 2007

A FEW WEEKS ago I bought a low energy, long-life bulb guaranteed to last a minimum of 10,000 hours. "Mind," I said to the shop assistant, "if this only lasts 9,500 hours, I want my money back!" She smiled (slightly patronisingly, as I recall).

On Wednesday the bulb packed up.

In the same week a hi-tech thief raided our theatre company's internet account and made off with a big bag of money (which the bank is now replacing).

Myself and technology, who are never the best of bedfellows, at present seem as well-matched a couple as Margaret Thatcher and Arthur Scargill (remember them?).

It is time to scuttle off to a place where a firewall is something you lay the kindling against, and megabytes give way to midges' bites.

How about the island of Jura?

Jura is not the easiest place to reach: a seven-hour car journey from Tyneside to the west coast of Scotland, circumnavigating various lochs, followed by a two-hour ferry to Islay, then a second short ferry to Jura itself.

There's no quick route. Few people live on the island, and there's only one road which stops five miles short of Barnhill, the remote cottage where, in 1946 to 1949, George Orwell (who was already dying of TB) exiled himself to finish his great novel 1984. Barnhill is the destination of my partner Kitty and me.

I have an affinity with George Orwell, having exiled myself for a winter on Holy Island some six years ago. This also led to a book which has sold slightly fewer copies than 1984, but hey – it's early days!

Orwell visited Jura more than 60 years ago, but the island probably looks little different now. The human population has declined to 200, though there are 6,000 deer. These splendid creatures attract regular visits from the unspeakable people who hunt them.

The original intention was to wing this column back from Jura, following the long tradition of Mortimer at Large finding its way home from all points of the compass.

Did I not, in my dedication to file copy, master the mysteries of a Yemeni internet cafe which every ten minutes changed my text into Arabic? Was the dateline only the other week not Minneapolis? Were there not columns from Rome, Ireland, Northern Italy, and yes, even Rotherham? Not to mention Ravenstonedale on the Cumbrian border, or deepest Bellingham.

But Jura has defeated me. Short of taking a carrier pigeon, the task is impossible.

Barnhill has no mains electricity, merely a battered old generator which might just have the strength to power the cottage's light bulbs (10,000 hours or not). No landline phone, no computers, no internet, TV or radio. To reach the island's only small village is a 20-mile journey, some of it over bumpy rough tracks.

Given the mountainous terrain (the three main mountains are vividly called The Paps of Jura), in many parts of the island you may as well hold an ice lolly to your ear as a mobile phone, for all the signal you're likely to get. So no Jura dateline.

Barnhill overlooks the sea close to Corryvreckan, the world's second most powerful whirlpool into which George Orwell was almost sucked.

This would have meant no *1984* – a very bad thing. But without that brilliant book, what would they have called those two television programmes *Big Brother*, and *Room 101*, for Orwell is their source?

For the seven days on Jura, it's probable we will not glimpse another human being.

This is an interesting thought, as the human species spends half its time desperately seeking out the sociability of others, and the remaining half trying to shun them.

Why we can both loathe and adore our fellow humans I am not sure.

I am the gregarious type, yet the loneliness and remoteness of Jura also appeals.

Is this pure romanticism? Or, after seven days will Kitty (who is much better at isolation than me) need to wheel me home in a Hannibal Lecter straitjacket, while I garble gibberish?

Possibly we may become hermits. Or start a novel called *2012*. Or arrive back home with a large (live) deer. More of this anon. Westward Ho!

No new baths for old on the island that time forgot

20th September 2007

THE ISLAND of Jura has defeated us humans; we retreat, admitting our failure to live with nature. In the 19th century there were once almost 1500 people on the island. Now it's less than 200 ; we've slunk off to cities and shopping malls, we've rushed away to stress ourselves out with hi-tec junk, traffic jams and credit card overload.

We look at Jura's staggering, if often harsh beauty, and say "aah!", put it in a picture frame and zoom off to live our crazy lives elsewhere.

London has a population density of 12,000 people per square mile. In Jura it's one. Not one thousand, just one, the least populated place in Europe.

It is the only large island round our shores without its own mainland ferry service.

In the remote cottage of Barnhill, George Orwell's home while writing 1984, and temporarily that of my partner Kitty and me, we stare at the deep claw footed cast-iron bath, and wonder if it's the same bath used by the great writer 60 years ago.

Of course it is. Imagine bringing another bath here.

More than three hours tortuous roads from Glasgow to the mainland ferry terminal. Two hours crossing to Islay, then another ferry across the sound to Jura, then 20 miles of Jura's only road, followed by five miles deep rutted track accessible only by a 4x4, on foot or by horse. A new bath ain't easy.

But then Jura ain't easy, its terrain often boggy and inaccessible, its weather wild and constantly changing; it has midge armies, its terrible tics lay siege to both us and Polly the dog. On arriving home I found yet another tic burrowing to lay its eggs in my navel.

And the cottage is no soft holiday home. The furniture is old and lumpen, the doors painted the same dull dark brown as the brackish water that coughs from the taps.

It is damp, and clothes (washed by hand) take forever to dry. The floorboards creak and groan, some of the poorly painted walls have strange growths. No mains electricity, no TV, no phone.

Yet after a few days this matters little. I sit in the same deep window where Orwell wrote his masterpiece.

I look down at the azalea bush he planted 60 years ago. Orwell came here to rediscover himself. For most of us it's probably too late.

The rough pasture land slopes down towards a boggy wood, and then the small bay and a sea of myriad shapes, patterns and colours, and beyond the empty sea, the wild Scottish mainland, drifting in and out of the mist like some half snatched memory.

The sea moves sideways here, tugged by the ferociously strong tides that journey between these islands.

Older inhabitants still speak of the islands, not as separate entities, but as 'linked by the sea'.

The white-washed Barnhill cottage is a speck in infinity, a tiny presence in a huge mountainous landscape unchanged in centuries, the silence so total and uninterrupted that our city-blasted ears invent noises in compensation.

A mile's rough walk to the only other house at this island's northern extremity throws up golden eagles, wild goats and a bobbing seal. By the track, the deep drainage ditch reveals black soil which glistens, sweats and drips, an island so saturated you fear it may sink.

Entrepreneurs try to drag Jura into modernity. Attempts to launch a direct ferry service have been resisted by locals, an insularity that both preserves and condemns them, depending on your stance.

In the island's only village, Craighouse, The Jura Hotel (accurately defined as 'the only place to drink on Jura!') learned the AA and RAC ratings could only be preserved if the bedrooms were fitted with televisions and phone. The manager declined.

Moves to install high-powered street lights were also resisted by villagers fearful of losing their unique pollution-free night skies, whose dimensions of stars stretch back to infinity.

Maybe Jura is an anachronism, side-lined by history, attractive only from a distance, a wild hostile place best left to documentary makers. Or maybe it teaches us we have lost something.

Whatever, after five days of basic frugal living, tics or no tics, both Kitty and I discovered new ideas for a book.

George O – thank you.

Big Top as against Big Brother in pursuit of a lost childhood

27th September 2007

OFF TO BEACONSFIELD, Tynemouth to see Uncle Sam's American Circus. Who actually was Uncle Sam by the way? The thought struck me at the show's end, when to a large musical fanfare, a 15ft high replica of the guy strode into the Big Top. The applause was muted. Maybe we Brits don't go in for this cheerleading stuff so much, or maybe it was Iraq.

When I was a kid, circuses were full of wild beasts, and smelt differently. Then came the campaign to stop 'cruelty to dumb animals'. Quite right too, but what did 'dumb' mean?

Not silent, surely. Dumb meaning stupid? Hey, which species exactly is threatening to wipe out our planet – performing seals or human beings? So careful with that adjective 'dumb.'

The animals have gone. I'm not sure the circus has found a suitable replacement.

Especially with no trapeze, or high-wire, without which the Big Top seemed – well, too big. It swallowed up the performers.

I once interviewed a lion trainer. I wish I hadn't. He had frayed cuffs, which somehow diluted the magic.

I later wrote a short poem, now to be inflicted on you.

The bearded lady's looking tired
The juggler is all spent
I caught the circus clown
Smoking Players behind the tent

As a spotty nipper, I marvelled at the circus film *The Greatest Show on Earth*, which starred the concrete jaw of Charlton Heston. I wanted to run away to the circus. Everyone did.

The school careers master was a dead loss, and suggested instead a job in the wages department of Boots head office, where most of we Nottingham laddos ended up.

Maybe we leave circus behind with childhood; there's a sense that every adult in the audience is merely a child escort, a detached observer, trying to respond in a way that being grown-up makes impossible.

Yet I'm intoxicated by this small travelling army of giant lorries and caravans, trundling round the country and pitching camp to raise their extraordinary marquee, performing, then moving on. They're medieval troubadours, gloriously out of time. I want to create theatre like this.

The clowns are as sinister as ever. I'm still frightened by their huge trousers, oversized grinning mouths, long boots curling up at the toe cap. I don't want them to come near.

Yet a couple of clowns here are no older than seven. Seven! Surely they should be doing normal kid things, drinking alcopops, brandishing knives?

In the interval the clowns move round the audience selling merchandise. This cheapens them somehow, but the circus has to make ends meet. Kids are also urged to get their faces painted, have their photos taken with Spiderman and Buzz Lightyear, (who don't really belong in a circus) or buy raffle tickets for £2, the prize for which is a giant cuddly toy. They parade around three giant cuddly toys as prizes, but the trick is only one gets won.

Another trick is the music, which sounds live, thanks to the presence of a drummer. But he's banging away alone. All the rest is taped. Do the children in the audience notice such sleights of hand? Of course not.

The ringmaster has no top hat. He's a small bullish man, bald head shaved at the sides, a pigtail, one gold earring. He has an outfit like some brash Las Vegas gambler (black shirt and trousers, gold lame waistcoat), the gravelly voice of Schnozzle Durante (remember him?) and the face of Spencer Tracey (how about him?). His accent is New York gangster, and he pronounces the word as "soicus."

The finale is extraordinary, a 3D Wall of Death as a trio of motor cyclists, like angry hornets, and rasping out blue fumes, criss-cross at high speed round the inside of a large ball shaped structure. We hold our breath for the inevitable collision. It never happens, because the timing is split second, the skill finely honed.

Finally we have our superhumans, those special beings who transcend our normal humdrum lives and take us onto another plane.

And we know that this is what circus is for, an experience that thrills the blood in a way that watching Big Brother somehow never quite can.

Future should lie between a Rock and a special offer

4th October 2007

OVER THE last week, the following unconnected incidents occurred. Firstly, I was approached in the splendid Avalon bar in South Parade by an individual who, shouting above the noise of the band *Crash* said, "I bet you can't get the word numbnuts into your column!"

He's right. I can't.

Secondly, a knock at the door revealed one Tricia Belcher, who delivers this esteemed organ (the *News Guardian*) in our street. She referred to last week's column which yearned for a travelling theatre company akin to a circus.

Tricia recalls such a creature visiting her native Staffs 50 years ago. It was called New Century Theatre, and consisted entirely of women.

Thirdly a letter arrived, chastising me on the improper use of 'myself' as against 'I' in 'myself and technology'. 'Forgive me for using a non-de-plume,' concluded the writer, 'but I fear your wrath, or even more, your ridicule.' It was signed 'A Chicken.'

Fourthly, a small incident in St Georges Road, Cullercoats, 10.30am Thursday last, with the visit of the council wheelie bin lorry. The contents of one shop bin were misjudged on the automatic lifter, and a pile of sand and rubbish was deposited in the centre of the road. Three bin men stared briefly at this unsightly mess, slapped the lorryside, and moved on, leaving the good shopkeepers to sort it out.

Meantime, I am moved to compare the recently troubled Northern Rock to the redesigned Co-op store in Cullercoats. How can he do that, I hear you ask?

I have mentioned Cullercoats Co-op before, and its legendary queues that suddenly appear in an empty shop, its second counter assistant, summoned only when the queue numbers nine, and dismissed again when it's down to six.

The store was famous for its elusive special offers, Two For One, etc. Stocks on such offers lasted maybe three minutes, and the display signs offering the same were inevitably accompanied by an empty shelf.

The Co-op recently distributed fliers through every local household, trumpeting its new look. The special offers are better; that apart, it looks little different.

The thing is, no-one really minds. Because it's the Co-op. And the Co-op isn't the same as the rapacious supermarket giants, who we suspect are part of the great multinational plot to take us all over.

We have a love-hate relationship with these stores; we drive there to buy mountains of goods while secretly wondering what their dreadful shopping malls are doing to our way of life, our small farmers and shopkeepers, our decaying city centres. Why are they bringing an avocado pear half way round the world encased in plastic, we ask, as we pop it into our trolley?

Somehow the Co-op escapes such mistrust. They're decent coves at the Co-op, they're part of our working history. Not dynamic, but decent.

Which brings me to Northern Rock. The reputation of banks has slumped drastically over the years, regardless of their glitzy advertising and slick brochures. We see them as predatory heartless multi-national corporations, distant impersonalised outfits whose branch managers we never know, who charge £20 to send us a letter, and £35 if our overdraft exceeds its limit for a nano second. Banks? We don't like 'em.

Yet here we are, all rallying round the bank Northern Rock. A major regional newspaper launches an appeal for support. What goes on?

For a start, there's the title, Northern. We like that. The head office is in Gosforth, not Bangkok. We like that too. Somehow the bank 'belongs' in a way others don't. Then there's the Northern Rock Foundation which has given more than £175m to good causes. The outfit is human, real, and more interested in helping those same causes than in promoting its own image. Thus ironically, its own image is much improved.

But now financial experts say the only solution is a take-over of Northern Rock. Our hearts sink. We hate take-overs. No take-over has ever been for our benefit.

Both Northern Rock and the Co-op are capitalist, but instinctively we feel they're not ripping us off. We want the rest to be like them, and if it means missing out on the occasional special offer, so be it.

How the sepia tints grow stronger on road to museum

11th October 2007

MORE FLAK for your correspondent. "Mortimer!" yells a strident voice as I am hitching up my trusty push bike outside the Rockliffe Arms in Whitley Bay. "You got it wrong!"

This is often the case, but what now?

"You wrote that Bacchus was the Greek God of wine!" The speaker is one David Beever, who continues, (displaying the kind of triumphant smirk known to gamblers who lay down four aces), "whereas Bacchus was the

Roman God of wine."

He is totally and utterly right. There was no Greek God of wine, a fact which no doubt led to those awful years under the Colonels. Still, the Greeks did have Plato and Socrates, who I prefer as philosophical icons to our own Ant and Dec.

Elsewhere I am reminded of that wonderful moment in the spoof rockumentary film *Spinal Tap*. The fading eponymous band is touring America, growing ever gloomier as their reputation slips into obscurity.

Suddenly on a leading US radio station, their greatest hit is playing. The band perks up, but at the record's conclusion, the DJ says, "That was *Spinal Tap* in our series, *Where Are They Now?*"

The same kind of thing just happened to me. My friend Pat rang to say, "Your photographs are all over the *Evening Chronicle* supplement!"

I rushed to the local newsagents. Was it a knighthood? The Freedom of Seaton Sluice?

But what if it were an expose? 'The Writer who could not identify the Roman God of Wine – We name names!'

This is simply part of Writer Paranoia; every writer suffers that occasional panic, that sense of being not a real author but a fraud. They fear that once the truth is revealed, they will be tarred and feathered, rolled down the main street in a barrel and banished. Being banished has gone out of fashion. In Shakespeare's plays people were continually banished, though the word was pronounced 'banish-ed.'

So many modern Brits continually moan about the country, and dream of a life in some rural French backwater, that being banished might be no bad thing. Despite a good deal of unstructured travel, I've never lived anywhere but my native country; and suspect I might miss the Marmite.

But I digress *(Oh, you noticed? – Ed)*

The newspaper supplement was called *Remember When*, and there, spread right across the nostalgic sepia of the front cover was your correspondent's photograph astride a somewhat sad looking donkey. I had long thick hair, faded jeans, an Afghan coat, a beard, and was waving in the air a wide-brimmed black felt hat. Given the humble beast, and the general hippy appearance, the photo evoked a sense of some hybrid: Jesus Christ mixed with the Grateful Dead.

The photo, dear readers, was a third of a century old, and there was a two-page spread of photos inside, plus a write-up. This involved my 1974 series for *The Journal, Travels With a Donkey* in which I meandered with the loveable but stubborn Doris, a 115-mile journey from Berwick to Durham, penning a daily diary en route.

Were people even at that moment staring at this photo, and with a wistful look in their eyes, saying "Aaah, those were the days!" before cocking their head to one side and asking "I wonder if he's still alive?"

Any published photo feeds the ego. But there was also the sense that suddenly I had become part of history. In one fell swoop I was half-way to Beamish Museum. Friends pointed at the photo and roared with laughter. I wasn't quite sure how to take this.

Had I been sucked into the nostalgia industry? Would people now talk about me mainly in the past tense?

Sepia photos are from another planet. They belong with jerky old black and white film fuzzy at the edges. They belong in fusty old albums discovered in attics, from whose surface a cloud of dust is blown before they are opened.

Mortality stared me in the face with that supplement. Coming unexpectedly across such a public spread from yesteryear, was like an ironic inversion of catching that sudden shop window reflection, and realising it is you.

Or in this case, once was.

No addiction for Polly Dog as television channels multiply

18th October 2007

MORE HUMILIATION for your correspondent regarding wine and gods. Both writer Valerie Laws and North Tyneside arts officer Mike Campbell point out that indeed there is a Greek God of wine, (this column last week) and his name is Dionysus. Ah! *In vino veritas.*

Other matters occupy my attention. The television packed in.

"The TV's packed in," I said to Polly the Dog, who rarely watches.

"Woof."

I suspected something to do with the freeview box, and those strange things called scart leads that look like large wafer biscuits.

I shoved the scart leads in, but they're ill-fitting, like cheap false teeth.

Surely they're too big and heavy? I wiggled them around. The picture on the TV changed from a white blizzard to a zig-zag pattern, like a creation of the pop artist Bridget Riley. Then nothing.

My technological competence is limited. I looked behind the TV at the writhing mass of cables and leads. Once there were two leads, one to the socket, one to the aerial.

Now they are endless; they come from and to the video player, the DVD player, the freeview box, the heart pacemaker (I made the last one up). Regularly I go through the ritual of disentangling these leads, my non-technological mind worried at the thought of all that electricity criss-crossing on itself. This disentangled state lasts no time at all.

When I am asleep, these same leads and cables come awake and go through a magical dance that criss-crosses them all once again. Tracing any one lead to its source is like those childhood picture puzzles tracking the wiggly line to the treasure in the middle of the page.

"Why do I need all this junk, Polly? What is my life about?"

"Woof."

Housemate Wilkie came to lend a hand. His technical competence is on a par with my own.

He once almost rewired a plug after a correspondence course. We both stared bemusedly at the blank eye that stared back at us. We affected an indifference. Like most people I claim to watch less television than I do. With a shock I realised I was already disturbed about missing the football and the late film. Why was I annoyed with myself?

For some reason, I took down my Oxford Dictionary and looked up the word 'addiction'. It read 'habitual or excessive use of a drug or the like.'

"Polly," I said, "what if our society is addicted to television, but no-one is admitting it, or doing anything about it?"

"Woof, woof."

"In some houses it's never off, Polly – addiction or what? People can't live without it."

Polly was nibbling away at her fur should any of those nasty tics be remaining from our Jura trip. Now my mind's racing. Tobacco addiction has produced strong legislation. Whole clinics are devoted to alcohol addiction, and that of other drugs. So what about the telly?

No government health warning advising against more than so many hours viewing a day.

"In fact," I say, and I believe I'm really impressing the canine now, "the policy with most addictions is to wean people off. Whereas here we are feeding the habit!"

"Woof."

"New rubbish channels come on line every day. Everyone once had one small set in the living room, now houses have tellys in the airing cupboard! Some screens are the size of football pitches. Giant TV sets assail us in our local pub. TV is pumped through our mobile phones, our computers and now the dealers are flooding the market with hundreds of new digital channels.

"Polly," I say, "why does no-one take to task those who feed our addiction?"

There is no answer. But my partner Kitty has partly fixed the TV, except it now offers only the terrestrial channels.

A moment of epiphany. I remember the words, "If there's nothing worth watching on five channels, do something else."

I disentangle and throw out the cables and scart leads. Who needs them? The TV is back to simplicity, I have weaned myself off scanning 20 pages of schedules daily. My addiction is less. Can I keep it up?

"It's a start Polly," I say, but already she is loping off. She has a need to do something else.

Pitmen Painters, Road to Jericho & unpredictable art of the people

25th October 2007

OFF TO Live Theatre, Newcastle to see Lee Hall's wonderful new play, *The Pitmen Painters*. This is heady stuff that makes you laugh, feel and think – and any art that does that gets my slice of plum pie. The play also brings back into public consciousness the defunct and mainly forgotten Ashington Group, that collection of north east miners/painters that made the art world sit up in the 30s and 40s and whose reputation was still big enough in 1980 to become the first exhibition of English art shown in China since the early 50s.

Your correspondent has two links to this show.

One of the show's actors, Chris Connel was simultaneously appearing in our own Cloud Nine production *The Purple Pullover* (which curiously enough has the same three initials), written by the veteran North Shields surrealist Leonard Barras. Veteran North Shields surrealists are a minority group.

At times Chris needed to take a high-speed taxi between our show and Newcastle Quayside. He also experienced theatre's two extremes. The Live production, which re-opened their theatre after more than a year's closure, sold out.

Our own humble offering attracted decent audiences as it trundled round North Tyneside for two weeks of lunchtime performances, but at Dudley People's Centre, no-one turned up.

That's right. Not a single soul.

We put up the set, the actors got changed, the seats were put out. Then nothing. We looked up the street for latecomers. Latecomers were there none.

The actors changed back, we struck the set, put it back in the van, poked our heads round the office door and said, "Well, we're off," and that was that.

Possibly surrealism and Dudley don't mix. Possibly the range of counter-attractions in this small isolated settlement was enormous. Possibly they all get up late.

But suddenly the subject matter of *The Pitmen Painters*, the obstacles of involving the working class in culture and art, seemed highly relevant. And Dudley of course is old mining territory.

My second link to *The Pitmen Painters* is that in 1980 I published a book by a 94-year-old retired Durham miner William Bell, called *The Road to Jericho*.

The manuscript was sent to me by the late great north east novelist Sid Chaplin. It was a barely legible tatty hand-written scrawl, but Sid enclosed a note saying, "please persevere with it Pete – it is remarkable."

So I did, and it was. Bell wrote nothing else in his life, but this account of growing up in the Durham coalfield round the turn of the 20th century, a time known to most of us only through history books, was among the most vivid, moving, humorous and closely detailed pieces of documentary writing I'd come across.

Bell captured every tiny detail of the mining communities' lives and work, and we decided to publish his work. Sid Chaplin wrote a fine introduction.

Our art editor Pete Swan suggested Ashington Group paintings would make a perfect accompaniment, so we included eight, printed in black and white (colour was too expensive).

By chance, *The Observer* around that time did a special colour supplement feature on the painters' group, and we persuaded them to give us 100 free copies.

Thus we also did a special limited edition, in which we cut out and mounted by hand four extra full-colour pages of Ashington Group paintings on specially inserted blank sheets. Each was signed by the author in that same shaky arthritic scrawl.

And like *The Pitmen Painters*, the book sold out, as did the reprint. Before the second print was off the presses, William Bell died. "He was," said his wife, "just waiting to see his book."

The book, and the group shared something, that potential for the common man (it was all men in this case) to create and celebrate art and ensure it's not the preserve of the privileged few, which for complex reasons is still too often the case.

That's at the heart of the play, *The Pitmen Painters*. It's something our own theatre company is pretty keen on too.

But, as I perused the rows of empty chairs, and considered Dudley's indifference to our efforts, I found myself wondering why it couldn't just be more simple.

Hello? Hello? Anyone there? Please signal if signs of life!

1st November 2007

THE HOUR goes on – or is it off? No-one is ever certain, nor whether clocks go forward or back. What is the whole thing for? I have no idea. Forward then back. Forward then back. It's like the Grand Old Duke of York. Why not scrap it?

Except it guarantees that many wage slaves will pass the next few months, Mon – Fri, without seeing their homes in daylight.

They leave for work in the dark. They return from work in the dark.

In centuries to come (should we survive that long) this will be seen as a primitive practice. Why did they do it, people will ask?

The answer will be, to boost the production of rubber flanges, or chiming door-bells, or to ensure the country's least loved institution, the call centres, are constantly manned. The questioner will shake his or her head, and pass on.

Meantime I am worried that a highly contagious disease has broken out in Cullercoats.

Do not be alarmed, (oh, alright, be alarmed). What is my evidence, you ask?

Only this. I have kept watch day and night over the seafront block of flats called Winslow Court, previously known as The Bay Hotel.

The Bay Hotel itself would have a regular influx and outflux: *(You just made up the word 'outflux'. This is a laziness we will not tolerate – Ed),* drinkers, diners, wedding guests, leek growers, residents. At any reasonable time of day or night, people would be stepping into or out of The Bay Hotel.

Not now. There are several doors at Winslow Court leading out onto the street. No-one uses them. My observations revealed zilch activity, zero toing and froing, no signs of life.

Such things upset a simple soul such as I, who believes there is such a thing as society, and is troubled by signs to the contrary.

I mentioned this to a friend, who replied: "It's the underground car park. Residents come down their stairs, get into their car, drive out through the automatic gates, and are not seen. They do the same in reverse when they return."

Another friend offers the following: "Residents of such places rarely go out. They return from stressful jobs clutching their Marks & Spencer dinner-for-one, eaten in front of the telly, then off to bed, then awake to return to their stressful jobs and so the process continues."

What to believe? My own alternative is almost more bearable: decomposing bodies, flies crawling in eye sockets, while a half-eaten low-fat chicken Madras slowly rots on the table, and the deadly virus spreads through the air ducts.

The theory is strengthened by the fact that not only are these people never seen to enter and exit the building, they are never, unlike say the residents of Beverley Terrace, seen at their windows.

If I lived in Winslow Court I would spend half my waking hours staring out to sea.

My friends stress that such people are often far too busy to stare out to sea. Here's a way to test for the truth.

Every wining, dining and social establishment on or near Cullercoats seafront can combine to offer a special discount to residents of Winslow Court.

Through every letter-box (any idea how to gain access to the letter-boxes?), will go a letter which reads:

Dear resident of Winslow Court,

Welcome to Cullercoats! We would love you all to be an active part of this historic and much-loved village, and as such we are offering a 15 per cent discount for all customers upon proof of your residency in the above block of flats. Please come and show your face!

The letter would be signed by The Crescent Club, The Community Association, The Queens Head, The Bilash, the Copper Kettle, the Watch House, Mamma Rosa's, Bruno's, Bill's Fish Shop, and Quality Pizza.

Maybe the car park's automatic gates will open, 40 residents will roar out in cars, drive the few yards to Bill's Fish Shop, pick up their fish suppers and roar back in.

Or maybe someone will walk out the door, stroll along the pavement, be seen in the village, and prove that life exists in Winslow Court.

Meantime we watch and wait.

A bout of hedonism coming on – phone for an ambulance!

8th November 2007

FRIDAY NIGHT, South Parade Whitley Bay, and a shiny ambulance was parked up. Not an unusual occurrence, you might say. The 'Special Offers' on the drinking strip (i.e. a bath full of Red Bull and vodka for a fiver) means apprentice imbibers often topple over cracking a skull, or are fuelled to sudden punch-ups on the hi-octane booze.

But this ambulance was different: in the back, flashing disco lights plus a lap dancing pole.

Outside, two flimsily dressed bimbos were wiggling and handing out leaflets enticing customers to take a trip for around £10 a time.

South Parade regulars are already familiar with the fire engine outside one bar. Such appliances are occasionally spotted in transit, crammed full of squealing and giggling females, given to mooning out the front window.

Mooning isn't new. According to that infallible historical source Hollywood, William Wallace's men did it (see *Braveheart*). It is though, slightly ridiculous. The mooner looks daft, and is in no position to witness the effect on the moonee, if I can coin such a word.

To return to South Parade; if both ambulances and fire engines are to join the mushrooming hedonist industry, can police vehicles be far behind? Barriers are breaking down rapidly, and all services, emergency or otherwise, are being urged to maximise income. The new mantra ('That which does not turn a profit shall have no place in our modern market economy'), is gaining force.

How about young revellers being invited for a spin along the coastal trip in a cop car at a fiver a turn? Two hundred trips a weekend would bring in £50,000 a year which is probably enough to ensure Whitley Bay Police Station stays open all the time.

Walk up South Parade Friday or Saturday and you'll spot the coppers secured in their cars or vans staring out at the passing revellers who, in true festive spirit, may give them the finger, or let down their tyres.

This is a kind of apartheid where the two sides meet only in the event of trouble.

You could get at least a dozen youngsters at a time into the back of a large police van for a bit of funky dancing while they are whizzed to Tynemouth Priory and back. And no reason why PC Plod should not act as a groovy DJ en route.

Plus which, instead of using cells to house malcontents (little profit there), same cells could host 30 minute discos on a Friday or Saturday night at a fraction of the cost of Deep!

However, this merging of public services and entrepreneurship does have potential disadvantages...

PHONE OPERATOR: Hello, 999, which service did you require?
CALLER: Ambulance! My husband's leg has just fallen off!
OP: One moment, I'll check availability.
CALLER: Do please hurry!
OP: We will have an ambulance available at around 5am.
CALLER: But that's six hours from now!
OP: Friday night, busiest time, we've got eight stag parties in Whitley and

Tynemouth alone booked for trips.
CALLER: Stag parties? But –
OP: They pay £100 every trip; your husband probably expects us to come out for free.
CALLER: Yes, of course, but –
OP: There you are then. Stands to reason. He has to wait his turn.
CALLER: Oh my God – his other leg's fallen off now!
OP: Perhaps your husband could walk to the hospital?
CALLER: Walk? With no legs?
OP: It would relieve the emergency services of some of the pressures.
CALLER: Are you insane?
OP: We all have to do our bit to help ease the present cuts. Hang on – a call coming through! (TAKES IT) Hello? An ambulance for ten revellers from Grimsby, for 30 minutes, to include lap dancers? No problem. Pick them up on the seafront, OK? I'll put that Seaton Sluice epileptic on hold, and I'm sure the collapsed old lady from East Sleekburn won't mind waiting a bit. Bye. Is there anything else caller?
CALLER: Well, I –
OP: Keep on the line for a recorded message; special discounted ambulance trips for Christmas, including a stripping yodelling Santa. Remember – hire an ambulance – because you're worth it (PHONE GOES DEAD. CALLER IS LEFT TO STARE AT HUSBAND'S DETACHED LEGS).

Cravat, whisky, Cockney maid and murder that never was

15th November 2007

OFF TO Cross Keys Community Hall, Monkseaton to see St Peter's Players perform the play *Something to Hide* by Leslie Sands. The occasion reminds me of the familiar formula for many amdram plays; they're middle class, with a drawing room set, and situated in a cosy south of England village.

Early in the first scene one of the characters will say 'God, I need a drink' and avail him or herself of the row of spirits set on the cabinet stage left.

Characters will continue to pour themselves gin or whisky almost every time they enter.

People in such plays drink so regularly, and at any conceivable hour of the day or night that the fact they (as characters) remain sober throughout the play is a minor miracle, and I suspect a committed method actor would fall off stage during act two if only in search of dramatic reality.

By the middle of act one, a maid will appear with a comic 'cor blimey!' Cockney accent; occasionally she will give humorous asides to the audience about her employers or their friends.

Someone will seem to be bumped off early on, but end up not being dead at all. Phone calls are made via the operator to such numbers as Climpton 236. There will be a police officer of droll wit, obviously of more working class stock than the rest of the cast (the maid apart). The main male character will probably wear a cravat.

Such plays exist in a kind of middle England that never existed, except as a kind of cosy security blanket for readers of the *Daily Mail*, and to provide amdram groups with suitable scripts.

There is also of course, that mainstay of amdram, the prompt (once known, in less economical days as the prompter). I once saw an amdram play so devastatingly under rehearsed, the cast so unfamiliar with the script, and requiring so many prompted lines, that it became almost a one-person performance, that person being a muffled voice from some hidden recess. As this was the person who had worked hardest during the evening, I felt she deserved a curtain call of her own.

What would happen if prompts were banned as from tomorrow morning 7am?

Would theatre collapse? I doubt it. A prompt induces a complacent mindset, a safety net where a forgotten line is not something an actor should use his or her skills in overcoming, but merely a hiatus till they hear the voice from the wings.

And once the audience hears that voice, all the brilliant illusion is shattered. We are no longer immersed in some carefully constructed dramatic scenario, some artistic creation that for two hours has ingeniously sucked us into its own world, but simply with a group of people in a draughty church hall who are trying to remember (and in this case forgetting) lines from a play.

There is no prompt in life (where we make up the words without a script all the time).

Why on stage? Amdram also often suffers the age problem. It is not alone in this. Many social societies, voluntary clubs etc. are increasingly run and supported by those of mature years, while the young watch Myspace or Youtube, or are blogging, or are on iPods. That social structure that brings people together into church halls or the upstairs meeting rooms to run voluntary societies is often irrelevant to the young. I recently gave a talk to a rambling group and was surprised to find the average age about 86.

And though age brings caution, not all amdram is conservative. Tynemouth Pageant for instance produces only new commissioned plays. Plus which the country does have a healthy youth theatre structure whose exponents are often hungry to explore new dramatic forms.

But where do those budding youth theatre thespians go in their 20s and 30s? Why are they not exporting more of their talents into amdram?

Possibly it's that cosy world of so many amdram plays that puts them off. Possibly they feel little curiosity about curtseying maids, cravated rotters, whisky and soda poured every ten minutes, plays which seem preserved in aspic, with little social or political hinterland outside their own plot twists and turns.

Maybe every amdram group should include at least one brand new play in its annual programme. Maybe we should have a one-week regional amdram festival where every group would produce an entirely new piece of work, some of which could come from the wealth of theatre writing talent in this region. Now there's a good idea. And you know, I thought of it totally unprompted.

They're the dead and the imaginary, so why not the living?

22nd November 2007

I'M MOVED to write about statues. No, this has nothing to do with Newcastle United's back four. The desire comes after reading about the new statues at the revamped St Pancras Station in London, a giant statue of a couple embracing, and a second of the nation's favourite (albeit dead) poet John Betjeman, staring skywards.

Both are very different from the statues of yesteryear, some pompous military git on a horse with a large moustache (the git, not the horse), or another pompous git clutching a scroll.

These statues were mounted on plinths and, if we discount defecating birds, were (are) totally ignored. The plinth presumably was to symbolise the person's superiority and was taken to extremes when statues were put on the top of columns half way to the moon.

Thus Lord Nelson in Trafalgar Square, Earl Grey in Newcastle, and Lord Collingwood in Tynemouth. Such statues may well have a missing ear or arm (true in Nelson's case), or have a plum pudding for a head, for the public is never close enough to check. Such statues are always of nobility, which says a lot about the British.

There was also a columned statue of Lord Nelson in Dublin, but the Irish had the good sense to blow it up.

North Tyneside is not well-endowed with statues. As well as Collingwood, there's the constipated Queen Victoria in Tynemouth, and in North Shields Stan Laurel, plus the fishwife in Northumberland Square, and the wooden dolly outside the Prince of Wales (it was the pub's former name). Let me know if I've missed any.

Just across the water at the river mouth in South Shields, you'll find one of the few examples of statues with a sense of humour, the dumpy figures of *Conversation Piece*.

As far as I can tell, if we discount those small figures on top of the Spanish City building, Whitley Bay boasts not a single statue.

I'm quite taken with the statues near the Central Station, Newcastle.

These are human unpompous figures at street level, and on a weekend night you can often find drunks engaged in serious conversation with them, even expressing undying love.

I'd also like to visit the statue of John Lennon in Havana, Cuba. Lennon sits at one end of a park bench on which you're also encouraged to sit and thereby feel some engagement with the great man.

When did anyone ever engage with the statue of Lord Collingwood?

Newbiggin-by-the-Sea, not normally the most fashionable watering hole, attracted a deal of attention to itself recently with its giant statues of a man and woman, who are both standing above the waves and staring out to sea. Engagement here though would cost you wet feet.

Mortimer has a spiffing idea for the coast, which no doubt will be treated to the total indifference afforded my previous flashes of genius.

Most statues are of people who are either famous and dead, or fictional. What's wrong with the living? Down on Whitley's Southern Promenade is the enormous paddling pool unused since the days of Ethelred the Unready.

Let's turn it into a People's Statue Park. Here's the whole project. Employ a sea-front photographer to spend the summer season photographing strolling holidaymakers (if any are still to be found). At season's end select at random 100 photographs and employ artists to make life-size ground level statues of them, then place in the resurfaced (empty) pool.

Like Antony Gormley's *Domain Fields*, these will be statues of the common man and woman or child (pet?), but out in the open, not in an art gallery. Each statue could have a short biography attached. This random gaggle of humanity would be unique and attract great attention. Maybe more statues could be added over the years.

Symbolically this statue park would return Whitley Bay as a holiday resort to the people.

Visitors could wander in and out of the figures, talk to them, touch them. The town's image would be transformed, without the use of a single consultant, developer, or town planner.

And it would bring back the usually deserted Southern Promenade to the land of the living – as it were. Plus which you yourself could become a work of art.

Another day, another postal delivery; more decisions, decisions, decisions

29th November 2007

AN UNEXPECTED package arrives through the letterbox. Inside are two CDs plus a hastily scribbled note saying, 'Might just catch the van with these if I hurry George! I hope they're OK!'

They're far from OK. In fact they're pretty boring, an endless list of names, addresses, bank account and national insurance numbers, and other dry information of no use to me whatsoever.

And here was me thinking it might be the latest White Stripes album! Trawling through these is no fun at all – the damned things go on forever – millions of them! Only one place for this lot – the bin.

Hang on though, there were four more letters to open, all with expensive envelopes, neatly typed.

I read the first one:

Dear Mortimer,

Your experience at writing your weekly column suggests you might make the ideal person to fill an important position about to become vacant.

Running Middlesbrough FC is a challenging job and we are sure you will be up to it. The best bus is the X10 from Newcastle, every hour, and please keep your ticket as proof of purchase. Should you buy a cheese roll on the journey keep the receipt for that also. Tell us when you'll be arriving at Riverside, and we'll leave the gate open, (the south gate of course).

Yours sincerely....etc

How flattering. I opened envelope number two:

My Dear Mortimer,

It is said that in your days managing Cullerbay Dynamikz FC (North-East Heating Trades Sunday League Div V), your team hardly ever let in seven goals. This would appear to be a strong recommendation for running Sunderland FC. We do anticipate a managerial vacancy in the near future.

We hope you will not mind the presumption of this direct approach. We realise you have a column to write, and a play half-finished, but we are sure you will see things in perspective. This is an important position and one on which any football lover would be Keane – sorry, keen. The job does come with free chewing gum.

Yours sincerely, etc....

Hmm. I nervously slit open letter number three:

Dear Mortimer,

It is well-known that you grew up supporting Notts County, for whom Sam Allardyce is a previous manager. We are often accused of the club having no policy of continuity, and wish to discount this by offering you the job of Newcastle United manager once Mr Allardyce (or Not Quite So Big Sam as he's affectionately known hereabouts) empties his desk and leaves, which alas will not be long in coming.

This will continue the links with the other (and of course original) Magpies, and prove that far from being a rudderless ship, Newcastle United has a recognisable and distinctive policy. Yours sincerely, etc....

PS We would prefer you didn't come in to work on your pushbike. Football managers (and players) don't do that kind of thing.

One envelope remained. With my souvenir Long John Silver letter opener, I slit along the top.

Dear Mortimer,

It has come to our notice that you passed French and German A Levels, (and Spanish O Level) which gives you just the kind of international perspective needed for running the national football team.

We could choose another Johnnie Foreigner (let's face it, they're much better at the damned job), but thought we'd give a Brit one last try. Best not let on that you're half Irish. You get to travel a lot in the job, though your hair falls out rapidly.

Hang on though, I see yours has already! In which case we anticipate no problems and hope you could turn up at Lancaster Gate next Tuesday to meet the FA committee. Please speak loudly when interviewed as some of our ear trumpets malfunction.

Yours sincerely.....

I considered them carefully dear reader, but concluded that whatever the attractions, and football's need of me in a crisis, such a calling could not rival sitting in my small study, and penning for you my weekly 700 words, fortified by the occasional Rington's ginger biscuit.

Thus, I turned them all down. Back next week!

Note: the government had just lost 25m people's confidential details in the post

Chance to make North Tyneside famous with a new slogan!

6th December 2007

YOU MAY HAVE read the news about the Scottish Executive spending £125,000 to think up a new national slogan. The idea is that this would cause people to say, "Gosh!" and be so impressed they'd immediately head north (or if they lived in Iceland, south).

Naturally consultants, PRs and marketing people were brought in, no doubt a clutch of young turks with gelled hair brainstorming round tables in expensive hotels.

They were encouraged to think outside the box, to push the envelope, to adopt a blue sky approach. Slogans such as 'Scotland – where the Mars Bars Fry Deeper' or 'The Irn Bru is Waiting for You' were unlikely to make it.

The project would require brilliant wordsmiths, talented alchemists conjuring pure gold from the base metal of our everyday lingo.

What they came up with was, 'Welcome to Scotland.' Yes, that's right, 'Welcome to Scotland'.

Pause a moment to absorb this trio of words. You may wish to consider the lyricism, the verbal cadences, the metrical beauty, the evocative echo that lingers. Here they are again: 'Welcome to Scotland'.

My immediate thought is that any graffiti artist worth his or her salt is likely to skulk out in the night and spray 'You Are' in front. Is it just me or does the slogan (which works out at £7,000 a letter) leave something to be desired?

My own home county, Notts has also come up with a new slogan. The previous one (this is Robin Hood country remember) was 'Our Style is Legendary', which has a certain ring to it.

The new slogan is 'N'. I'd better repeat that in case you think there's been a computer glitch. Notts Co. Council's new slogan is the single letter 'N'. The good news is that this came out £5,000 cheaper than Scotland. It cost only £120,000 to think up 'N'.

Here's what Scotland and Notts should have done. They should have said to their tourist board staff, "We need a new slogan and there's a bottle of single malt for the person who comes up with the best one by Friday week."

My suspicion is that the results would have been less dull than 'Welcome to Scotland', less impenetrable than 'N'.

It reminds me that I once thought up such a slogan. Travelling up the A19 I passed a large sign advertising Wearside. I immediately thought of WEAR on your SIDE, and straightaway did nothing about it.

But it reminds me that maybe it's time we gave the boot to expensive and useless consultants, and asked the people.

Which is why Mortimer (roll of drums please) is about to announce yet another of his breathtaking competitions.

At present North Tyneside has only one slogan. This is 'Working Closer with Communities'. It's honest, reassuring and down-to-earth, and no doubt does its job in bringing some small reassurance to us residents of the borough who like to think we're both part of a greater whole, and are being looked after.

But on the larger map it's unlikely to cause potential visitors from New Zealand to jump up and shout, "That's the place for our holiday next year Sheila!".

And it may be that all such slogans, like most advertising, are pure nonsense. But at a time when we are told Whitley Bay is about to undergo a cultural renaissance, should we not be thinking of trumpeting our advantages to the world?

So I'm looking for an eye-catching slogan for our borough.

Think of the unique features we have: the coastline, St Mary's Island, Tynemouth Priory and Castle, North Shields Fish Quay, the river mouth, Cullercoats Bay, to name but a few.

So any good slogans out there? Previous challenges from this column have proved your creative ingenuity, so I'm confident of some eye-catching responses. I will publish any half-decent ones, and send them to the relevant North Tyneside council offices. Who knows, your slogan could soon be blazoned across the world?

Drop them into the *News Guardian* office, post them, or e-mail them to sue.slattery@northeast-press.co.uk

There is (provided entirely at my own expense!) a bumper size box of liquorice allsorts for the slogan I think the best. It's not £125,000, but I suspect the result will be better than 'N'.

Cheer up! Falling house prices can't go on forever!

13th December 2007

ALAN FIDDLER informs me of two more North Tyneside statues (this column November 22) – the Duke of Northumberland at Master Mariners Tynemouth, and G B Hunter (the big boat builder) at The Green, Wallsend. Ta.

Meantime letters flood in on the falling house prices, likely to lead to a recession.

'Dear Mortimer, does a recession mean they are less likely to build new airports, or put fewer cars on the road?

Then bring it on! My house is to be demolished either for a new airport runway or to widen a motorway, which will be choked again in three weeks. So I say let house prices drop even further if it means I can keep mine. I dream of a detached house in Darras Hall priced at £100. What's wrong with that?'

A second correspondent writes:

'Dear Mortimer, I am told the possible coming recession and drop in house prices is something to do with poor people in the USA failing to pay their mortgages. Please excuse my ignorance in not understanding this.

My neighbour scoffs and says it's just as likely to do with his budgie being off its food, his leaking drainpipe, or having allowed his custard to go cold. Would it help the possible recession if I sent a small donation to someone in Iowa?'

More correspondence follows.

'Dear Mortimer, we have been dreaming of owning our own property for more than ten years, but to qualify for a mortgage our incomes would need to equal the Saudi Royal Family's annual outlay on new Rolls Royces.

If house prices came down we might just be able to afford our own little dream home and give up this uncomfortable lifestyle in a cardboard box on the town moor. Should we feel guilty at putting our own welfare before the economic wellbeing of the nation, and urge prices to rise again? Should we beat ourselves with birch twigs for such thoughts?' And more.

'Dear Mortimer, please help me with my confusion. We are constantly told by experts that unless western nations change their excessively consumptive and indulgent lifestyle, the less well-off countries will continue to starve and the effect on global warming will see us all drown from melting ice caps within 30 years.

Yet we are now told that falling house prices may see the GNP drop next year from 3.2 per cent to 2.8 per cent, a fact that has caused several economists and financial experts to jump from high windows or leap off bridges while wearing concrete feet. You have an economics degree from Sheffield University, so please explain.' Another letter.

'Dear Mortimer, I have been reading about the crisis with falling house prices and possible recession, and am wondering just how big an effect this will have on my lifestyle. I would be panicking if I thought it might prevent me from buying the new Apple mobile phone that can (a) iron my trousers, (b) spray skunks with a pleasing fragrance, (c) automatically choose the orange coloured Smartie, and (d) play the theme tune from *Big Brother* backwards. Perhaps you could advise me. I wouldn't say I was suicidal, but life could soon lose all meaning.'

And more.

'Dear Mortimer, all this talk about falling house prices. What about falling houses themselves? Ours just collapsed around our ears and we are left in the rubble of what once was a beautiful fitted kitchen – although only 6ft x 4ft in size.

We live on one of those new estates (Elysian Fields) that have sprung up throughout the region, and were urged to get on the property ladder as soon as possible, despite it being a huge drain on our resources. We did not expect the house to fall down, but it has done, along with those of several neighbours, and in the rubble we discover that the walls are mainly made of discarded Weetabix packets, and the roof timbers are used Swan Vestas.

All this, despite firm verbal assurances as to the construction quality from the builders, whose name is Roy Rogers Ltd, (catchphrase 'Howdy pardn'r!').'

I shall reply to all letters in due course. Meantime happy house hunting! Really sorry that it could cost you less.

The people have spoken! Let the borough's coast be reborn!

20th December 2007

SEASONAL GOODWILL has swept over me to such an extent this week that I am offering not one but two (yes TWO!) large boxes of liquorice allsorts for the first readers who can solve the following brace of teasers.

There is a clear mistake in Fenwick's Christmas window display, Newcastle. The first reader to identify the mistake gets the first box of sweeties. Here's a clue: it has nothing to do with the model animals, and mistake apart, they've got everything off to a 't'.

Secondly, identify the name of the well-known Christmas carol from which these two lines are taken: 'Radiant beams from thy holy face/With the dawn of redeeming grace.' Answers to this office, or e-mail to sue.slattery@northeast-press.co.uk

This was among the carols sung last week at Cullercoats Community Centre, with the visit of the Caedmon Choir. The choir sang, the audience too.

People are starting to sing in increasing numbers (there's a major campaign in schools) and I understand why. It costs nothing, is classless, and, while not wanting to appear overblown, makes a celebratory statement about our common humanity.

I lived one winter on Holy Island and joined the local choir (there wasn't much else to do). It was addictive, and I found myself eagerly anticipating the weekly two-hour session where we were all released through filling our lungs. How about multicultural choirs in Iraq and Afghanistan? It's hard to blow someone's head off after harmonising with them.

Meantime there's my search for the best slogan for North Tyneside (this column December 6), for which yet another box of liquorice allsorts is on offer (headline – 'Mortimer Column Sees Liquorice Allsorts Shares Soar!')

The competition convention is to say "We were inundated with entries!" This is not exactly true. I have spent most of my life not being inundated, and the pattern continues. A respectable number of highly literate personages did enter, and you might like to read what they had to offer.

Paul Agnew of North Shields suggests 'North Tyneside – Uniting History, Beauty and Opportunity', and writes a spirited letter in support. From George Richardson of Wallsend, comes 'North Tyneside – this is Civilisation', or 'North Tyneside –T.I.C' to which he adds, slightly defensively, 'at least it's short'.

Mrs Ivy Kerr of North Shields has the following, 'INvigorating, INspiring, IN the North-East', with a suggested picture of St Mary's Lighthouse and sketch of the sea and beach.

The ubiquitous and alliterative Ronald Rumble suggests among others, the punny 'North Tyneside – Feats Ahead', and (tongue-in-cheek I suspect), 'North Tyneside – It's What's Written on the Bins!'

From Brian Teasdale, the author of *A Plea for Whitley Bay*, come three entries, namely 'The Welcome Way in Whitley Bay Every Day', 'The Whitley Bay Way Makes Every Day a Holiday', both a bit on the long side, but I am taken by Brian's third effort, 'Make my Day in Whitley Bay'; echoes of a famous film line, a certain insistence and a great sense of self-confidence.

Maggie Longton (again e-mail address only) offers no fewer than nine entries of which I think the best are 'Whitley Bay – Dream Village by the Sea', and 'Whitley Bay – Widening Horizons' where the word widening can be either a verb or an adjective.

Cullercoats stalwarts, Colin and Cath Bowman sent a plethora of entries, with Colin freely admitting an addiction to liquorice allsorts since childhood, when, he says, they were sold cheaply as mis-shapes.

Colin concludes his letter, 'I look forward to seeing everyone's efforts, in the full knowledge that they will surpass those of the overpaid plagiarists (consultants)', and I say hurrah to that.

Try some of Colin and Cath's slogans: 'The Cool Place to Chill out', 'Thousands of Sea Birds Can't be Wrong', 'Slow Down; Stop; EXPLORE' or the intriguing, 'Lose Yourself – Find Yourself'.

Finally it came down to a choice between 'Make my Day in Whitley Bay', and 'Lose Yourself – Find Yourself', with the latter just marginally shaving it. Many thanks to everyone who entered. Sweeties en route to Colin and Cath Bowman and all entries have been sent to Steve Forshaw of North Tyneside Council for reactions. Watch this space!

Over-sized Christmas cards, and deteriorating windows

27th December 2007

LATE ENTRIES arrive for my North Tyneside slogan competition (alas, already with a winner decided). Mike Rigby is disqualified – his slogans are for the North-East whereas our subject is North Tyneside.

Janet Roper emails to say her mother Dora Clarke of West Monkseaton won the original slogan competition back in 1963 and received 15 shillings for, 'Miles of Curving Golden Sand, Whitley Bay, Northumberland' which was then franked onto all outgoing mail for ten years. 'North Tyneside is on the Go – We Know, We Know, We Know!' is Dora's offering 44 years on.

Her original slogan was before the dreadfully named Tyne & Wear. We have since given this metropolitan authority the boot, though the name lingers like a bad smell. I blame the Post Office. Throw it out, use Northumberland on your address.

Talking of the Post Office, those of you lucky enough to take the long (and difficult) trip to the PO sorting office of North Norham Road (conveniently situated miles from main bus routes and metro station), may have been intrigued to see a whole clutch of elderly people wandering round in a bemused state.

Each had received a card stating under-stamped mail was awaiting their collection. They took the long journey, possibly avoiding frostbite en route, to discover such mail was merely Christmas cards to which the sender had, quite justifiably, attached either a second or first class stamp, but which under the new Post Office size regulations, was not enough!

No matter that the payment may have been only a few pence short, the festive cards were returned to the sorting office, where, after a 48 hour delay, same addressees could walk, bus, bike, or travel by car to pick them up, paying more than a quid per card surcharge. This kind of thing fills a poor pensioner's heart with glee, causing him/her to sing out, "And a happy Christmas to you too!" and delve into a small purse to cough up the necessary.

Added to this, the queue outside the sorting office at Yuletide is longer than those for the soup kitchens during the Russian Revolution, and my partner Kitty queued 45 minutes to pick up a package which the PO had failed to deliver three days previously. After a ten minute search she was informed that it had still not made its way back to the sorting office.

Where could the parcel have spent those three days? What circuitous route had it taken for the three mile journey?

I have written about this fabled sorting office before, a column that produced an unfavourable reaction from my postie, who scribbled the following words after my name on one letter 'who does not like postmen'.

This is not as extreme as the reaction from the local window cleaner after my somewhat tongue-in-cheek column on the curiosities of his profession. Three months after the column I realised I could no longer see the trees across the street, a shortcoming created not by sea fret, but by windows that had not been cleaned in the interim.

I finally tracked down the window cleaner, to discover he had taken umbrage at my column, and in protest had withdrawn his labour, which remains withdrawn to this day. Secretly I felt quite pleased my words produced such an animated reaction, though efforts to find a replacement have proved abortive. I now clean my own downstairs windows and upstairs the view grows more hazy as the neglect continues.

We columnists obviously require a thick skin (not to mention a tall ladder). Only last week I was hailed across the street by a man who asked, "Has Prince Harry been round to officially declare your gate open yet?"

This was a reference to a Mortimer column way back in Spring 2003. What a memory! The man further endeared himself to me by saying "I did like that column", though all good feeling evaporated in an instant when he added "mind, they've been rubbish ever since," and walked away.

This column, rubbish or otherwise, is written well in advance of normal deadlines to meet seasonal requirements. Thus at time of writing I have no idea if my two mini-competitions will draw any response.

Note - they did.

"He threw me in the lake"

Postscript

A Moderately Known Literary Hack interviews the Author

HACK When did you start writing?

AUTHOR That would be about two thirty

HACK There must have been early influences?

AUTHOR My elder brother influenced me at an early stage

HACK How exactly?

AUTHOR He threw me in the lake

HACK I understand you wrote other newspaper columns before the *News Guardian?*

AUTHOR Undoubtably

HACK And eventually were sacked from all of them, I'm told?

"One man posted a sock through my letterbox"

AUTHOR   Your sources are impeccable

HACK   How would you see the role of the contemporary newspaper columnist? Is it to poke fun at authority, to question the great issues of the day, to champion the causes of the unsung, to recount some amusing anecdotal episode in the columnist's life, to satirise the pompous and the self-inflated, to expose humbug, or to complain about the price of fish fingers?

AUTHOR   You couldn't have put it better yourself

HACK   Is there much reaction to your column on North Tyneside?

AUTHOR   One man posted a sock through my letterbox. I took this in the spirit intended

HACK   Which was?

AUTHOR   Single malt whisky

HACK   Does writing a weekly column bring any weight of responsibility on your shoulders, a sense of public duty, an historical imperative?

AUTHOR   You have a way with words

HACK   Where do you get your ideas from?

AUTHOR   Please don't end a sentence with a preposition

HACK   Very well. From where do you get your ideas?

AUTHOR   As one writer put it, if I knew that, I'd go there more often!

HACK   I don't suppose you would have any advice for a promising new writer who relishes the challenge of penning a weekly 700 word column for his or her region's periodical?

He shouted 'Your column's rubbish' "

AUTHOR	That's exactly right
HACK	What brought you to North Tyneside?
AUTHOR	The number 308 bus. You can catch it in St. Marys Place, or Eldon Square Bus Station, Newcastle. The latter suffers more diesel fumes
HACK	I imagine you are often engaged in lively intellectual discourse with your readers
AUTHOR	Only last week I was hailed across the street in Whitley Bay by a passing fellow
HACK	What did he say?
AUTHOR	He shouted, "Your column's rubbish!"
HACK	Reader response must be very valuable to you, even creatively instructive?
AUTHOR	Another reader wrote to say that in some columns she had no idea what I was talking about
HACK	Did you reply?
AUTHOR	Naturally
HACK	What did you say?
AUTHOR	I said, *moi aussi,* (that's French)
HACK	Upsetting some people must come with the job
AUTHOR	Less than that of a traffic warden, which I hear has a better pension, and you also get a free hat and pencil, which for some reason you're expected to lick before you write out the ticket. The pencil, not the hat. Licking hats is an unsavoury habit

"I once visited the Pencil Museum in Keswick"

HACK You have written more than 200 columns for the *News Guardian* –

AUTHOR The number changes every week

HACK And the future?

AUTHOR A distinct possibility

HACK The life of a writer is sitting at a desk, alone; do you not sometimes crave the social company of a normal job?

AUTHOR I often get up and whistle. And there is always the pencil sharpener

HACK Pencils again?

AUTHOR I once visited the Pencil Museum in Keswick

HACK You obviously live life on the edge

AUTHOR Will that be all?

HACK Yes. Thank you very much

END